WAGNER AND THE ROMANTIC HERO

Few major artists have aroused the ire and adulation of successive generations as persistently as Richard Wagner. The centre of controversy during his lifetime, when he died he was the most idolized man in Germany. Little has changed since then. In this book based on lectures delivered at the Bayreuth Festival, Simon Williams explores the reason for this adulation and antipathy by examining one of the most contested aspects of Wagner's work, his treatment of the hero. He begins by defining heroism as it was understood in Wagner's time and then explores the phenomenon of heroism and the hero in all thirteen of the stage works. He concludes with a survey of how the Wagnerian hero and the idea of heroism has been interpreted on the modern stage. Williams offers a theatrical and cultural reevaluation of one of the most enduring and controversial figures in the history of the arts.

SIMON WILLIAMS is Professor of Dramatic Art at the University of California, Santa Barbara. He is the author of *German Actors of the Eighteenth and Nineteenth Centuries: Romanticism, Idealism, and Realism* (1985), *Shakespeare on the German Stage: 1582–1914* (Cambridge, 1990), and *Richard Wagner and Festival Theatre* (1994).

WAGNER AND THE ROMANTIC HERO

SIMON WILLIAMS

CAMBRIDGE
UNIVERSITY PRESS

PUBLISHED BY THE PRESS SYNDICATE OF THE UNIVERSITY OF CAMBRIDGE
The Pitt Building, Trumpington Street, Cambridge, United Kingdom

CAMBRIDGE UNIVERSITY PRESS
The Edinburgh Building, Cambridge, CB2 2RU, UK
40 West 20th Street, New York, NY 10011–4211, USA
477 Williamstown Road, Port Melbourne, VIC 3207, Australia
Ruiz de Alarcón 13, 28014 Madrid, Spain
Dock House, The Waterfront, Cape Town 8001, South Africa

http://www.cambridge.org

© Simon Williams 2004

First published 2004

Printed in the United Kingdom at the University Press, Cambridge

Typeface Adobe Garamond 11/12.5 pt.   *System* LATEX 2$_\varepsilon$ [TB]

A catalogue record for this book is available from the British Library

ISBN 0 521 82008 1 hardback

For
Pene and Clive

Contents

Acknowledgments

This book is based upon talks that I delivered at the Bayreuth Festival between 1998 and 2000 and I am grateful to the Wagner Society of New York for their kindness and courtesy in inviting me to speak in the lecture series that they sponsor. I have also delivered much of this material in various forms to several Wagner Societies, opera-houses, opera guilds and leagues, and university departments in the United States, Australia, and Europe. I am indebted to far more individuals than I can possibly list here for their hospitality and their unfailingly challenging questions on Wagner, his works, and their place in the modern world. My research was greatly aided by a grant from the Senate Research Committee of the University of California, Santa Barbara. I am particularly indebted to the Interdisciplinary Humanities Center at UCSB for tolerating, during my directorship of that institution, the frequent absences when I was away lecturing on Wagner. After I had stepped down, I thought the Center would have been pleased to see the back of me, but it generously provided me with a grant that enabled me to complete this project in a timely fashion. As always I am deeply indebted to my wife Euzetta for her love, support, and willingness to sit through more productions of Wagner than she ever bargained for.

Note on abbreviations of sources

All references to Wagner's prose writings are taken from two editions: Richard Wagner, *Gesammelte Schriften*, ed. Julius Kapp, 14 vols. (Leipzig: Hesse & Becker, n.d. [1914]), which is abbreviated in the notes to *GS*, and Richard Wagner, *Prose Works*, tr. William Ashton Ellis, 8 vols. (London: Kegan Paul, Trench, Trübner & Co., 1893), abbreviated in the notes to *PW*. All translations from *GS* are my own. Extensive reference is also made to *Cosima Wagner's Diaries*, ed. and annotated by Martin Gregor-Dellin and Dietrich Mack, tr. Geoffrey Skelton, 2 vols. (New York: Harcourt Brace Jovanovich, 1978–80), abbreviated in the notes to *CD*.

Introduction

Heroism is, at best, a dubious quality. We admire heroes because they embody all that we consider most admirable in ourselves. Heroes are possessed of an excess of human energy, which has a propitious effect on the world around them. They display greater courage than regular people do, they know what they want and are fearless in achieving it. Through their exploits we glimpse, however briefly, images of human perfection and, depending on our beliefs, of something divine. But heroes are not easy to live with. The moment we try to incorporate heroism into our everyday lives, we play down whatever is individual about it and lay stress on its social virtues. Community newspapers encourage readers to nominate as "local heroes" those whose selfless labors are a benefit to the community. We designate as heroes people who help us, set us good examples, and save us from our worst selves. But, as Emerson put it, "the heroic cannot be the common, nor the common the heroic."[1] The heroic in our mundane world can be positively oppressive, especially when it claims authority over us. Our leaders may conceive of themselves as heroes, but the moment they do so, we find ourselves obliged to deny them. We hem them in with bureaucratic limitations and reduce them to our own size or smaller by insisting that they are models of indecision and inefficiency. We may be unjust in these judgments, but, even if we are, we show good sense in making them, for our pragmatic instincts resist the idea of anyone having authority over us on the strength of personality alone. Hence while we admire heroes, we must consign them to the sidelines of life: to sports arenas, where they can engage in heroic feats that have no tangible impact on our lives; to religious cults, where if we subject ourselves to charismatic authority, we do so entirely as a matter of choice; or to popular movies, where action-heroes feed our fantasies by evincing a singular freedom from the moral and physical restraints that normally confine us. Our aversion to public heroism has its downside. Our over-rationalized society promotes inaction, and we often call for people of heroic stature who might clear the logjam of procedures and regulations that seem to stand in the way of commonsensical action. Once such people have acted, we tell ourselves we will be able to work with a renewed sense of freedom. But heroism like this is rare and even more rarely allowed.

If we can measure the attitudes of different generations to heroes and the heroic, it is likely that our own time displays a greater degree of skepticism toward the viability of the heroic in public life than any previous age, and for good reason. The millions who died in two World Wars, in the Holocaust, and in dictatorships in several parts of the world were victims of political forces that were in many instances nothing but hero-cults, as consideration for the glory of one leader, ethnic group, or national interest overrode all human rights. If the apocalyptic history of the twentieth century has resulted in anything positive, it should be a relentless and abiding mistrust of any claim to heroic privilege and authority. It should have led too, one might think, to an equal mistrust of that composer and dramatist whose works have been taken as the supreme articulation of heroism as a formative power in public and private life, Richard Wagner.

Wagner's works have never found uncontested acceptance. When he was alive, he polarized audiences and critical opinion; now, 120 years after his death, he has lost none of his power to divide the public. Each generation discovers a Wagner to outrage it. The last *fin de siècle*, encouraged by the febrile imagination of Friedrich Nietzsche, projected onto Wagner's works its intense fear of sexuality; Max Nordau charged Wagner "with a greater abundance of degeneration than all the degenerates put together."[2] During the first half of the twentieth century, as Europe's obsession with the nation-state reached its climax in the rise of fascism, Wagner came to be seen as "the most important single fountainhead of Nazi ideology."[3] Our own generation, committed to the rights of ethnic minorities, has subjected the anti-Semitic aspects of Wagner's work to withering and persistent scrutiny. Wagner, more than any other canonical figure in the literary, visual, and performing arts, has demonstrated an unerring capacity to serve as a lightning-rod for each generation's anxieties about itself.

What is remarkable about these anxieties is the intensity with which they are expressed. This may arise in part as a reaction to the unabated enthusiasm the music-dramas continue to generate in the opera-house. Those who suspect Wagner might claim that the response his music-dramas receive represents covert endorsement of political ideologies and sexual attitudes that have been long discredited. But opera audiences are not notably illiberal and it is more likely that they are responding to the heightened atmosphere of the music-dramas which, as Thomas Mann put it, "implies that the highest and best available to man is a life cast in the *heroic* mould."[4] The heroic ambience often weakens the ironic aspects of the action and thereby has the effect of suggesting that all issues arising from the action are put forward for our admiration. The idiom of opera, as Herbert Lindenberger has written, "can draw us temporarily out of our individual selves and raise us to what we take to be a higher form of consciousness, in the process of so doing . . . lead[ing] us to think ourselves greater than we are."[5] If this is true, then we should remain always aware of the causes of this self-aggrandizing process, especially in the case of Wagner, whose heroes may often stand for ideas we have difficulty in coming to terms with today.

This book, which comprises an examination of the workings of heroism and the heroic in Wagnerian music-drama,[6] is not so much about the ideas in Wagner's work as about the dramatic action and theatrical mechanism by which they are set into play. Through a discussion of the literary, theatrical, and operatic culture out of which Wagner's work came, I identify two modes of heroism, romantic heroism and epic heroism, which were to be central to his entire oeuvre, and a third, messianic heroism, toward which his thought was tending, but which was only treated as a viable phenomenon in his two last music-dramas. The heroic experience lies so close to the heart of his music-dramas that Wagner was induced to devise innovative uses of the stage-space to give it theatrical expression. This initiated several modern developments in the use of the stage, which I often touch upon. I divide Wagner's career into three phases, in each of which romantic and epic heroism play discrete but interlocking functions. The first phase, after the apprentice works, comprises *Der fliegende Holländer*, *Tannhäuser*, and *Lohengrin*, music-dramas governed by the dramaturgy of the early nineteenth-century theatre, in which action is centered on either the alienated romantic hero or the epic hero who cannot find acceptance in society. The hero remains essentially an outsider in the central work of Wagner's career, *Der Ring des Nibelungen*, in which concepts of romantic and epic heroism compete in a tragic universe. In the final phase, which comprises *Tristan und Isolde*, *Die Meistersinger von Nürnberg*, and *Parsifal*, Wagner attempted progressively to incorporate the hero into society as a messianic figure, an undertaking with questionable implications as the hero begins to acquire an authority that, in the traditions within which Wagner was working, had been denied him. The three modes of heroism I have identified in Wagner's music-dramas are associated exclusively with male characters, but their viability is often challenged by the hero's female partner, whose selflessness in sacrificing herself for the man she loves displays a moral power that has greater force than that of the male hero, a circumstance most apparent at the end of the *Ring*. As the modern world is not at ease with Wagner's heroism, I conclude my study with an examination of how it has been represented on the modern stage. In my discussion of contemporary productions, I comment only on those I have seen.

Modes of heroism in the early nineteenth century

The age in which Richard Wagner grew up had little time for heroes. After the turmoil of the French Revolution and the Napoleonic Wars, Europe entered upon an uneasy and somnolent peace. During the period of "Restoration" that followed the final defeat of Napoleon in 1815, royalist governments attempted to return to the pre-revolutionary status quo, so there was little encouragement of critical and progressive thinking among artists, academics, or political radicals. In the German Confederation especially, curbs on freedom of speech were imposed by techniques prefiguring the modern police-state and applied by ever-expanding, impersonal bureaucracies. Through the Carlsbad decrees of 1819, freedom of the press was suspended, universities placed under rigorous state supervision, and political protest banned. Although these proscriptions were not applied uniformly and prison sentences were not always harsh, whoever challenged public authority did so at their peril. But this was not the worst of times. The post-war economic boom resulted in an expanded middle class and improved standards of living, so for those who enjoyed a modicum of prosperity, life was not unpleasant. Germans turned to the cultivation of their personal and professional lives, and their culture of this time, known to us as "Biedermeier," expressed itself in modest, sentimental artistic forms that celebrated the family and cozy domesticity and avoided the uglier aspects of life. In Biedermeier art, the city was represented as an extension of the pastoral world, not as an arena for the incipient industrial revolution. If Biedermeier idealized any period other than its own, it was the Middle Ages, which represented for many the apogee of the organic urban community in which all individuals had their allotted place. Biedermeier also fostered public culture through the founding of institutions of art, education, recreation, and public health in cities large and small.[1] For those with some protection from economic hardship, there was a touch of the idyllic in Biedermeier life, but for those excluded by necessity or choice from its intimate family circles, life was harsh and channels of protest against these circumstances difficult to come by.

Censorship did not entirely silence dissent, which was heard through clandestinely published periodicals and pamphlets. In the mid-1830s the loosely associated group of writers known as "*Junges Deutschland*" ("Young Germany") published novels protesting against social complacency and advocating a more progressive dispensation, which would allow, among other liberties, free love. But their work was suppressed and some authors imprisoned. For the most disenchanted writers, such as Heinrich Heine, survival was possible only in exile, in the more cosmopolitan environment of Paris. In Germany, any radical social schemes and political ideologies were forged through private dialogue among radicals, scholars, and writers, not in public debate. Nevertheless, nothing could suppress the growing sense of alienation among the disenfranchised, underprivileged, and indigent in what was for them an impersonal, oppressive society. In fact, the muzzle placed on the public expression of dissent only served to augment it, so that the quiescent surface of public life was twice shattered by civil disturbances of exceptional violence, the revolutions that swept Europe in 1830–32 and 1848–49. As they were driven by the ideologies of socialism, liberalism, and nationalism, these revolutions gave rise to forces that would shape the future world. In retrospect, the age of Biedermeier bred more change than its tranquil surface suggests. It was an age that looked backward and forward, in which "the juxtaposition of old and new appears to be extremely intense, when values, ideas, habits, and institutions seem to be torn between two orders . . . when some people lament an old world in decline, while others yearn for a new one waiting to be born."[2]

If there was any sign of incipient change in Germany, it was the nationalist cause. For centuries, the political fragmentation of Germany had ensured the country's weakness internationally and backwardness internally. The idea of a unified nation offered the Germans prospects of greater influence in Europe and freedom from restrictive provincial governments. Nationalism gave the Germans a sense of common origin and a common direction. As Thomas Nipperdey has written, "the nation transcends the world of daily notions to constitute something primal and something still to come . . . it is a dynamic principle, which triggers actions and emotions. In the epoch of political faiths, the nation acquired something like a religious character . . . eternity and a future fulfilled, sacredness, fraternity, sacrifice, and martyrdom."[3] German nationalism first arose as a symptom of German opposition to Napoleonic occupation and flourished during the

Prussian-led war of liberation against France. In abeyance for over a decade after the fall of Napoleon in 1815, when it was regarded as a potentially revolutionary movement, nationalism enjoyed a vigorous revival during the 1830s and 1840s as public perception of the political advantages of unity grew. But the strength of this revival, which articulated ambitions for a single state, was an extension of the idea of a cultural or folk nation,[4] which had been fostered in Germany since the late eighteenth century. German national identity had been formed from a wide range of writings, from Johann Gottfried Herder's anthropological essays, through romantic poetry and prose, to Johann Gottlieb Fichte's popular *Lectures to the Nation*, delivered to enthusiastic audiences of students in French-occupied Berlin in 1807–08. From these multiple sources emerged the image of the Germans as a race distinct from their French, Latin, and Slav neighbors. The Germans considered themselves to be the original folk of Europe and insisted their language was pure as it had not been corrupted by foreign admixture. They claimed to be distinguished by the simplicity of their lives and the honesty of their dealings. Germans saw themselves as a people who prized inwardness, as individuals free to develop their own personality, and "the concept of individuality, unique and self-contained, was transferred from the individual to the national community."[5] German culture was deemed distinct from that of the classically oriented French, which had dominated Europe during the Enlightenment. It had its roots in primeval nature, it prized feeling and instinct more than pure rationality, and German society was considered to have achieved its apogee in the organic communities of the Middle Ages in which communal and individual interests had been at one. The romantics revived the literature of the Middle Ages with the intent of creating a foundation for German national literature in the medieval epic, *Nibelungenlied*, the collection of folk-songs *Des Knaben Wunderhorn* (published 1804–07), and the translations of the songs of the courtly Minnesänger. By the 1830s and 1840s, the cultural ferment earlier in the century had been transformed into demands for national unification.

Wagner's entire work arose from the cultural and political tensions of the Biedermeier period of his youth and early adult life. Like the writers of *Junges Deutschland*, with whom he was acquainted, he found it impossible to acquiesce in a society that tolerated the mediocre and offered no place to an art that was individual or unorthodox. At the same time, he was temperamentally unsuited to the anti-romantic liberalism of *Junges Deutschland* and to the acerbic and often ironic tone of their writings. In his youth Wagner had read widely in early romantic literature and he returned to it in the 1840s when he was establishing himself as a composer of national stature. He was therefore agreeable to the romantic image of Germany as a pastoral land where individuals were free to cultivate their inner life. But he also needed a means of articulating his bitterness and sense of isolation from a world in which he had little part. He found it in the literature of later romanticism, which confronted the fallibility of the ideals of the earlier romantics and the failed ambitions of the age of revolution. His ideas of heroic action as a means of saving humanity from the materialism, fear, and lovelessness that were destroying it arose first from this literature and were later enhanced by his return to an earlier romanticism oriented around nature. But they also derived from his reading, in the 1840s, of medieval epics, whose heroes were embodiments of human strength and courage. While the heroes of his early operas and music-dramas, up to and including *Der fliegende Holländer* and *Tannhäuser*, are based on the prototype of the late romantic hero, by the time he wrote *Lohengrin* he had fully incorporated notions of epic heroism as well. Consequently, to determine the origins of the Wagnerian hero, we should explore first the romantic then the epic hero.

THE ROMANTIC HERO

The romantic hero displayed a multiplicity of characteristics and purposes, but all manifestations of the figure have three qualities in common: a deep reverence for nature, a tendency to respond to the world through feeling rather than rational cogitation, and the insistence that the world can only be understood when viewed from a subjective viewpoint. "The romantic," as Lilian Furst puts it, "invariably apprehends the outer world through the mirror of his ego."[6] These three qualities have, of course, been constant traits in human beings, but they are so persistent in romanticism that they became central to the movement. Wagner not only shared these values, he centered his work around them.

Although some scholars have seen the romantic hero as originating in the "sentimental hero" of eighteenth-century drama and fiction,[7] it was in Rousseau's conception of "*l'homme sauvage*," "savage" or "natural" man, that the romantic identity of humanity with nature was first unambiguously asserted. Rousseau argued that humans had been happiest in primal or near-primal states, existing solely in nature or small communities close to nature, desiring only what they needed, and living content when those needs were met. In nature, the human "heart is at peace and body is healthy,"[8] and peaceful coexistence is assured by the primary emotion of compassion. This serenity is, however, thrown into disorder when humans claim property and engage in competition, which inevitably constrains their freedom. Rousseau sees history as an accumulating process of enslavement and corruption until order can be maintained only through dictatorship. Society is the condition which indicates that humans have abandoned their naturally virtuous state. As long as humans remain within society, their natural goodness is lost, but if they can detach themselves, become wholly individual and nothing social, they can in part recuperate their lost virtue.[9] So they would do best by retreating to pure nature, where, Rousseau claims, "we can call ourselves happy, not with a poor, incomplete and relative happiness, such as we find in the pleasures of life, but with a sufficient, complete and perfect happiness which leaves no emptiness to be filled in the soul."[10] Such happiness arises only when isolated individuals are entirely sufficient to themselves, and they can cultivate the inner world of the mind and imagination until it acquires a reality more complete than that of the objective world. Rousseau also initiated romantic concern with subjective vision, his autobiographical *Confessions* being postulated on the assumption that the unique and individual self was a realm of legitimate enquiry.

The Rousseauian romantic hero is unproblematic so long as he exercises a benign influence over those with whom he lives. Frederick Garber posited a model of romantic heroism in which the "glories of the self" enable the romantic hero "to expand outward in all directions, absorbing and thereby affecting more and more of what is outside oneself."[11] But such a hero, perhaps best realized in Wordsworth's projection of himself in his autobiographical poem, *The Prelude*, is in fact relatively rare. Wagner was familiar at least with one instance of him, the hero of Novalis' novel, *Heinrich von Ofterdingen* (1802), a fictional medieval poet, who feels an intrinsic closeness with nature, which feeds his imagination and forms his creative mind. Heinrich apprehends the world through aesthetic not moral perspectives. He learns that humans were happiest when they lived in a state close to that envisaged by Rousseau, one of "idyllic poverty," in which they possessed few material goods, but whatever they owned was functional and had iconic value. Later, more prosperous ages were characterized by greater monotony and uniformity in their cultures. Heinrich realizes that the function of the poet is to bring harmony to the social world by connecting the present with the past and recalling times when "nature must have been more alive and meaningful than today."[12] The creative act benefits the poet as well as his listeners, as his imagination allows him to develop an inner world that resists the stressful pressures of the outer and substantiates the romantic ideal of solitude as the most desirable human state. Romantic love is the only agency that can penetrate that solitude and intensify the pleasure it offers, and through it the poet becomes aware of a "higher world" and beauty beyond human senses. To recapture this in poetry is the goal of the poet's life. In *Heinrich von Ofterdingen*, Rousseau's "natural man" becomes the romantic artist.

But characters like Heinrich are rare in romantic literature. More common is the romantic hero who feels a "sickness unto death . . . when the direction of energy is reversed and the world impinges on the self,"[13] and his preoccupation with the self and his difference from others becomes so intense that it consumes him. The most celebrated of early romantic heroes, Werther in Goethe's *Die Leiden des jungen Werthers* (*The Sorrows of Young Werther*, 1774), commits suicide as he cannot consummate his love for Lotte. His feelings for her are identical with his worship of nature and idealization of simple country life, but they vitiate his natural goodness. Werther is partly a victim, as marital custom and social convention stand in the way of his desires, but Goethe does not unambiguously endorse his hero, leaving it an open question as to whether his suicide results from self-pity and self-dramatization or is dictated by tragic necessity. The aristocratic hero of Chateaubriand's popular short novel *René* (1802) lives most happily in solitude, where he can nourish "the innermost feelings of his soul."[14] However, his final retreat to the American wilderness is not willingly chosen, but an escape from what he longs for most, an incestuous union with his sister, the most forbidden, yet most desirable relationship, as through it brother and sister can most fully experience oneness with nature. Nature can destroy those it nurtures, and living solely within it can as well express *Weltschmerz* as love of solitude.

During Wagner's youth, the most familiar guise for the romantic hero was that of a wanderer. Traveling in romantic literature rarely indicates progression toward a fixed goal or ideal, but declares isolation from others, so the hero's ceaseless wanderings become a metaphor for the soul unable to find peace either in itself or in settled society. René, whose travels to distant countries and ruins of ancient civilizations are metaphoric for life as a voyage away from childhood, comes to the bitter conclusion: "Happy are they who reach the end of their travels without ever leaving the harbor."[15] The most celebrated of romantic wanderers, who possessed the imagination of readers throughout Restoration Europe, was the hero of Byron's *Childe Harold's Pilgrimage* (1812–18), an infinitely self-conscious figure, burdened by guilt from a past he cannot reveal and nostalgic for a transcendent love, which cannot be fulfilled. He wanders without tangible goal, sardonically observing a world debased by corruption, in which the weak are exploited by the strong and wealthy. He contemplates ruins attesting to the decline of humanity from earlier states of strength and social harmony, but harboring intimations of a slumbering energy that, if awoken, might return abject humanity to its former greatness. While Byron's poem won readers because of its quality as a travelogue, the journey expressed radical alienation of the hero from society.

The romantic hero was not entirely supine. In the earliest phase of romanticism, the German *Sturm und Drang* (Storm and Stress), he could be a titanic rebel. The hero of Goethe's *Götz von Berlichingen* (1773) struggles for the rights of a peasantry oppressed by a cruel feudal system and corrupt church. The most celebrated rebel, Karl Moor in Schiller's first play, *Die Räuber* (*The Robbers*, 1782), champions the poor by defying law and property rights, but the energies that drive him also implicate him in acts of brutality that obliterate his radiance. In the latter days of romanticism, Byron crafted the idiom of social revolt. His poetry caught well the alienation of those who fretted at the restrictions of Biedermeier life and the freedoms he advocated touched that society's most intimate nerves, for the site of his rebellion was the boudoir. Byron's scandalous sexual liaisons allowed his readers to fantasize transgressions they would never attempt in actuality. "Many people," as Prince Pückler-Muskau put it, "make the sign of the cross when they so much as speak of [Byron], and though women's cheeks glow with enthusiasm when they read him, even they are violently hostile in public to their secret darling."[16] Above all, readers were drawn to the figure of the Byronic hero, which comprises most romantic models and conceptions of heroism, including Rousseau's "natural man," rebellious figures from *Sturm und Drang*, the "Gothic Villain" and "Noble Outlaw," ubiquitous in popular melodrama, and anguished, alienated heroic characters, living in outright defiance of God and human law.[17] No other writer responded so effectively to "the social climate of doubt and questioning" as Byron, who fascinated the first half of the nineteenth century with his "rejection of established ties, his cult of the self, his love of adventure, and his ironical distrust of his own emotions and beliefs."[18]

The brooding Byronic hero, be he Childe Harold, one of the piratical heroes of the Oriental tales, or the guilt-wracked Manfred, reminds us how close the romantic hero comes to villainy. One influential interpretation of romanticism, centered on the erotic, even argues that the great figures of unadulterated evil are heroic, purely because they oppose aspects of conventional society and morality.[19] But heroism is not only a life lived to the extremes. One of its essential components is the altruistic impulse to further the interests and well-being of others, so while the romantic hero may be afflicted by that *mal de siècle* aptly described by Furst as "the solipsistic self-absorption that entraps him in a vicious circle,"[20] he is not vicious in himself. Ultimately even the most alienated romantic hero sheds some benign influence on the world from which he is never entirely separated. This is not a sign of moral excellence, but comes from sources of natural energy beyond conventional morality. Nevertheless, society and the moral code that holds it together can only be renewed when they are open to those energies released by the hero.[21] If the hero's obsession with himself blocks the conduit between nature and society, then it must be cleared before his heroic function is fulfilled.

The most immediate influence on Wagner during his youth was E. T. A. Hoffmann, in whose stories the mundane is uncannily mixed with the supernatural and the imaginative world entered by his artist-heroes confounds the senses and transforms the surfaces of life into nightmarish configurations. The realms opened to the artist's imagination do not bring union between humanity and nature, but are separate domains, which require total withdrawal from everyday life. In Hoffmann, passion for absolute aesthetic beauty can destroy life not nourish it. "The Mines at Falun," a story Wagner once considered adapting as an opera, offers dark insights into this theme.[22] The mines, which draw the young sailor Elis from the freedom of life on the ocean to labor deep within the earth, are not a fabulous extension of nature. They lure the artistic imagination not by bewitching flowers, animals, and magical creatures in constant transformation, but by those forms hardened into metal and precious gems. Those who succumb to their fascination are destroyed. Few writers could equal Hoffmann's capacity to portray the enclosed, cozy, urban world of Biedermeier, but even fewer could so effectively undermine the sense of stability that gave Biedermeier such a solid foundation. Hoffmann's artist-heroes dwell both in social routine and in a demonic and unpredictable world of the imagination. Like the solipsistic heroes of Byron, they occupy the outer limits of asocial experience, and are even less likely than Byron's to return to the world.

The self of the romantic hero can as easily become a prison as a site of freedom. This means that romantic writers should be identified with the figures of their imagination only with caution, as they not infrequently viewed them ironically. Even so, romantic heroes still maintain heroic standing, not only because of the extremity of their sufferings, but because they possess the potential to transform the society of which they are, however tangentially, a member. Such change can occur through their arousing a transcendental vision of beauty among and within those who are imprisoned by the obligations, obsessions, and petty desires of everyday life. Their visions are aligned with nature and apprehended through the imagination, that mental facility that fosters individuals and enables them to escape from the social world. This is possibly why the transcendental dimension of a romantic hero's mission is one that may only fully be realized after death.[23]

The degree to which the romantic hero embodied national character traits is difficult to establish. Although romanticism was identified particularly with German culture, it was a continental phenomenon. "Natural man" originated in French literature and the Byronic hero came from England; both served as prototypes for writers from various European countries – de Musset, Vigny, Sand, Lermontov, Pushkin – as well as Germany – Büchner, Lenau, Heine. But romanticism also provided images, imaginative environments, stories, and characters that came to constitute the stock-in-trade of Germans' understanding of themselves. The romantic hero was, however, ill-suited to serve as a mouthpiece for burgeoning German nationalism. That function belonged more to the epic hero.

THE EPIC HERO

Like many wanderers, Wagner only began to feel attached to his native land after he had left it. The years of destitution in Paris intensified his loathing of a commercially oriented world, which offered no support for his work and no chance of public recognition. Returning in 1842 to a Germany that showed signs of accepting him, he found himself open to the romantic aspects of the countryside, especially as he passed the Wartburg, a castle of particular significance in the revival of medieval and national culture. But even in Paris, he had begun to look on Germany "in a wholly new and ideal light,"[24] drafting there a five-act drama on the Hohenstaufen Emperor Friedrich II while dipping into writings on the Wartburg and the legend of Lohengrin.[25] Once he had settled in as Kapellmeister in Dresden, he embarked on a systematic reading of medieval Germanic epics and romances, the main purpose of which was to expand his understanding of the culture of his native land.[26] From this he acquired the subject matter for all his later music-dramas. After completing *Tannhäuser* in the summer of 1845, he chose the epic of Lohengrin as the source for his next drama, wrote a preliminary draft of the plot for *Die Meistersinger*, and encountered, not for the first time, the figure of Parsifal and the theme of the Holy Grail.[27] By this time he had already embarked on the extensive reading that would result in the *Ring*, the first scenario of which he completed in October 1848. Although he did not decide on the composition of *Tristan und Isolde* until

1857, the library he assembled in Dresden contained three editions of the Tristan myth.[28] With the exception of *Meistersinger*, all the music-dramas from *Tannhäuser* on were based on the heroic literature of the German Middle Ages.

But as Wagner's knowledge of heroic German literature grew, his faith in contemporary Germany was waning. He soon realized that the forces of commercial interest, political convenience, and artistic mediocrity were as characteristic of Dresden as they were of Paris. His disaffection reached its peak with his involvement in the brief revolution against the Saxon monarchy in Dresden in May 1849, which led to his eleven-year exile from the German Confederation. There is no ideological consistency in the development of his thoughts in the months leading up to the revolution. In his scant writings at this time, he borrows ideas from Bakunin's anarchism and Marxism, but his political theory is idiosyncratic in the extreme, as evidenced by his speech to the Dresden Vaterlandsverein. In this, like a good socialist, he proposed that the people should be free to live off the fruits of their own labors, but that the monarchy also should be "emancipated" from the aristocracy that presently encumbers it, allowing the king to lead his people forward to a new radical republic.[29] One can only assume that with this highly tendentious statement, Wagner was trying to appease both his revolutionary friends and royal master. But when it came actually to effecting social change, he may have had other solutions in mind. At approximately the same time as the speech, he published an essay, *Die Wibelungen*, "a world-history as told in the saga," recounting the decline that followed when the inheritance of the great kings and tribes of the heroic era was divided into property and became subject to trade. He ended his first draft of the essay by looking back to the heroes of the past, to Friedrich Barbarossa asleep in the Kyffhäuser and to the hero of the first part of the *Nibelungenlied*, Siegfried, and called for them to return "to smite mankind's evil, gnawing worm."[30] Heroic action rather than systematic revolution seemed in his mind to be more efficacious in undoing the ills of society. The epic hero might save a world dying from its own corruption.

Wagner's attraction to the heroic milieu of the medieval Germanic epics and romances and the Scandinavian sagas, which he was also reading by the late 1840s, is not difficult to fathom. He was growing acutely aware that the individual counts for little in a society where all interests were becoming increasingly subordinate to commercial prerogatives. The romantic hero, faced with this predicament, took refuge in isolation, where his contact with society was limited and any influence he had upon others mainly encouraged them to remove themselves from society too. But in the world of the epics and sagas, the hero exercises a more active function.

The epic hero, almost invariably a male figure, is distinguished by the degree to which he corporealizes the most admirable of human traits. His elemental feature is his immense strength and courage and his greatest ambition is to prove himself superior to all other men. The epic hero defines himself not by thought but action and celebrates human strength. He has some connection with the divine. However, while most heroes can trace their origins back to divinity – in Germanic and Scandinavian, as in other mythologies, heroes are often the offspring of a liaison between a god and a human woman – their actions epitomize human autonomy. They do not employ magic. They may kill hundreds of enemies or wild animals single-handedly, deeds that are clearly outside the realm of possibility, but these are nonetheless represented as extensions and celebrations of human strength, not as instances of gods intervening on behalf of humanity. Hence even though heroes recall the power of the divine in their action, they stand also for freedom from it. The hero "redirects us continually to the Sacred as it can be found in vitality and the power of choice, not in the Beyond or its promises."[31] The lives of the heroes may even be, as Jan de Vries argues, "repetitious and imitations of the lives of the gods,"[32] but they are so only to display how the hero is equal to the gods. If the hero has about him an aura of religious power, it surrounds and celebrates the body. In antique communities, the tomb of a hero was considered to bestow a blessing on the community within which it was placed. The hero thereby becomes akin to the saint, "a dead man who has grown far beyond ordinary life . . . a man who raised himself to the level of the gods."[33] The hero connects humanity with the divine, on humanity's terms, not the gods'.

Although Wagner, in the *Ring* especially, would draw on material that described humans in conflict with nature alone, most of his music-dramas, including the *Ring*, are based on sources recording more advanced stages in civilization, in particular the age of chivalry in which the hero dedicates his services to interests or ideals beyond himself. He is unquestioningly devoted to his feudal lord; as a warrior, his exploits guarantee the lord's military power; and, as a devotee of the cult of courtly love, he champions principles of honor that ensure a peaceful domestic life and a stable social order. This dedication to causes outside himself does not lessen his vitality. As a hunter and warrior, he is driven by a superabundance of energy, which

guarantees he never acts out of partisan motives, but simply from the pleasure action gives him. "The hero is never power-mongering, sanctimonious
or self-righteous . . . He confronts situations, he does not embrace causes.
If he takes sides at all, it is for the challenge of the occasion, not for ideological reasons."[34] Hatred is never a motive that drives him. For example,
he recognizes that his enemy in battle is as bound to the cause of his own
lord as he is, so he is in a way his brother and if both die in combat with
each other, ideally they do so in each other's arms. The more powerful this
brotherly enemy the better, for the hero's ultimate goal is to win a glorious
and early death, which will ensure him eternal fame.[35] It will also glorify
the family or lord in whose interests he acts.

But though the epic hero is the champion of social ideals and norms, he is
still isolated. Despite the admiration he arouses, he is an outsider and in this
is similar to the romantic hero. This is clear from the predicament he faces
if he does not meet an early death. Maurice Bowra observes that although
the hero acts in the service of a lord or king, once he actually becomes lord
or king, his heroic strength wanes.[36] Lord Raglan, in an influential analysis of heroism, constructs an abstract for the hero's life from twenty-one
epic heroes from several national cultures. Most heroes are born of royal
parents with some kinship to a god; they are usually spirited away to be
brought up in obscurity, and make their mark on the world by "a victory
over the king and/or giant, dragon or wild beast" and marry a princess as
reward. But the moment the hero becomes king himself, the energy that
has driven him flags, his rule is uneventful, and once he leaves or is driven
from the throne, he dies an obscure death.[37] Kings are capable of heroic
deeds – King Gunther, for example, goes out in a blaze of glory at the end
of *Nibelungenlied* – but once he is king the hero must rein in his overwhelming energies. The epic hero is an epitome of freedom, of primordial
energies. He, no more than the romantic hero, can be subject to social
conditioning. Even though his energy is vital to society, he remains himself
asocial.

THE MESSIANIC HERO

Both epic and romantic heroes are figures of paradox. They work for the
benefit of individual and collective humanity, but only to the degree that
they stand outside social life. They must, because if the heroic impulse is
allowed free rein in society, it destroys all that holds society together; if
society curbs it, then the strength of the hero is sapped and his efficacy

weakened. Also, while epic heroes especially materialize values that society holds as foundational, they serve as constant reminders that the practices of society at any given time are inadequate to the heroic spirit that embodies ultimate value. Heroes reveal how being is a process of constant change. Joseph Campbell's description of the mythological hero as "the champion not of things become but of things becoming" and his statement that "the hero-deed is a continuous shattering of the crystallizations of the moment"[38] apply to both epic and romantic heroes.

But the most celebrated exegete of heroism in the first half of the nineteenth century, Thomas Carlyle, would have nothing to do with the separation of the hero from society. Deeply influenced by German culture – he was its principal exponent in Britain during the 1840s – Carlyle's writings did not fall into Wagner's hands until the 1870s, but once they did, the Scottish polemicist was never far from his thoughts. Wagner cited Carlyle at the head of his introduction to a new edition of "Art and Revolution,"[39] and from Cosima's *Diaries* we learn that he was among the most frequently read contemporary authors at Tribschen and Wahnfried; there is even a suggestion that Wagner valued Carlyle as much as he did Schopenhauer.[40] Carlyle's deep discontent with his age, the 1830s to 1850s, parallels Wagner's. In apocalyptic prose, Carlyle thunders against a world that has lost direction due to its obsession with material wealth, its preoccupation with the trivial details of life, its skepticism, and its slavery to the ballot box. His popular lectures, *On Heroes, Hero-Worship, and the Heroic in History*, delivered in Britain, then translated several times into German, first in 1853, argue that salvation will come not through a restructuring of society, but only through unquestioning trust in great men or heroes. Carlyle's understanding of heroism owes much to romantic thought. "The Great Man," he announces, "is a force of Nature; whatever is truly great springs-up from the *in*articulate depths"[41] and the Hero "is he who lives in the inward sphere of things, in the True, Divine and Eternal, which exists always, unseen to most, under the Temporary, Trivial."[42] The hero will lead humanity to an awareness of whatever is essential in life, he will reveal reality, standing "upon things, not shows of things."[43] The heroic mentality, which will once again give humans access to sources of primal energy, is marked by passionate sincerity and is possessed mainly by geniuses of rugged temperament, as it has no respect for the smooth surfaces of contemporary life and fashion. The artist too has heroic stature. Like Novalis' poet, Carlyle's hero-artist will reveal "the sacred mystery of the universe" to humanity; from his work humans will come to recognize the coherence of all things and the essential truths that lie behind the icons and idols of the modern age. For Carlyle, ideas did not energize society, human presence and action did, a power labeled by Eric Bentley as "Heroic Vitalism."[44]

But while the epic hero was primarily a figure to be called upon in times of war and the very existence of the romantic hero indicated crisis as he had to live outside the pale of conventional society, Carlyle conceives of the hero as having a tangible impact upon everyday life. Modern civilization, according to Carlyle, has obliterated one of the essential virtues of humanity, an innate nobility that leads every individual to search for something beyond their own ease and happiness. Hero-worship, he argues, was one of the most fundamental of human traits, the deepest of all human instincts, an instinct leading to social cohesion: "No nobler feeling than this of admiration for one higher than himself dwells in the breast of man."[45] In contrast to epic and romantic heroes, Carlyle's hero offers sterling moral examples. All exemplary figures selected by Carlyle grew up in obscure circumstances and by their sheer courage, energy, and unswerving devotion to what they see as the absolute truth have risen to exercise sway over thousands or, in the case of prophets and political leaders, millions of people. Carlyle's hero is essentially the Victorian self-made man writ huge. But in his final and most complete manifestation of the hero, the "Hero as King," Carlyle brings him in from the freedom that is his element, to become "the Commander over Men; he to whose will our wills are to be subordinated, and loyally surrender themselves, and find their welfare in doing so. [He] may be reckoned the most important of Great Men."[46] He is, in effect, the hero as messiah, one who will lead society to utopia. Carlyle came to imagine his messianic hero, such as his own mythical "Plugson of Undershot," as one who would harness the material wealth of nineteenth-century society to the great benefit of the masses, a union of heroic charisma and energy with the material forces of society that has no truck with bureaucracy, democracy, elections, and all the impeding paraphernalia of modern society. It is a worrying vision, dismissed by John Lash, who writes that the "fanatical and uncritical endorsement of the 'transcendental admiration of great men' was a terrible nadir for the hero and effectively prepared the atmosphere for the Nazi–Aryan cult of male supremacy."[47]

Lash may be right, with regard to Carlyle, but his comments may not apply to Wagner. For a start, Wagner's admiration for Carlyle was not uncritical. Late in life, he decided that Carlyle, along with Hoffmann, was one of the "great eccentrics,"[48] implying that his ideas, though possibly engaging, could not effect social transformation. Furthermore, Carlyle's vision of a hierarchical society saved and unified by its unquestioning admiration of the messianic hero at its apex is not a model that conforms with either romantic or epic heroism, nor does it conform to the motivational forces that drive the action of Wagner's works. Carlyle came to Wagner's attention late in life, after all the music-dramas had been conceived and most of them had been written and composed. Carlyle's messianic heroism cannot therefore have exercised an active influence upon them. Only *Parsifal* was written entirely after Wagner had read Carlyle.

2

Wagner and the early nineteenth-century theatre

For Wagner, the arts had a heroic purpose. His belief in theatre and music as agencies that allow us to free ourselves from the circumscriptive and corrupting conditions of everyday living was the overriding intellectual preoccupation of his life and the central concern of his major theoretical and critical writings. His vision of theatre's power to transform audiences grew from his impatience with the all-prevailing mediocrity he discovered in the smaller German opera companies where he began his career as a conductor in the 1830s. It was intensified by his stay in Paris, when he came to the conclusion that the most influential theatre in Europe was dominated by routine, egotistical display, shallowness, and indifference to artistic worth. What he saw in Paris was theatre devoted solely to commercial gain; what he came to envision was theatre released from all financial obligation, a place where individuals could achieve freedom by seeing works that led them to understand how they are part of a natural community, a community of the folk. This conception of theatre germinated during his years in Dresden and came to maturity in the great essays written during his first years of exile in Switzerland.

THEATRE AND FREEDOM

Wagner's critique of contemporary opera underwent few modifications in his lifetime. In his earliest essays, we find him complaining that artists have lost touch with their public, that no one knows how to give life to the voice of the folk on stage, and that librettists cannot instill their works with a poetry that provides the dramatic figures with an "organic core of life." Characters on the contemporary opera stage have no passion; they are mere "musical-boxes" for the melodies placed in their mouths by the composer.[1] In his journalistic writings from Paris, he continued to assail theatre as a medium without passion and poetry, though the occasions for complaint in Paris were more various than in Germany. Performances in opera are centered, he claimed, around the "distracting individuality of the performer," who is more concerned to display a polished technique than give "a pure and perfect reproduction of [the] thought of the composer."[2] This leads to a loss of dramatic coherence and stage performance becomes a mere recital in costume. Operatic theatre is dedicated primarily to the production of musical and scenic effects that cause a momentary sensation but have no intrinsic relation to the action. Works in both the musical and spoken theatre are churned out with a numbing regularity. In the theatre as a whole, the prevailing rationale for production is profit. Alexandre Dumas and Daniel Auber, he asserts, are bankers first, artists second, and are bored by their own works. Meanwhile Eugène Scribe, the most prolific of all playwrights and librettists, the "man of the exhaustless rents, the ideal of productive force in weekly numbers," is interested only in money, claiming large sums from the performance of works for whose success he should take little credit.[3] The commercial purpose of art is nowhere more nakedly apparent than at the Opéra, where "each director finds it his duty to treat the art institute confided to him as a machine, a sort of steam-press for minting money as fast as possible."[4] The consequence of this widespread venality is an art that tires rather than rejuvenates, and performances that are little more than "a tangle of tactless vapidities."[5] This is a theatre at the furthest extreme imaginable from those works of art intended to nurture and arouse a sense of identity among the folk.

Wagner's ire against the modern theatre industry reached its climax several years later in the first of his great essays, *Die Kunst und die Revolution* (*Art and Revolution*, 1849), where he denounced it in tones worthy of the most radical revolutionary:

This is Art, as it now fills the entire civilized world! Its true essence is industry; its ethical aim, the gaining of gold; its aesthetic purpose, the entertainment of those whose time hangs heavily on their hands. From the heart of our modern society, from the golden calf of wholesale speculation . . . our art sucks forth its life-juice . . . [and] descends to the depths of the proletariat, enervating, demoralising, and dehumanizing everything on which it sheds its venom.[6]

Wagner's notions of an ideal theatre were developed in reaction to commercialized French theatre and in response to nationalist ideas of Germany as a community in touch with its primeval roots. The model he used was the Festival of Dionysos in ancient Athens, perhaps the only instance in the history of Europe when the theatre occupied a central position in the life of the community. He envisaged a throng of thirty thousand people abandoning their occupations and trades to witness the fate of Prometheus, one of those prodigious heroes who stood as a bridge between humanity and the divine. In his suffering they "see the image of themselves, . . . read the riddle of their own actions, . . . fuse their own being and their own communion with that of their god."[7] This theatre took the audience back to myths in which they sensed a common identity, which gave them strength and confidence and aroused an awareness of their roots in nature. It also celebrated the purely human, for "art," Wagner argued, "is pleasure in itself, in existence, in community," and is a clear testimony that humans have been created "for a happy and self-conscious life on this earth"[8] and not for a world in which they live in slavery. But ever since the Festival of Dionysos, he argued, the theatre has been exploited for antithetical purposes. Successively, the Christian church, absolutist European rulers, and, in Wagner's own time, the forces of commerce have used the theatre to further their own interests, thereby binding the people to their power, rather than leading them toward the freedom they can discover in their identity as a folk. Wagner had too acute an historicist sense to assume that the Festival of Dionysos could literally be recreated in contemporary Germany, but it gave him an understanding as to how theatre could be used to represent human beings as a natural community and so give them a romantic vision of their potential freedom. As it was, in his time, Wagner found theatre to be nothing but the "efflorescence of corruption, of a hollow, soulless and unnatural condition of human affairs and relations."[9]

If the theatre were free to achieve its fullest potential as an institute of the folk, it would assume a role in society not unlike the one in which the hero stands toward the society whose ideals and aspirations he embodies. Like the epic hero, theatre by representing myths should make audiences aware of their common origins as a folk and of a life-view they have in common behind the temporal concerns of social life; like the romantic hero, theatre returns the audience to a sense of their natural being[10] and provides them with glimpses of an ultimate beauty. As Wagner's conception took on tangible form with the founding of the Bayreuth Festival, he came to realize that his theatre, like the hero, cannot fully exist within society, but must be withdrawn from or outside it.

LIMITATIONS OF THE THEATRE

While Wagner inveighed against the contemporary theatre and the operas it staged, he was, like it or not, still a part of it. His early music-dramas did not originate in a vacuum, but stood in the romantic and grand operatic traditions of the early nineteenth century. However, they departed from these traditions by focusing on the primacy of heroic aspiration as a motivating factor in the action. Epic heroism was a concern of neither the musical nor the spoken theatre of Restoration Europe. There were institutional and technical reasons for this. Theatre in post-Napoleonic France was centered on Paris, a city undergoing massive population explosion, rapid commercialization, and a transfer of political and economic power from the aristocracy to the *haute bourgeoisie*. Theatre catered to this new urban society by producing a drama in which the interests of the individual were subsumed by the whole, and, with the exception of some romantic plays of the 1830s and early 1840s, it infrequently challenged social or aesthetic norms. Its stages offered no site for epic heroic action. Neither did those of the German theatre, which, during the 1830s, was uniformly stagnant and mediocre.[11] The great age of theatrical growth in Germany had passed, and the romantic movement that had aspired to transform the theatre failed to do so. The ideology of the Enlightenment that had cultivated theatre as a means of educating a civic population still provided the fundamental rationale for all court and municipal theatres. Even Wagner, in proposing a National Theatre for Saxony early in 1849, was reduced to citing the words of the Habsburg emperor Josef II as a justification for theatre as a public institution: "The theatre should have no other purpose than to work for the ennobling of taste and manners."[12] The "ennobling" theatre of the Enlightenment had achieved much. At its best it had been, according to Schiller, a place where "higher justice" is recognized, "a great school of practical wisdom, a guide for civil life, and a key to the mind in all its sinuosities."[13] Early in the nineteenth century, it had also begun to promote a sense of national identity. But despite substantial patronage from royal and civic authorities, theatre still had to pay attention to box-office receipts,[14] so the demands of the consumer for pure entertainment, which often militated against these high ideals, could never be ignored. Hence the easily accessible dramas of Kotzebue rather than the tragedies of Goethe, Shakespeare, and Schiller dominated the spoken theatre, and as Kotzebue's plays faded from the repertoire in the 1830s, French drama took their place.

If the theatre in France and Germany was no place for the disruptive energy of epic heroes, neither was it congenial to the romantic hero. Theatre in the eighteenth and nineteenth centuries was preeminently a realistic medium, not always in the sense that the sets and production were designed in a way that literally reproduced the appearances of real life, but it was based on the fundamental assumption that whatever one saw on stage, however stylized, should be understood as a reflection of that real world. The stage setting was, therefore, universally regarded as a surrogate for the natural and social environments in which people lived and dramatic action was accepted as phenomenally the same as life outside the theatre. Symbolic value might be invested in certain scenic elements, but no attempt was made systematically to use the scenery and staging as a metaphor for the inner life of the hero. But it was precisely this inner life that was the proper domain of romanticism. In Goethe's *Faust*, perhaps the most characteristic romantic drama, the protagonist attempts to reconcile the two souls of earthly love and heavenly aspiration at conflict within him, and the action, as well as all aspects of staging, setting, and characterization, can be understood as figurative of his inner life as he strives to resolve this. Metaphor rather than plot, and poetic meaning rather than the practical demands of a realistic theatre, determine the composition of the play, which represents the being of the romantic hero. But Goethe, who had much experience of the practical stage, was always ambivalent about whether *Faust* should be produced at all, and when it was, in 1829, the text was radically pruned and the action adapted to the realistic conventions of the time.[15] Although romantic themes abounded in popular melodrama, whose Gothic settings can be read as indicative of the darker impulses that impel both romantic heroes and villains, the morality of popular theatre tended to sustain the sentimental values of the Enlightenment. In brief, any attempt to represent on stage the romantic hero's subjective view of the world lay beyond the conceptual limits of early nineteenth-century theatre.

What Carl Dahlhaus has observed about romantic opera can be said about romantic theatre as a whole. There is no distinctive romantic genre in early nineteenth-century theatre, though romanticism as "an aesthetic idea and a set of features that can be rendered in different and even sharply diverging genres"[16] thrived within it. Elements of romanticism can be found as readily in grand opera as in the *Singspiel*, in the fairy-plays of the Viennese theatre as in the popular comedies and melodramas of Iffland and Kotzebue. They can be identified in medieval, exotic, and rural settings, in rebellious heroes defying the forces of oppression, in the exaltation of romantic love against the predations of coldhearted villainy, in thrilling, spectacular climaxes, and in a ruggedness and disunity that owes more to the irregular plays of Shakespeare than the canons of neo-classical drama. But a thoroughgoing romantic work that externalizes the inner experience of the romantic hero was a rarity and never performed. One of the major outcomes of Wagner's concentration on romantic heroic experience was the creation of such a stage.

There was something distinctly schematic in the way Wagner prepared himself to become a music-dramatist. After he had completed his first opera, *Die Feen* (*The Fairies*), in the idiom of German romantic opera, he wrote to his friend Theodor Appel of his ambition to "write an Italian opera." After this he will turn to Paris, where he will write a French opera. "God knows," he added, "where I'll end up then."[17] This resulted in *Das Liebesverbot* (*The Ban on Love*), written primarily in the style of Italian bel canto, and *Rienzi*, an ambitious exercise in grand opera, which brought Wagner his first success with the Dresden and later the German public. Of these three apprentice-works, *Liebesverbot* has the least to do with heroism as we have so far defined it. Although the romantic hero is central in the operas of Donizetti and Bellini, the theme of Wagner's opera, a free adaptation of Shakespeare's *Measure for Measure*, is the demand for free love, not a central concern of either romantic or epic heroism. But *Feen* and *Rienzi* each offer extended representations of these modes of heroism.

GERMAN ROMANTIC OPERA AND *DIE FEEN*

While Weber's *Der Freischütz* is commonly regarded as the first instance of full-fledged romanticism on the German operatic stage, Spohr's *Faust* (Prague, 1816) and Hoffmann's *Undine* (Berlin, 1816) were important precursors.[18] *Faust*, a standard repertory piece until the middle of the nineteenth century, bears only a fleeting resemblance to Goethe's drama. Spohr's Faust, like Goethe's, is torn by conflicting forces: he wishes to use the powers he has gained from Mephisto for good, but this impulse is invariably subverted by his ungovernable sexual desire. His spiritual and emotional dilemma is represented in his love for two women, one a rural girl of spotless purity, the other a dazzling aristocratic beauty, whom he abducts on her wedding night. This makes for a diverting melodramatic intrigue and an unexpectedly tragic ending when the country girl commits suicide, but it is presented within a moralistic framework which makes the innocent victims of Faust's miscreant behavior the sole objects of our sympathy. Spohr and his librettist harbor some awareness that Faust's inner turmoil is an emotional condition that morality can do nothing to modify, but this is articulated only in the overture, not the action itself. A prefatory note to the libretto states that the overture describes Faust's life and how he is divided between impulses to good and evil.[19] His sensuality has an energy that propels the music forward; the central section of the overture represents his more conscientious self which has a damping effect upon the high spirits, but when sensuality returns, it is heavier and more threatening. But Faust's inner conflict is not sustained in the action itself. He is more a moral cipher than a character driven by irresistible and contradictory impulses, while

Mephisto's apparatus of magic is merely a bag of theatrical effects, not a materialization of the demonic energies driving Faust. While the complex finale is reminiscent of Don Giovanni's descent into hell, one never feels, as one does with Mozart's hero, that the world has lost something with his demise.

Undine occupies more familiar romantic territory. Although Hoffmann was the young Wagner's favorite writer, he would have known *Undine* by reputation only, as the opera disappeared from the repertoire after the sets and costumes of its first production were destroyed in a fire that burnt the Berlin Royal Theatre to the ground. In *Undine*, the supernatural world is both an extension of human imagination and its own plane of being. The supernatural arises from and is made evident through nature, which is not passive or benign in the tradition of Rousseau, but a phenomenon that is active, all-embracing, and impossible for humans to evade. If they attempt to deny it, it turns hostile and destroys them. The settings divulge the difference between humanity and the natural-supernatural. In the water-logged natural world, nature and Eros are one, and the music and spectacle of the spirits prevail; meanwhile, humans live in castles and cities, though the physical security these afford is an illusion because water, the element of the spirit-world, permeates everything and reaches them wherever they are. The natural-supernatural world demands acceptance and unquestion-ing surrender to feeling in an immersion that obliterates human values. Humans, fascinated though unsettled by the erotic allure of nature, com-promise their emotions and become fractured, vulnerable to the ruthless insistence of nature. While human and spiritual worlds are distinguished scenically, musically they are interwoven; off-stage choruses of spirits and the malign goblin Kühleborn join in the ensembles of human voices, both as a sinister background and as voices of the unconscious fears or desires of the human characters. Dramaturgically, Hoffmann's *Undine* provides the foundation for romantic opera though musically it is less significant, as music neither sculpts the action nor penetrates the mind. Although the fascination Undine exercises over her errant husband Huldebrand disturbs and moves, the *Liebestod* he suffers as Undine embraces and drowns him in the midst of his second wedding to Berthalda lacks climactic power.

Hoffmann in *Undine* touched on the core of German romanticism, which resided in the affinity of individuals with an organic world encom-passing human life. Nature and the supernatural, either in conjunction or apart, were the commonest means to realize this asocial realm, and those individuals in contact with them could be nurtured or destroyed by their powers. The dangerous ambivalence of the romantic experience caught the popular imagination in Carl Maria von Weber's *Der Freischütz* (Berlin, 1821), an opera for which Wagner always had the greatest admiration. Its stage world is quintessentially romantic – a seventeenth-century peasant community in the heart of the Bohemian forest, ruled by a feudal prince and ministered by a benign hermit – but the peace and order that should reign in such an idyllic setting are threatened by powers arising from the closeness of humans to nature. The action centers on the huntsman Max, a romantic hero whose disaffection ensues from the curiously bad luck he has recently encountered in his shooting, which puts him in danger of losing the woman he loves, Agatha. He knows no cause for his trouble, is possessed by a fear he cannot understand, and is isolated in the community that once admired him. Max is not the only misfit. Agatha is a melancholic for whom love is a cause more for anxiety than happiness and whose most characteristic statement is an ecstatic aria to the moon as the object of infinite longings. Kaspar, the villain, lives in terror of the numinous powers that inhabit the forest. The strength of *Der Freischütz* lies in Weber's treatment of the forest as a serene romantic landscape, a site of supernatural threat, and a figuration of the disturbed mental conditions of the characters. For example, Samiel the "black huntsman" appears whenever Max expresses his despair, but vanishes as his thoughts turn to Agatha. The forest and its creatures are a living extension of the human characters. As the omen-laden action progresses, a sense of poison grows within the community, which needs to be purged. This is achieved in the midnight encounter of Max, Kaspar, and Samiel in the Wolf's Glen. The Gothic spectacle and tumultuous music made this the most celebrated scene in romantic opera, but, as John Warrack has observed, "it is [its] close association with human personages that elevates the scene above the conventionally picturesque, since it becomes a projection of their own disturbed emotions, their most appalling night fears." Although the scene once terrified audiences and can still be thrilling, even in Wagner's day it aroused condescending smiles. Nevertheless, it is a milestone in romantic theatre, for "not only has nature . . . become part of the action instead of a decoration, but the horrifying is made part of human consciousness."[20] The conditions for representing the romantic heroic experience on stage were at hand. The success of Weber's combination of nature and the supernatural as a metaphor for the human psyche was one that a young opera composer might wisely follow.

But Wagner, despite his enthusiasm and sense of personal connection with Weber, looked more widely for inspiration when he wrote his first completed opera, *Die Feen*. He was perhaps more directly influenced by the romantic operas of Heinrich Marschner, especially *Der Vampyr* (*The*

Vampire, Leipzig, 1828) and *Hans Heiling* (Berlin, 1833), both of which entered the repertoire of the Würzburg theatre where he was employed while writing *Die Feen*. In Marschner, the supernatural is conveyed not through a metaphorically rich natural environment as in Weber, but by an underworld of demonic earth spirits that exists in active hostility to humans.[21] But Wagner's major source was the fantasy comedy *La donna serpente* (*The Serpent Woman*) by Carlo Gozzi, a work from mid-eighteenth-century Venice. His choice was not arbitrary. Gozzi was popular in Germany during the early nineteenth century, especially as a source for operatic material,[22] and the self-conscious interplay of human and fairy worlds in his plays had strongly influenced Hoffmann in the composition of his stories. Gozzi's plays are also akin to the dramas of the popular Viennese theatre, which had produced *Die Zauberflöte*, which Wagner considered, along with *Der Freischütz*, to be the most complete achievement of German popular theatre.[23] Although Wagner's enthusiasm for *Die Feen* stimulated him to complete the score with alacrity, he does not seem to have set much store by it and, after it had been refused production in Leipzig, he abandoned it. This could be because it is one of only two of his works that he based upon a pre-existing drama – *Das Liebesverbot* being the second – and the only drama in his entire oeuvre in which he did not radically alter the plot of his source. He changed the setting, from a desert somewhere near the Caucasus to a vaguely Nordic environment, but did little else.

This trust in his source material was unwise. Gozzi's intricate dramatic situations, which require passages of detailed exposition, do not adapt well to operatic treatment when all words are sung, and in the few places where Wagner did rearrange Gozzi's plot, he confused matters rather than clarified them. But more tellingly, Wagner's theatre was incompatible with Gozzi's. The Italian playwright wrote pantomimes arguing for the retention of traditional culture and social order in face of the rationalism of the Enlightenment. Their characters are the archetypes of *commedia dell'arte*, in which low comedy and high pathos are mingled in a theatrically self-conscious manner. It is a theatre that reveals the separateness of its parts. But as early as *Die Feen*, Wagner's theatrical instincts were leaning toward synthesis rather than separation, toward compatibility between the different parts of a work rather than their divergence. He turns Gozzi's *commedia* figures into realistic courtiers, royal companions, and warriors of the kingdom of Tramond, but still tries to retain something of their Italian origin. This gives rise, among other anomalies, to a charming *buffa* duet, a skilful pastiche of Papageno and Papagena, but it does not suit the romantic idiom of the rest of the opera.

Die Feen introduces some of Wagner's most characteristic themes. Here love is posited as a state of perfect trust and the sacrifice of oneself for another affirmed as a supreme good. In Arindal, Wagner presents his first romantic hero. The original of this figure in Gozzi, Farruscad, is driven solely by sexual desire; in fact with Gozzi, all love is purely physical. But the emotional landscape of *Die Feen* is richer. The story becomes, in effect, an inversion of the myth of Undine, in which the human king Arindal enjoys eight years of wedded bliss with the fairy, Ada, but in fairyland, not among humans. The division between the fairy and human worlds symbolizes a polarity between aesthetic existence, in which love is cultivated solely for pleasure, and the human political world, where love is a means of cementing dynastic power. When Arindal is forced to return to his kingdom, it is apparent that his sojourn among the fairies has unfitted him for the public world. Consumed by self-pity over his loss of Ada and bereft of all joy, he is incapable of expressing delight in his people's pleasure at his return and has lost all will to defend his kingdom in battle. Love, when it comes to participating in the social world, is a crippling not an empowering force: it depletes rather than feeds human energy. But, as the tortuous plot unfolds, the demands of love assume for Arindal a greater reality than the world of political and military action. Ada is eventually restored to him by a series of tests which, while they have their parallels in Gozzi, more immediately suggest the trials of Tamino in *Die Zauberflöte*. However, while Tamino undergoes his trials in the company of Pamina, Arindal fights alone, and while Tamino, with Pamina, advances toward virtue and the total humanity required of the wise ruler, Arindal proves nothing but his love for Ada. It is a love that finds its voice in song, for in the final stage of his trials Arindal, Orpheus-like, sings Ada back to life. Wagner does not explore the properties of song that enable it to rekindle life, but he introduces what would become a recurring pattern in his dramas: song as a means of arousing love in the person who has inspired it. But in his first opera, this conjunction exists separate from the world of practical affairs. The first romantic hero in Wagner emphasizes how unbridgeable the gap is between romantic heroism and the social world.

GRAND OPERA AND *RIENZI*

Wagner's uncompromising denunciation of contemporary theatre in the theoretical works of the late 1840s and early 1850s is deceptive. It is, perhaps, more a stalking-horse behind which he could construct his own ideal of theatre, than a scrupulously accurate reflection of his opinions

of contemporary theatre. The reviews from Paris, which he published in
Europa and the Dresden *Abend-Zeitung* in 1841, show him to be a shrewd
critic, well aware of the entertainment a modern metropolis requires of its
theatre. He had come to Paris to launch his career as a composer of grand
opera, a genre that reached its zenith in the 1830s and 1840s, and his attitude
toward opera in the city was more ambivalent than his diatribes against theatre and his later theoretical works suggest. As a critic he acknowledged the
technical expertise with which the Opéra staged its productions, and found
genuine strengths in the major grand operas. His admiration for Auber's *La
muette de Portici* (*The Mute Girl of Portici*, Paris, 1828) was lifelong: "Here,"
he claimed later, "was a 'Grand' opera, a complete five-act tragedy clad
from head to foot in music: yet without a trace of stiffness, hollow pathos,
high-priestly ceremony and all the classical farrago; warm to burning, enter-
taining to enchantment."[24] He was equally enthusiastic about Halévy's *La
juive* (*The Jewess*, Paris, 1835) with its "strong emotion, incisive and profound, quickening and convulsing the moral world,"[25] and he was even
capable of writing with great warmth about the despised Meyerbeer's *Les
Huguenots* (Paris, 1836): "It is impossible to conceive that anything higher
can be achieved in this line: we feel that the culminating point has been
reached in the most precise sense of the term."[26] At the same time, he
felt much was lacking in grand opera. The action was often smothered by
ostentatiously lavish production and devolved into mere effect: "nothing,"
he complained of Halévy's *La reine de Chypre* (*The Queen of Cyprus*, Paris,
1841), "springs from a higher spiritual idea, no inner swirl has carried the
writer away, no glowing inspiration lifted him from out himself."[27] There
was, despite its exotic locales and historically momentous actions, something prosaic and unheroic about grand opera. For Wagner, this was due
in large part to Scribe, whose unbroken stream of plays and vaudevilles
satisfied the constant demand of the growing city for new repertoire and
who wrote the libretti to most grand operas. Wagner was not unsparing in
his attack on Scribe; he was prepared to grant that he was "the cleverest
and best equipped"[28] of the journeyman writers of comedy in Paris, but he
would concede little more.

Scribe's principal contribution to dramatic history was the "well-made
play," a genre that enjoyed an immense vogue in Europe throughout the
nineteenth century. The well-made play operates on the assumption that
audience attention is most readily held by means of suspense. Well-made
plots are centered on a secret, the answer to which may be known by the
audience from the start: the dramatic action is driven by the confusion
the secret causes, and the audience is held by the playwright's ingenuity

in working out the plot. The play begins with a complex exposition, during which all characters are introduced, after which the action is set in motion. The main body of the play is structured around a series of causally linked crises that mount in intensity until they reach a climax, the *scène-à-faire*, a confrontation that has been anticipated from the start, followed by the denouement. Throughout the unities of time, place, and theme are rigorously observed. The whole is a well-constructed machine, in which all aspects of character are subordinated to the smooth running of the action. Above all, the well-made play operates on the principle that individual endeavor can have no impact upon public affairs and that, as one of Scribe's characters puts it, "great effects are produced by small causes."[29] In Scribe's world, heroic action has no part.

Although most of Scribe's grand opera libretti do not comply rigorously to the demands of the well-made play – only in the dramatically taut *Juive* does an unresolved secret determine the action to the last moment – they do display that genre's attitude toward individuality. Many of the central characters of grand opera are passive creatures; the lovers Raoul and Valentine in *Les Huguenots* are ignorant of the world in which they live, are misled by appearances, and incapable of exercising any influence over the events leading to the St. Bartholomew's Day massacre, to which they fall victim. When characters find themselves thrown into the role of leader, as does Masaniello in *Muette*, they are driven not by the injustices and oppression suffered by the people, but by personal grievances. Masaniello leads an uprising solely because his sister has been seduced by the aristocrat Alphonse. Both he and the people in whose name he is nominally acting are portrayed not as potential revolutionaries but as charming figures of folklore, best characterized by the lilting rhythms of the barcarole. The action reaches a cataclysmic conclusion, but legitimate authority, which is Catholic and royalist, restores order. The romantic triangle upon which the action of *La juive* is built provides the central intrigue and diverts attention from the larger potential issues of religious intolerance and anti-Semitism. Individuals have no effect upon the events in which they are caught up; the social machine will inevitably destroy them. If characters display selflessness, it betrays rather than succors them; Masaniello's henchmen turn upon him because he respects the laws of hospitality, while the Comte de Nevers in *Les Huguenots* is slain because he refuses to participate in the massacre. Grand opera does not believe in individual heroic action.

Wagner provided a just commentary on this phenomenon in his essay *Oper und Drama* (1853), where he describes vividly the atmosphere of revolutionary exaltation conjured up by Scribe and Meyerbeer in *Le prophète*

(Paris, 1849). In this work, Wagner insists, a hero "in the full radiance of his deeds of glory" must arise to unify the folk and through his leadership make them "conscious of the god within them." But instead of a leader, they are given John of Leyden, a "characteristically-costumed tenor" who sings "as charmingly as possible" and is nothing but "a poor devil who out of sheer weakness has taken on the role of trickster" and is characterized primarily by mendacity.[30] Grand opera never produced the disturbingly attractive hero who was the protagonist of some contemporary French romantic dramas, especially those of Victor Hugo, in which good and evil, the divine and the earthly, redeeming love and vile corruption were mixed. Eléazer in *La juive*, who is prepared to allow his (foster) daughter Rachel to be burnt when he could save her, is among the few potential romantic heroes in grand opera, but he is deprived of all freedom of will by a plot that relentlessly pursues him to his death. What Anselm Gerhard observes about Meyerbeer's characters applies to grand opera as a whole; they are "passive figures and never embody a utopian dream reaching beyond the confines of the dramatic action."[31] Grand opera is grand in its external landscapes, but the inner life of its characters is limited.

Not all grand opera denied heroism. In fact, its great decade of the 1830s was framed by two works about popular leaders in which the personality of the individual does have palpable effect on the world around him: Rossini's *Guillaume Tell* (Paris, 1829) and Wagner's *Rienzi* (Dresden, 1842). Rossini's opera, while based on multiple sources, borrows its setting and plot from Schiller's play of the same name. But the view of heroic action it projects is antithetical to that of Schiller, whose Tell is one of the few successfully realized romantic heroes in early nineteenth-century drama. While bravery, selflessness, refusal to tolerate oppression, and deep love for family and country turned Schiller's Tell into a national hero for the Swiss, under the cruel rule of the Habsburgs these very virtues make him unfit to be a public hero. He is a Rousseauian natural man, happiest living in the mountains and hunting chamois, a man who wishes his only ties to the human world were his family, a figure chasing an ever-changing ideal, to whom action on the social plane is inimical. Tell is an intense, reticent character; he is absent from the Rütli scene where the cantons unite against the Austrians; he shoots the apple from his son's head at a moment when attention is deflected elsewhere; his murder of Gessler has no influence on the events that overthrow the Austrians; and the last scene in which he plays a major part suggests he is wracked by remorse. *Wilhelm Tell*, far from being a drama about national heroism, explores the compromises implicit in social action and the need of the hero to be distant from the society he inspires.

In Rossini's opera, by contrast, Tell is the active, national leader, to the fore in inciting revolution among the Swiss and present at the Rütli where he is hailed by the cantons as the inspiration for their struggle. Tell's deeds are pivotal to the drama, and, unlike later heroes of grand opera, he is never swamped by the ever-present chorus; indeed, the ensembles that make up so much of the opera are structured to mark his preeminence. Rossini and his librettists anticipated the passive protagonist in the figure of Arnoldo, who is swept up by events he cannot control, but the viability of an active heroism that can form and guide the social world is constantly present in the figure of Tell.

Although Wagner's antipathy toward French grand opera grew during his stay in Paris, it did not prevent him from completing *Rienzi*, nor from submitting it to the Dresden Court theatre where it had a tumultuously successful premiere. In some regards, grand opera was a natural for Wagner. While the inner lives of its characters were constrained, as each new opera appeared it offered "yet more exciting action, yet larger and more colorful orchestral music, yet wilder mass scenes and stage effects, yet longer acts, yet higher tenor roles, yet deeper bass roles, yet more reckless coloratura, all in five acts."[32] Grand opera had become an art of extremes and Wagner, whose work would always explore the further reaches of human psychology and action, was naturally drawn to it. He wrote *Rienzi* to accord with the expansive ethos of grand opera. "Grand Opera," he would write later, "with all its scenic and musical display, its sensationalism and massive vehemence, loomed large before me; and not merely to copy it, but with reckless extravagance to outbid it in its every detail, became the object of my artistic ambition."[33] But although Wagner modeled *Rienzi* on grand opera, it would be a mistake to see it as a mere imitation of Meyerbeer and his school. *Rienzi* certainly displays all the formal features of grand opera – massive choruses, processions, public prayers, ballets, riots, off-stage battles, and a conflagration to conclude it all – but when it comes to the relationship of characters to the action, it is far in spirit from French grand opera. Indeed, had the score of *Rienzi* ever found its way to the desk of the director of the Paris Opéra, it would never have moved from there to the stage.

By the early 1840s, confrontation of vulnerable individuals with the formative forces of history, usually in the form of inflamed mobs and murderous armies, had become standard in grand opera. In *Rienzi*, however, the individual has a strength that potentially exceeds that of the crowd. Indeed, the Roman leader gives evidence that even though Wagner's reading of Carlyle was some decades in the future, the messianic hero was already present in his imagination. Rienzi exercises a charisma that confounds his enemies and galvanizes his supporters, the common folk of Rome, and he dominates the stage like no hero of grand opera since Rossini's Tell. Like Masaniello, his crusade against the oppressive class arises from injury to his family, the murder of his brother, an act duplicated in the opera when the nobles attempt to abduct his sister. But his cause acquires an ideological intensity surpassing its personal origins. He has a task, articulated in the haunting trumpet call that introduces the overture and heard intermittently throughout the action, to restore a past glory, in this instance the old Roman Republic. He acts as leader of the folk, whose freedom from the ruthless nobles will be regained by a return to older republican ways. Rienzi devotes himself entirely to the society he is called upon to lead and conceives of Rome as nothing less than his bride. He has a utopia constantly before his eyes, which seems constantly on the point of achievement were it not for the unrelenting treachery of the nobles. But while Rienzi sustains Wagner's initial vision of him as a hero with "great thoughts in his head, great feelings in his heart, amid an entourage of coarseness and vulgarity,"[34] he also degenerates. The reasons why are never specified. Rienzi is apparently very vain – at one point he inexplicably appears in outlandish garb – and allows private considerations to affect decisions he should make for the public good, which leads to his eventual downfall as the folk suspect that he is in collusion with the nobles. But, more tellingly, the intellectual basis for his ideology is uncertain at best: what freedom means to him and how it is to be achieved is never made clear. Instead, with wearisome regularity, he exhorts enthusiastic, then hostile crowds, to be free, but never expands upon what that freedom is. As these calls are persistently delivered to militaristic music, they sound as denials of the very spirit of what they claim to be celebrating.

Rienzi's nature has aroused much critical suspicion because Wagner's attitude toward his hero is never clear. For most of the time, the unrelieved furor provides no opportunity for insights into his character, so Wagner may be encouraging us to accept the identity of the man with his rhetoric and politics. Hitler must have taken it this way when he claimed, notoriously, that it was at a performance of *Rienzi* that he first conceived those ideas that would lead to his own rise to power.[35] Adorno has subsequently argued that the "self-praise and pomp" displayed by Rienzi are in fact "features of Wagner's entire output and the emblems of Fascism."[36] He may be right as far as fascism is concerned, but their application to Wagner is doubtful. In *Rienzi*, Wagner's powers of characterization were at their lowest ebb; he glorifies the heroic individual, but provides no account of what is individual in that hero; we can discover nothing of the private man that allows us to judge the authenticity or otherwise of the image he presents to the public. To the degree that totalitarian thought is based on the denial of difference between private and public or the individual and the social, *Rienzi* might display tendencies that foreshadow fascism. The action, uncharacteristically for Wagner, is unclear and poorly constructed. The tortuous political situation – the exile of the papacy from Rome, the election of the Holy Roman emperor, and the precise knowledge Rienzi and the nobles possess of these matters – is only alluded to, never explained. The climactic point where Rienzi's fortunes are suddenly reversed by his excommunication from the Church is unanticipated and so lacks dramatic force. In his later music-dramas, Wagner planned such moments meticulously. Ironically, the lack of clear exposition and structured action means that *Rienzi* makes its impact primarily through the piling up of stage-effects, which was Wagner's most devastating criticism of Meyerbeer.

But *Rienzi* cannot be simply dismissed as a botched grand opera. John Deathridge has come to Wagner's rescue by imaginatively suggesting that our ignorance of the political context draws our attention to the more sinister aspects of Rienzi's character. Consequently his rise to power becomes the sole subject of our attention and we become aware of Rienzi's manipulating spectacle to achieve "mass pathos."[37] He points out that the presence of Baroncelli and Adriano encourages us to question Rienzi so that we understand his venality more clearly. Further factors extend this questioning of Rienzi's political power. Wagner's opera resembles *Guillaume Tell* as the eponymous hero stands at the apex of the work, but is not technically the protagonist. Instead, Arnoldo in *Tell* and Adriano in *Rienzi* execute this function. Both are exemplars of the indecisive hero torn between love and duty to party, country, or family, but while Arnoldo's dilemma generates nothing but displays of indecision, Adriano's requires him to display considerable courage. Adriano may be placed in confusing positions, but he is never ignorant of the forces in conflict, nor does he reveal frailty of character in attempting to resolve them. As the action progresses, he rises in stature until he has a dramatic presence almost equal to Rienzi's. Admittedly, the grounds for his action are not especially compelling because, like the passive hero, he is driven by his love for Rienzi's sister. But Wagner abjures here any representation of the erotic, which could serve as a foil to the impersonal forces of society in grand opera. Nevertheless, while Adriano, like Rienzi, lacks character, in him some hope is offered that the individual might have a tangible influence on the external world.

Adriano also acts alone, a key attribute of the hero. Isolation is also the state in which Rienzi eventually finds himself. For most of the opera, he acts with the support of the masses and only in the final act, when he has been abandoned by them, do we encounter him as a private man and find ourselves drawn to him. The moment is marked by his prayer, the melody of which provides the memorable first theme of the overture, written after the completion of the opera. Its prominence there and the powerful sensation of recall when it is sung suggest that Rienzi's greatness lies not in his leadership, but in his capacity to stand alone. The action for the first time has reached a point of rest, and we are reconciled with Rienzi as a human being, not as a political despot. This lends the conclusion of the opera unexpected power. It is copybook grand opera: the conflagration recalls the eruption of Vesuvius in *Muette* and the onslaught of the nobles on the people the massacre that ends *Huguenots*. But while those operas conclude with the spectacle of humanity as supine victims of their own or nature's violence, in *Rienzi* the final moments focus on a man and his sister who have chosen their deaths. Death, therefore, appears as an assertion of human will, not as inevitable destruction by the mechanical power of an inhumane society. The heroic stature of the individual lies not in the achievement of supreme power, but in defiance of it. It is a conjunction that Hitler, had he been paying attention more to the action of the work than to its rhetoric, might have been forced to acknowledge. It is also indicative of the hero's relationship toward power in many of Wagner's subsequent music-dramas.

3

Early music-drama: the isolated hero

All Wagner's heroes are, to a greater or lesser degree, travelers. They come from outside society and are surrounded with an aura that suggests they possess special knowledge and exercise unusual powers. Those who encounter the heroic stranger find his presence either invigorating, as through him they grow more intensely aware of their own inner life, or disquieting, as he disrupts their settled ways. Whatever wonder or anxiety the hero arouses, few can open themselves to him unconditionally, and he must eventually leave the world because it is incompatible with him. His death is not, however, an unmitigated defeat, because as with the epic hero of myth, it intensifies rather than cancels the potency of his heroic aura. Nevertheless, in Wagner, the glory is rarely the hero's alone, for it is often shared by a woman who dies with and for him, and, by her very act of self-sacrifice, she not only vindicates his heroic stature, but evinces her own mode of heroism, based upon pure altruism. In each case where that altruism prevails, it embodies values superior to those for which the male hero stands.

This progress of the hero through Wagner's music-dramas reflects, in most instances, his own emotional and artistic concerns and crises. Indeed, his work was unique in his time, first because it employed the stage as a means of representing personal crisis, secondly because none of his stage-works was ever written on commission, all were written out of personal need. Wagner admitted as much in his autobiographical essay, "Eine Mitteilung an meine Freunde" ("A Communication to My Friends"), which he began by insisting that he could only be understood as an artist by friends who sympathized with him as a man.[1]

This chapter is devoted to exploring his first three music-dramas, which he considered to be linked by a single preoccupation: the bleak predicament of the exceptional individual in the face of an uncomprehending society. Each of Wagner's heroes is isolated from society and each longs to be reconciled with it. While this isolation arises from the absolute value each hero stands for and believes in, it also indicates a solipsistic condition out of which the hero wishes to escape so that he can grow through life with others. In fact, Wagner shows himself to be increasingly skeptical of the condition of the romantic hero. In *Der fliegende Holländer* (*The Flying Dutchman*), the pathos of the hero's predicament goes largely unchallenged, but in *Tannhäuser* doubts surface about the authenticity of the figure, while in *Lohengrin* Wagner achieves a new objectivity that allows us to look at the predicament of the hero with unwonted irony. But the importance and quality of the early music-dramas resides in their representing more than just the personal predicament of their creator. *Holländer* can as readily be interpreted as a drama about the desolation caused by ruthless commercial practices as about the torments suffered by an isolated man; *Tannhäuser*, the only early music-drama specifically about the artist, questions the workings of art, sexuality, and religious atonement in personal and social life; while *Lohengrin* is not only the tragedy of a man of higher sensitivity, but a reflection of German politics prior to the revolution of 1848.

While *Rienzi* had brought Wagner to the attention of the German public, for some decades after its first performance in 1843, *Holländer* made little impression, because the simplicity of its action and the gloomy figures of the Dutchman and Senta had minimal appeal. Both singers and régisseurs had difficulty in giving life to the music-drama. Faced with public indifference and incomprehension, in his next music dramas, *Tannhäuser* and *Lohengrin*, Wagner used the more familiar dramaturgy of romantic and grand opera, which established him as the preeminent German opera composer of his day, *Lohengrin* even becoming generally acknowledged as a culminating work in the development of German romantic opera.[2] Nevertheless, neither music-drama offers a mere repetition of the characters, themes, and situations of contemporary opera; both, rather, combine these elements to explore the phenomenon of heroic isolation. Because of this, Wagner's early music-dramas are among the first viable theatrical expressions of the subjective apprehending and understanding of the world that had been one of the central concerns of the romantic movement.

THE FLYING DUTCHMAN: VAMPIRE AND WANDERER

Some of Wagner's heroes travel through life with an ostensible purpose, but most are embarked on a journey with an unattainable goal or no goal at all. As they rarely find a place to rest, they are wanderers more than travelers. They meet constantly with rejection, which intensifies the repetitive solipsism of their inner life and prevents them from experiencing growth. The familiar wanderer of late romanticism stands at the center of

Der fliegende Holländer. There are multiple ties between the Dutchman and the figure of the wanderer as he appeared in current literature and in myth, in the guise not only of the legendary Flying Dutchman, but of Odysseus, Ahaseurus, the Wandering Jew, and others.[3] For Wagner's contemporaries, the most familiar paradigm for the late romantic wanderer was, as we have seen, Byron's Childe Harold, whose travels through poetic landscapes evocative of the fall of humanity from an earlier state of glory caught the European imagination like no other romantic metaphor. While the four cantos of the *Pilgrimage* appealed primarily as travelogue to those bound by Biedermeier domesticity,[4] readers found the figure of the Childe highly attractive – aloof, self-consciously wrapped in a cloak of doom, alienated from the world by his inability to love, and happy only when alone in nature. As Liszt observed, the fusion of *Weltschmerz*, loneliness, and heroic stoicism in Wagner's Dutchman recalled most readily the heroes of Byron.[5]

Wandering is a theme that lends itself more to epic than dramatic treatment and Byron was distinctly less successful as a dramatist than as a poet. In dramas like *Manfred*, where the wanderer is the principal figure and the action a quest to discover a haven from his own torments and a hostile world, Byron so ignored the conventions of realistic theatre that his plays could not be performed. When he did conform to the spatial limits of realistic theatre, he adopted a neo-classical structure that led him to abandon temporarily the central theme of his poetry. But Wagner, whose theatrical sense and experience would far outweigh Byron's, articulated the theme of wandering through a compact dramatic structure, which utilized the scenic setting and each component of the action. Thus the theme of wandering is realized on a metaphorical rather than a literal plane, as the stage-world centers on the hero and his predicament. Among the early music-dramas, *Holländer* most completely represents the inner life of the romantic hero.

The success of Wagner in crafting a romantic theatre in *Holländer* can be best measured by comparing it to another romantic opera to which he was indebted, Heinrich Marschner's *Der Vampyr* (*The Vampire*). Wagner had conducted *Der Vampyr* in 1833 and had even added an allegro to one of its arias.[6] Marschner's opera occupied a salient position in late romantic culture as it was among the most successful of those stage-works that fed the craze for vampirism that gripped popular literature and theatre in the 1820s and 1830s. The vogue originated in a short story, published in 1819 by Byron's doctor, John Polidori, in which an English aristocrat, Lord Ruthven, sucks the blood of two innocent women and drives his companion Aubrey, who is the lover of one of the women and the brother of the other, insane. Polidori's work is little more than an effective piece of hack writing, though it created quite a stir at the time. Although Polidori openly admitted authorship, the myth spread that it was by Byron, though Byron loftily disclaimed all interest in vampires and none of his characters ever display vampire-like tendencies. The story spawned a profusion of theatrical offshoots, notably in Paris and London, where adaptations by Charles Nodier and James Planché played to packed houses in 1820. Although these and other dramatic assays on the theme of the vampire that cropped up throughout Europe in the 1820s are minor works at best – most being medleys of melodramatic thrills, folksy comedy, and romantic spectacle interlaced with popular songs – the underlying attraction of the vampire figure is apparent through the trivia. He is the acme of the self-destructive sexual predator who violates all social norms and embodies the most extreme manifestation of romantic disillusionment. The hopes aroused by the French Revolution, which had infused early romanticism with energy and optimism, had been confounded and in its final phase romanticism turned in upon itself, not in the spirit of Faust to explore the inner world, but as withdrawal from a society lacking in color, value, and idealism. Late romanticism expressed despair at the failure of the Revolution.

Marschner's opera is taken directly from Polidori's story; according to the playbill, the action was "nach Byron." While the work is no towering masterpiece, it is no mere curiosity of operatic history either. It held the stage for most of the nineteenth century and was even given sixty performances in one season in London. Although vampirism was traditionally associated with central Europe and Greece, the action is set in Scotland, because of the country's romantic associations and picturesque landscapes. The libretto, by Wilhelm August Wohlbrück, is unusually well constructed. To win an extra year of life, Ruthven must drink the blood of three virgins within twenty-four hours. Aubrey is in love with the third virgin, Malwina, the daughter of the Laird, who is forcing her to marry Ruthven. The plot is a race between Ruthven's lust for blood and Aubrey's desperate attempts to fend off the dreaded moment when Ruthven will marry Malwina. Eventually Aubrey wins and Ruthven, in another scene reminiscent of the finale of *Don Giovanni*, is consigned to the flames of hell.

Marschner's opera is superior to other vampire dramas as it represents sexual desire with unusual immediacy. In earlier stage-versions, the heroines escaped the vampire's fangs and only Ruthven died, but two of the three victims in Marschner succumb. Also, Ruthven is no melodramatic villain, but a complex figure whose horror at the sexual forces driving him lets us view him as a quasi-tragic character eliciting pity and fear. *Der Vampyr* is distinguished by some genuinely funny comedy. Four characters, Gadshill, Scrop, Green, and Blunt, escapees from Shakespeare's London, provide genial speculations on the need to drink throughout the year and sing a hilarious quintet with one of their aggrieved wives. Marschner also made primitive use of the leitmotif and composed finales more continuous than any previously heard on the operatic stage. Much of the work is now dated. Several ensembles are of the type Gilbert and Sullivan would later take delight in parodying and Marschner lacks the melodic gift of Weber, while the dispute between a father and daughter over whom she should marry is wearisomely familiar. Furthermore, the settings are conventional. But, as an expression of romantic disillusion, *Der Vampyr* was among the best the operatic stage of the 1820s offered.

On first sight, Wagner's resort to the milieu of the romantic *Schaueroper* is puzzling. By the early 1840s, the historicist spectacle of grand opera had supplanted romantic opera in the tastes of the German public, so that one contemporary critic even thought *Holländer* predated *Rienzi*.[7] But Wagner adapted the ambience, situations, and forms of romantic opera to craft a drama that transcends its period. In contrast to Marschner and Wohlbrück's relatively simplistic representation of the battle between good and evil, Wagner produced a dramatic action that gives effective theatrical expression to romantic selfhood. Although Hans Pfitzner's description of Marschner as John the Baptist to Wagner's "music-dramatic Christ"[8] might be too extravagant for modern tastes, there is a progression from the older music-dramatist to the younger.

This is first apparent in the difference between the protagonists of the two works. Ruthven and the Dutchman are both facets of a Byronic world, ghostly emanations from the night-side of life, outside the pale of society, yet exercising an eerie influence on it. Both are demonic, both yearn for redemption by women. But while Ruthven is technically a dead man who longs for life, the Dutchman is a live man longing for death. If Ruthven lives, women must die for him; the Dutchman cannot die without the willing participation of his female companion, which he is averse to use. While Ruthven clings abjectly to life, the Dutchman wishes to be either reconciled or done with it.

The Dutchman is a more positive figure, and his inner life has greater reality as it is expressed *through* the medium of the stage, not merely *on* it. His opening solo, "Der Frist ist um" ("The time is up"), discloses the torment caused by the predicament of eternal wandering and the unfulfilled desire for salvation; in his despair he envisages cessation from the misery

of never-ending repetition only being achieved at the day of judgment that
will destroy him and the world. His personal crisis is enunciated through
music associated with the storms of nature, so we connect him imaginatively
with the tempestuous elements and the landscape of the stage becomes the
landscape of his soul. The depressingly sardonic opening of the solo leads to
a wild outburst of anger in which his inner turmoil is enunciated through
the restless sounds of the whistling wind. In contrast, an anguished melody
expresses his longing for salvation, but any hope of redemption is dispelled
by a final brass fanfare which transforms the music of the storm into the
trumpets of doom. As the solo concludes, we understand the Dutchman
as both a tormented human being and an element of the natural world. At
this point, the drama takes place solely within his soul, for which the entire
setting is metaphorical. This connection was clearly in Wagner's mind, as,
when giving instructions for a performance of *Holländer*, he insists upon
"an exact correspondence between what happens on stage and what happens
in the orchestra . . . The ships and the sea," he wrote, "demand from the
régisseur an unusual amount of care . . . the opera's first scene has to bring
the spectator into that *Stimmung* in which it becomes possible to conceive
the mysterious figure of the Flying Dutchman himself."[9]

The unity effected between the Dutchman's inner life and the visual and
sonic aspects of the drama is strengthened by Wagner's use of other popular
dramatic elements. In *Der Vampyr*, as in most operas of the time, the chorus
substantiates the human landscape in which the action occurs and provides
a bed of sound upon which the drama of individuals in conflict is played.
The chorus witnesses the events of the drama and serves as a mediator
between action and audience. But in Wagner the chorus participates in the
drama and embodies the inner conflict of the Dutchman. The chorus is
not entirely alien to the predicament of the Dutchman. We first hear of
the storms of life through the opening chorus of Norwegian sailors, and
in act 2 the spinning chorus of the women suggests that eternal recurrence
is as much part of a humdrum social life as it is of the wanderer's exile.
The chorus, like its Greek forebears, projects the themes of the drama
onto a symbolic plane. In the great choral scene that opens act 3, we see
and hear a conflict, monumental in its proportions, between two opposed
ways of life, between community and isolation, between the domestic and
the unsettled, between Biedermeier and late romanticism. Through the
chorus, Wagner extends the conflict of the Dutchman beyond the realm of
the purely personal and natural.

Marschner in *Der Vampyr* had proved himself a resourceful manipulator
of comedy. His drinkers are genuinely funny, but they only provide comic

relief, they have no bearing on the fate of Ruthven or his victims. In Wagner the comedy of life is integral to the action. Daland is the oppressive father and grasping merchant familiar from two hundred years of comic drama and *opera buffa*, and he gave Wagner the opportunity to satirize the venality of the merchant class. But there is a gracious side to his character. He may be greedy but he is no monster, he is as much a generous host as a rapacious businessman. His and the Dutchman's worlds are not entirely incompatible, as we hear at the end of act I when their voices unite effortlessly in a duet of agreement. As the duet ends and the wind changes, the Norwegian sailors rejoice in the prospect of returning home. The orchestra depicts the ships climbing the crests of waves and plunging into the troughs, so that we feel an exuberance that reflects the Dutchman's change in fortune. When Daland arrives home, the melody in which he asks Senta to welcome the Dutchman is elegant, poised, and generous. This compatibility between the pathos of the Dutchman and the comedy of Daland gives the social world dramatic credibility. Therefore we understand and sympathize with the Dutchman's attraction toward it and come to see the Norwegian village as a reflection of the Dutchman's desires – in this case his hope for salvation – just as the storms of nature reflect his torment.

The unity of Wagner's drama is also apparent in the contrast between the ballads at the center of both *Holländer* and *Der Vampyr*, the idea for Senta's ballad having been occasioned by Emmy's ballad in *Der Vampyr*. In Marschner's unsubtle foreshadowing, Emmy, the second of Ruthven's virginal victims, conjures up a vision of a deathly pale lover who will bring her death. Both Emmy's and Senta's ballads provide moments of stillness at the heart of their operas, both describe the numinous world beyond human senses, both have a mesmeric melody repeated three times, and Wagner's ballad fragmentarily echoes Marschner's in word and tone.[10] But Wagner's ballad is more closely tied to the action. Emmy just repeats a folk-tale told by her mother, unremarkably expressing fear at the vampire with no awareness that the story she tells will soon be hers, so the ballad only creates a creepy atmosphere. But each stanza of Senta's ballad is introduced by the leitmotif of the Dutchman and concludes with that of redemption. As both have been prominent in the score from the start of the overture, the ballad indicates that Senta has foreknowledge of the Dutchman. But most notably, the final stanza concludes with an unanticipated outburst in which her voice soars dramatically upwards, breaking out of repetitions as if she is escaping the monotony of the obsession that has hold of her. In so doing, she demonstrates that she will be the one to save the Dutchman as her ability to cast off the dreary round of routine and introspection might help him escape from his more tormenting solipsistic condition. Hence, she becomes as much a protagonist of the drama as the Dutchman.

Through Senta, the Dutchman will be saved. In act 1 he is the Byronic hero, a gloomy outsider fated to wander the world indefinitely, wracked by personal anguish, and his dark aura is reminiscent of the vampirism that was still considered characteristic of the Byronic hero in the early 1840s. But as the drama unfolds, the Dutchman sheds his Byronic guise, transformed by his growing awareness of Senta's love. Romantic love by its very nature involves the process of transformation. Not only do lovers feel themselves changed by their love for each other, they sense that the world in which they live has changed too. How it has changed is of secondary consideration; what really matters is the phenomenon of transformation, for, through it, the individual, caught in the circle of repetition, has the illusion of release into a freer state of mind and participating once more in the world outside him. Moreover, as mutual compassion is an important element of romantic love, transformation dissolves the isolation in which the two individuals have previously lived to create the illusion of a more companionable world.

Romantic love also makes those sources of energy that lie beyond immediate human consciousness, usually accessible to the hero alone, available to both lovers, and, through the conduit of their love, this energy passes into society, a transference that occurs in the great love duet at the center of the drama. The duet begins with the Dutchman singing of Senta as one who connects him to an intuited past:

> As from the depths of long forgotten times,
> this girl's image speaks to me.[11]

In a long mesmerizing melody, he sings how she reminds him of a time when he did not suffer as he does now, a time out of time, known only through dreams. His attraction to her is not erotic. Far from it, he concludes that his love is caused by her willingness to sacrifice herself, not from physical attraction. As Senta's vocal line intertwines with the Dutchman's, her feeling for him strengthens until compassion becomes her sole motive and the release that it will bring him becomes the central purpose of her life. Both are possessed by the sensation that their feelings come from beyond immediate consciousness. As the duet progresses, the music becomes increasingly animated. In the second section, the Dutchman and Senta answer each other with contrasting melodies that indicate fluctuating emotions – uncertainty, premature hope, and growing confidence – and effect the transition to the triumphant final section. In this they sing exultantly over the jubilant surges of the orchestra, which announces that their union will not drive them into further introspection and isolation, but social integration. At the height of their rapture, Daland enters to an exuberant march, as if the wedding celebrations are already under way and the clamorous trio that follows is no separate number, but the natural conclusion to the duet. The devotion and compassion the Dutchman and Senta feel for each other give new energy to the ceremonies of society.

The Byronic hero exists in spite and in defiance of society, but the Dutchman's feelings for Senta have released him from despair and self-pity. Through compassion and a mutual desire for constancy, his wandering has reached a point of rest and the end of their duet declares that their union will have a cohering and invigorating influence on society. The positive outlook does not contradict the way in which social reality is represented in the drama. Far from condemning the society of the Norwegian sailors and villagers, Wagner represents it with consistent sympathy. In act 1, the sailors have sung only of their longing for home and loved ones, as if they suffer, in modified form, the same pangs as the Dutchman. Once they reach shore, they celebrate their return to good food, wine, and their families with infectious energy. Their gossipy, home-bound women may be marginally less sympathetic, but even then their thoughts are mainly of their men at sea. Although Daland is greedy, his vocal line consistently establishes him as a generous, if slightly overbearing host and in their union, the Dutchman and Senta feel close to him. This issue is pointedly stressed in the duet, when Senta, in a notably confident melody, answers the Dutchman's question as to whether she is against her father's choice of him as her husband:

> Whoever you are, and whatever the fate
> to which cruel destiny has condemned you,
> and whatever I may bring upon myself
> I shall always be obedient to my father.[12]

Here Wagner specifically renounces one of the most familiar themes of domestic drama, conflict between parent and child, to highlight instead the desire of the romantic hero and the woman he loves to reach accommodation with society. So while *Holländer* initially bears the mark of romantic revolt, by the end of act 2 the urge to rebellion has been modified and the desire for reconciliation, even conformity, takes its place.

Wagner's benign representation of the Norwegian sailors and villagers is neither sentimental nor incidental. On the contrary, it explains the tragic ending. The reasons why the Dutchman and Senta cannot be united are never directly stated, but the choral confrontation between the Norwegian

sailors and the Dutchman's crew, which in performances without intermis-
sion follows immediately after the love-duet, dramatizes the incompatibility
of the bourgeois and romantic temperaments and so reflects on the different spheres from which the lovers come. In this scene, for the first and
only time in the drama, the dark forces that are reminiscent of the older
vampire drama appear on stage. As the ghostly crew of the Dutchman is
an amplification of their captain's condition, this scene announces that he
will never be capable of a settled life.

But the drama is not resolved on incompatibility between two characters or even two ways of life, and in this resides its principal weakness. The
only external obstacle to the Dutchman and Senta's union is Erik's love for
Senta. His feelings for her are expressed in eloquent, slightly over-elaborate
melodies, which make it difficult for us to see him as the "stormy, impulsive
and somber" character Wagner claimed him to be,[13] but he does achieve
genuine pathos when he realizes he is losing Senta, and at this point our
sympathy for the bourgeois world from which he comes is strengthened
rather than weakened. While his music has little force in contrast to the
compelling melodies that draw the Dutchman and Senta to each other, it is
easier to understand Erik's love, for although we are moved by the intensity
of the Dutchman and Senta's devotion, the feelings that compose it elude
us. This is partly because we are given little opportunity to understand
them, as they are alone on stage so briefly; they sing their love duet and the
next time we see them together, the Dutchman is heading out to sea. Here
is the flaw in the drama. While the inner life of the Dutchman and Senta
is the drama's action, the only plot device Wagner uses to advance their
relationship is a hackneyed one out of the dramatic tradition from which he
was freeing himself: a misunderstanding caused by someone incompletely
overhearing another's conversation. This grants us no further insight into
their relationship, nor does it provide any opportunity for the characters'
relationship to change and grow. So while we are presented with the spectacle of Senta redeeming the Dutchman by sacrificing herself, we are mainly
in the dark as to the personal motives that drove her to it. While the ending
is effective on the symbolic plane, it is inadequate as the conclusion of a
psychological drama, which *Holländer* substantially is.

This may be why Wagner was so uncertain about the ending of *Holländer*.
The final moments are intensely dramatic as the Dutchman summons up
visions of eternal damnation and, as he tells the world who he is, reminds
it of the dreadful legend he embodies. Senta meanwhile throws herself
from the cliff in an act of pure self-sacrifice. The couple then ascend from
the waves to the skies, a sign that compassion is a more powerful force

than the embittered alienation of the Dutchman. Their transfiguration, the most difficult of all Wagner's endings to stage credibly today, makes obeisance to a dramatic inheritance that incorporates works as disparate as Goethe's *Faust Part II* and popular melodrama, in which the tribulations of the hero and heroine on earth may be rewarded with a beatific union. In the earlier "Dresden" score, the apotheosis is uncertain and the drama concludes abruptly with heavy chords, allowing for only the briefest of spectacles. But in 1860 when Wagner effected revisions to the score at the same time as he was revising the overture for a Paris concert,[14] the ending is extended, concluding with an elaborate statement of the redemption theme followed by a figure high in the strings accompanied by the harp, which glorifies their union. When Wagner wrote *Holländer*, his faith in the powers of redemption by compassion seem to have been uncertain; the first score indicates that he still shared the bitterness and despair of late romanticism. The 1860 score in contrast expresses faith in the capacity of love to ameliorate the human condition. It also gives greater prominence to Senta's self-sacrifice and emphasizes the completion of the symbolic pattern of the drama.

TANNHÄUSER: SEXUAL TRANSGRESSOR AND ARTIST

Tannhäuser is the only early music-drama explicitly about an artist, who is a musician and singer. As an exploration of the sources of the artist's desire to create and the effect of his song on others, the work has historic importance, as it is among the few serious treatments on the operatic stage of a highly characteristic theme of the romantic movement. But Wagner was never at ease with *Tannhäuser* and subjected it to more revisions than any of his other music-dramas. He made the first changes immediately after its premiere in Dresden in October 1845, then he entirely rewrote the part of Venus and much of the opening scene for the ill-fated Paris production of 1861, but although this improved the balance of the conflict, he still was not satisfied that he had resolved the issues of the drama. He introduced further change for productions in Munich (1867) and Vienna (1875)[15] and, at the end of his life, he still felt he owed the world another *Tannhäuser*.[16]

The causes of his concern were multiple. No doubt they arose in part from the transitional nature of the work. *Tannhäuser* was the first music-drama in which he did not indicate separate numbers in the score, but he still had a long way to go before finding a suitable musical idiom for continuous dramatic action. But there are problems too with the protagonist.

He is, as Wagner observed, a profoundly divided man, constantly swayed by the demands of the moment. "Tannhäuser is nowhere and never 'a little' anything, but each thing fully and entirely."[17] The huge shifts within his character threaten the coherence of the action as they occur with an abruptness that makes it difficult to account for them dramatically and to understand the crises they indicate.[18] Furthermore, *Tannhäuser* lacks thematic unity, because while the sources of artistic creativity and the power of art itself are major concerns in the first two acts, in act 3 Wagner seems to have lost interest in them and adopted an attitude toward his protagonist that is unaccountably at odds with how he has treated him earlier in the work.

The association of creativity with sexual desire was a terrain that had been well mapped by romantic poets, but had infrequently been taken up on stage. Wagner had already addressed the issue in the unperformed *Feen*, but the subtle relationship between creativity and erotic love could not be adequately treated within the conventions of Italian lyric opera or French grand opera, which had provided the models for his next operas, *Das Liebesverbot* and *Rienzi*. But the use in *Holländer* of stage setting and elements of performance as metaphors for the inner life of his characters suggested a theatrical medium in which the theme could be effectively treated.

Wagner's enthusiasm for the Tannhäuser legend was stimulated by the view he and Minna caught of the Wartburg on their return to Germany, by his initial readings in medieval Germanic literature, and romantic versions of those tales. The theme of sexual transgression had traditionally been associated with the medieval minstrel Tannhäuser, who had indulged himself in the arms of Venus and then sought forgiveness from the Pope, who told him that the possibility of his receiving penance was as remote as the chance that the staff then in the Pope's hand would sprout leaves. Soon after this announcement the miracle occurred, but Tannhäuser had already returned to Venus. Wagner knew the original medieval ballad, Tieck's darkly romantic tale, "Der getreue Eckart und der Tannenhäuser" ("Faithful Eckart and Tannhäuser," 1799), and a satirical poem on the subject by Heine. He was also familiar with a story by Hoffmann on the Battle of Minstrels, which occurred during the thirteenth-century reign of Landgrave Hermann in the Wartburg. As the historical Tannhäuser had died some fifty years prior to this, Wagner exercised artistic license in associating him with the Wartburg.

While the contingency of creativity and sexual desire had been rarely treated in the theatre prior to Wagner, the situation of the romantic hero caught between heaven and hell had exercised a potent appeal upon audiences. Wagner could once again exploit the well-tried ambience of operatic supernaturalism to expound his theme. But although the interrelation of the human and supernatural was the distinctive territory of German romantic opera, the work that had most effectively caught the imagination of European audiences had originated in Paris, Meyerbeer's *Robert le diable* (*Robert the Devil*) to a libretto by Scribe. Premiered in 1831, it was among the most frequently performed of all operas until well after the middle of the century. Wagner came to know it in 1833, when he was in Würzburg and a decade later, when he was trying to distance himself from Meyerbeer, whose musical eclecticism he despised, he still had not forgotten its piquant mixture of supernatural fantasy and historicist realism. The egress of supernatural powers into the Gothic settings had proved to be a combination few audiences could resist, and its influence can be felt in the ambience of *Tannhäuser*. But while the milieu of *Robert* was employed as a setting for an uncomplicated tale of good and evil, Wagner confounded conventional values and used a similar setting to explore the emotional dynamic of the romantic hero and to dramatize the crisis of an artist in conflict with himself and society.

The title *Robert le diable* is something of a misnomer for the protagonist of Meyerbeer's opera, Robert, a Norman duke, is no devil but a Faustian figure over whom the forces of good and evil do battle. Evil is embodied by Robert's sinister companion Bertram, an emissary of the devil and, as it turns out, Robert's father, while the good resides in the Sicilian princess, Isabelle, who loves and is loved by Robert. The moral compass of the opera is the same as that of popular melodrama. Robert, who is visiting Sicily to woo Isabelle, is kept from achieving his goal by the intervention of Bertram, who has been charged by the forces of darkness to lure Robert into hell. Bertram goads Robert into gambling away his money and armor, then tricks him into missing a tournament where he would have competed for Isabelle's hand. He persuades Robert to pick a magical branch from the tomb of St. Rosalie so that he may gain access to Isabelle, a ruse that succeeds, but, through a series of complicated circumstances, leads to Robert's arrest. Salvation comes not through any decisive act by Robert, who is the nonpareil of vacillation to the end, but through Bertram being swallowed by the fires of hell, as he was about to secure his son's soul for the devil. Robert acquires Isabelle's hand, but through chance rather than by will. Good wins out over evil, but human choice has little to do with it.

It needs some imagination to understand why *Robert le diable* was so popular in its time. Although Scribe was the acknowledged master of tightly wrought plots, the libretto, by his own standards, is poorly structured and does not follow the laws of causality. Each act ends with Robert facing disaster, but when the next opens he is free because some agency, either the generosity of Isabelle or the guile of Bertram, has extricated him from the dangerous situation. The effect is to relieve Robert of responsibility for his actions and deprive the plot of consequentiality. The one suspense device Scribe does use, a letter to Robert from his dying mother warning him against Bertram, carries no dramatic weight, while the lack of foreshadowing makes for a strangely aimless plot. Meyerbeer's score is pleasant but hardly compelling. Never a master of atmospheric music, he could not conjure up sinister atmospheres like the German romantics. Highlights include the vigorous and elegant ballet music, Isabelle's aria "Robert, toi que j'aime," one of the great hits of nineteenth-century opera with its poignant refrain in which she begs her lover for mercy, and the final trio in which Robert is torn between the voices of heaven and hell, effectively his mother and father. The opera's appeal depended mainly on the theatrical flair with which the forces of darkness intertwined with humanity in an alluringly Gothic setting. Above all, it was celebrated for the notorious ballet in which dead nuns rise from their graves to reenact the carnal sins they had committed prior to being consigned to the convent. This mixture of the spiritual and profane, which in its day bordered upon the salacious, made *Robert le diable* the *succès de scandale* of its time.

The stage world of *Tannhäuser* owes much to *Robert le diable*. Wagner's music-drama has a medieval setting in which the forces of good and evil are in conflict. They display themselves in *Tannhäuser* as they do in *Robert*: evil comes about through illicit sexual indulgence and good through the compassion and faith of the woman loved by the hero. Both works place this woman in a position where rivals are in competition for her hand, and in this way the conflicting values of the action are expressed. But Wagner also creates a protagonist in conflict with himself, and it is here that he and Meyerbeer part company.

Wagner indicated the point of departure in an essay on how to perform *Tannhäuser*. Here he wrote about the fundamental divisions in Tannhäuser's character and urged the tenor not to represent the minstrel as if he were Meyerbeer's hero; if he does, he will turn him into "an undecided, vacillating, weak, and unmanly character," similar to Robert.[19] Instead Wagner instructed the singer to embody with wholeness and conviction the contradictory aspects of Tannhäuser's character. While the distress that Robert undergoes must, by the nature of his opera, be only lightly sketched, in *Tannhäuser* the mental conflict of the protagonist *is* the action. If the tenor cannot fully realize the divisions in the character, the opera becomes incomprehensible. Indeed, this is precisely what it was to its initial audiences in Dresden, because Tichatschek, who had been a perfect Rienzi, displayed no understanding of the dichotomies in Tannhäuser's character. As in *Holländer*, Wagner employs the scenic environment and dramatic action to represent the hero at war with himself and the world around him. The action can be read as moving from the recesses of Tannhäuser's mind at the beginning of the drama into the social world that occupies the stage for the majority of act 2, to retreat into his inner world at the end. In this progression, it becomes apparent that Tannhäuser is torn between two ideals of love, the sexually promiscuous and the chaste, and between two realms of experience: sensual indulgence, symbolized in the Venusberg, and the moralistic world of social convention, materialized in the Wartburg. Because Tannhäuser is unable to resolve his inner conflicts and his relationship with the social world, his life ends in apparent devastation. While he begins the drama as a Byronic hero, by the end he suffers a defeat that Byron would never have countenanced.

The changes that Wagner incorporated between the Dresden and Paris versions of the music-drama suggest that only after the first performance of *Tannhäuser* in Dresden did he become fully aware of the implications of his dramaturgy. Tannhäuser's sojourn with Venus in her exotic grotto is a fairly decorous affair in the Dresden version, but in the extended ballet written for Paris, the post-*Tristan* chromaticism offers erotic music as intoxicating as any he would write. His heightening of the dramatic profile of Venus and the voluptuous splendor of the domain over which she rules, depicted on the stage of the Opéra in a spectacle worthy of Makart, makes the Venusberg into a force equal in power to the Wartburg. Consequently, Tannhäuser's dual personality that will not allow him to rest in the enjoyment of the senses emerges more clearly. The dichotomy set up in *Die Feen* between sexual pleasure and the world of human affairs is taken up again. Sexual congress occurs in an underworld, away from the activities of everyday life. But after the wild ballet, Wagner centers on only one aspect of the Venusberg's unfettered sexuality, its capacity to smother the human desire for freedom. Tannhäuser has lost all sense of time and the boundaries of his identity. Like the existential wastes in which the Dutchman has roamed, the Venusberg is a solipsistic hell of eternal repetition, where no growth is possible. Despite its ravishing surfaces, it is stale, something strikingly evoked in the repeated stanzas of Tannhäuser's hymn of praise to Venus. His art has been congealed into a form that does not change. His hymn increases in urgency at each repetition, rising a semitone from the previous stanza, which underscores his plea to be released from a sensual indulgence that prevents him from being the artist he wishes to be.

The sudden transformation of the Venusberg into the countryside around the Wartburg implies a curious and, with regard to Wagner's entire work, important step back into an earlier phase of romanticism. Wagner's contemporaries, familiar with the morality of grand opera, would have agreed with Baudelaire that "*Tannhäuser* represents the struggle between two principles that have chosen the human heart for their chief battlefield; in other words the struggle between flesh and spirit, Heaven and Hell, Satan and God."[20] But subsequent critical literature has conferred a greater wealth of symbolic meaning upon the Venusberg, so that it stands now for more than sexual indulgence. It recalls Hoffmann's mysterious mines at Falun and the depths the imagination must plumb to bring to light its most exalted visions,[21] it embodies the "paradis artificiel" of those Parisian drawing rooms to which Wagner was so rarely granted access,[22] it glorifies the senses and harks back to the liberal ideas of *Junges Deutschland*, and in its orgy we can find vestiges of Goethe's classical Walpurgisnacht, reminiscent of a long tradition of Dionysiac revel.[23] But through Tannhäuser's suffocation and satiation the Venusberg also articulates the *Weltschmerz* of late romanticism. Although the reasons for his initial flight to the Venusberg are never specified, hints dropped in act 2 suggest that he was trying to escape the conventions of the court. Now rebellion has lost its attraction and Tannhäuser is yearning for a new freedom. He discovers it in the idyllic landscape outside the Wartburg where he finds himself after his expulsion from the Venusberg. This freedom for which he had been yearning is potent, a German nationalist idyll that combines rural peace and medieval community, which also recalls the early phases of romanticism, deeply influenced by the naturalistic vision of Rousseau. This is a moment when the dualistic conflict within Tannhäuser is maintained in perfect balance, in the juxtaposition of pagan and Christian sounds. The pagan is heard in the pipe-playing of the shepherd-boy and his invocation of Frau Holda, the Teutonic parallel to Venus; in this landscape sex is not repressed, but is a simple function of nature. The Christian is heard in the song of the elder pilgrims who sing of the need to expiate their guilt by repentance. But pagan and Christian are not in conflict. Atonement does not inhibit sexuality, as is clear from the harmony of the pilgrims' chorus with the shepherd-boy's song to Holda. Rather they sound as if they comprehend each other. It is a moment of great peace, where conflict has been stilled, though not obliterated.

In *Robert le diable* the conflict between the sensual and the religious only attracts attention in the visual synthesis of the nuns' ballet; otherwise the polarization is unremarkable and goes unquestioned. But in *Tannhäuser*, the hero needs to acknowledge his sexual appetite and to live in a manner that satisfies his desire for purity and pious devotion, a polarization that will never be reconciled if seen in a moralistic perspective. In Meyerbeer, the boundaries between good and evil are clear, and the pietistic ending leaves us in no doubt that we are to rejoice in Robert's salvation from the flames of hell. In contrast, Wagner at first sees little relevance in concepts of good and evil, and morality, when it does appear in the form of the court of the Wartburg, confuses rather than resolves the dilemma of the hero.

Tannhäuser's all-too-brief moment of equilibrium is disturbed by the arrival of the Landgrave and his hunting-companions, though initially the society of the Wartburg appears benign rather than hostile, and the hunting horns of the Landgrave and his courtiers even sound as if they are complicit in the idyllic state in which Tannhäuser finds himself. When the hunters enter and see him in prayer, their arrival is even welcome, and their ensemble of greeting sounds like an amplified and ennobled form of Daland's greeting to the Dutchman. Their swell of enthusiasm at Tannhäuser's return, which concludes act 1, rises to genuine exaltation at the start of act 2, when Elisabeth welcomes him back into the hall of song where he had once ruled. The hall potentially serves as a metaphor for Tannhäuser's inner self, for it is here that he will sing of the ideal balance of pagan and Christian, the sexual and the chaste. His meeting with Elisabeth confirms that this is the direction in which his life is moving. Elisabeth is based on the legendary St. Elisabeth, associated with the Landgrave and the Wartburg, whose reputation invoked ideas of purity, compassion, and self-denial.[24] But when she first enters, in one of Wagner's most exhilarating solos, "Dich, teure Halle, grüß ich wieder" ("Once more I greet you, dear hall"), she is a young woman anticipating the fulfillment of a distinctly sensual promise. Her life in the Landgrave's court has been torpid and dull since Tannhäuser left, but the prospect of his return fills her with vitality, and when he enters it is eminently apparent that their attraction to each other is physical. As Elisabeth recalls their earlier time together, she sings of her love being kindled by his singing, which aroused in her a "strange new life":

> But what a strange new world of feeling
> awoke in me when I heard you!
> At times it seemed I'd die of sorrow,
> and then my heart would burst with joy,
> with feelings I had not experienced
> and longings I had never known![25]

Tannhäuser's song had been delightful seduction and, as the wan phrases that conclude her solo betray, she felt his departure as sexual betrayal. Creative art, here specifically song, is a function in the emotional interplay of human beings. It is a liberating force, as it brings to consciousness emotions that are otherwise inaccessible and sexual desires that have been slumbering. It is an agent of nature, a biological power, and if it were to be fulfilled in the love of Elisabeth and Tannhäuser, the state of harmony Tannhäuser had reached at the end of act 1 might be perpetuated. But it is not. From this point Elisabeth and Tannhäuser's fortunes go rapidly downhill.

This is because the life-giving properties of art are not universally prized. Much of the ceremonial in act 2 explores the social rather than the personal function of art. That the Landgrave's court is a highly cultivated institution is at once apparent from the formal entry of the guests. The excitement of the trumpet fanfares, the measured confidence of the sweeping melody of the march, and the climax of the chorus' festive greeting to the Landgrave, fills the stage with a tangible sense of nobility and community.[26] That this can be attributed to the power of music and poetry is apparent in the Landgrave's subsequent welcome of the minstrels to the competition. He expatiates an Enlightenment view of the arts as a means of cultivating society and bringing peace into an otherwise troubled world.

> The art of song has played its part in battle.
> For virtue and our ancient customs,
> for chastity and true religion
> you fought beside us with your art,
> and won a victory no less great.[27]

But the pedestrian rhythms and stately melody of his solo lack life after the fireworks of Elisabeth's aria and her moving welcome of Tannhäuser. This suggests that art as an incitement to virtue and faith is a compelling priority for neither Tannhäuser nor Elisabeth, whose emotions are entirely different from those imagined by the Landgrave.

The song contest, on the subject of love, reconstructs in reverse the states of mind that Tannhäuser experienced in act 1. Wolfram advocates love, and the art that expresses it, as a mode of piety that goes beyond adoration to self-sacrifice, a condition related in spirit to the idyll in which Tannhäuser found himself, though without the pagan element of sensual love. It is this absence that infuriates Tannhäuser, precipitates him from the equilibrium he had achieved, and drives him to deliver a paean to physical love, ending with his hymn to Venus, which in the hall of the minstrels sounds even staler than when he first sang it in the Venusberg. He has reverted from the freedom offered by the fusion of Holda and the pilgrims back to the stifling repetition of the Venusberg. But in the confrontation that follows between Tannhäuser and the court, the nexus between creative art and sexual desire is forgotten. Instead, the quarrel devolves upon the horror of the Landgrave and the court over Tannhäuser's damning of his soul by sexual indulgence.

At this point, *Tannhäuser* begins to lose clarity. A moralistic response is to be expected from the court, as, like the Biedermeier society for which it stands, it is smug and tightlipped about sex, and Wagner still displays some loyalty to the liberal ideas of *Junges Deutschland* by casting, through Tannhäuser, a critical light upon it. But there are two inconsistencies. First the excessive harshness, even hysteria, of the court's reaction to Tannhäuser's apostasy is inconsistent with the urbanity they had previously displayed and the benign philosophy articulated in the Landgrave's speech on art. Secondly, their response triggers an unaccountable change in Tannhäuser, who swings from swaggering libertine to groveling penitent, an oscillation for which it is difficult to find psychological motivation. It tells us that Tannhäuser's instant remorse over singing about the Venusberg in Elisabeth's presence shows he cannot reconcile his sexual desire with his longing for piety; therefore the equilibrium he had achieved at the end of act 1 was impossible for him to sustain. But his collapse bears no relation to his previous character. Until now, his character has developed from inner necessity, so a response to social disapproval that makes him into an abject creature of the society he had previously defied is unaccountable. His subsequent surrender to an asceticism that includes no admixture of desire can be read as an instance of the extremes over which his character ranges, but it is nevertheless arbitrary. It therefore appears to arise not from inner necessity, but from the desire of the Wartburg to force individuals into the mould of their own prescriptive morality. In making Tannhäuser so easily and completely abase himself to this, Wagner seems himself to be making a moral judgment on Tannhäuser's previous life and, as there is not a touch of irony in Tannhäuser's assumption of religious asceticism, he seems to be aligning himself with the Wartburg, not with his hero.

Wagner's dissatisfaction with *Tannhäuser* may have arisen from his awareness that, by sending his hero to Rome and imposing on him an excruciatingly painful yet fruitless penance, he was sharing in the prejudices of the coercive powers of social convention. In act 3, the discourse on art and sexuality has been entirely abandoned. Instead, we return to the landscape of act 1, the country around the Wartburg, but in autumn now not spring, a time of decay not growth, of divided and conflicting impulses not unifying and complementary ones. Sexuality is obliterated and piety a grueling torment. Tannhäuser, once a vigorous and defiant figure, reveals himself in the narrative of his pilgrimage to Rome to be passive, helplessly torn between the desire for oneness with God and frenetically grasping at whatever scrap of security the Venusberg can offer him. In the abasement of his despair, he no longer determines his own life.

At this point, as in *Holländer*, the agency for action passes from the nominal hero to the compassionate woman. Wagner's preparation of Elisabeth for this role has been more deliberate than it was for Senta. For much of act 2, Elisabeth embodies the tension between desire and the urge to purity and religious devotion, a personification of the values of the romantic landscape of act 1. While she is forward in admitting her feelings to Tannhäuser, she is also the icon of Biedermeier modesty when she rushes to bury her face in the Landgrave's breast. But at the height of the song contest, she abandons bashfulness; we are told in the stage directions that as she reacts to Tannhäuser's song she is "torn between delight and alarmed consternation." Then in the fracas following the quarrel of the minstrels, she takes a commanding role. The phrase in which she begs the courtiers to have mercy on Tannhäuser, "Ich fleh für ihn" ("I beg for him"), leads to the climactic ensemble of the act, rising to a level of pathos unequaled elsewhere in *Tannhäuser*. She emerges as a voice for reconciliation in a divided society. But in doing so, she, like Tannhäuser, must renounce the sexual feelings that gave her life meaning and vitality and, by insisting that he humble himself in atonement, endorses the rigid and unconvincing prudery of the Wartburg, which denies the principle of opposites that has driven Tannhäuser.

Tannhäuser is saved at the end by Elisabeth's compassion, which is expressed through single-minded devotion to an ideal beyond human life, a devotion that denies duality and leads only to death. The juxtaposition of Elisabeth's funeral and the announcement of the miracle of the Pope's staff bursting into leaf indicates that Tannhäuser has been saved through her sacrifice, but salvation has come about through an annulment not a resolution of the conflicts within Tannhäuser. He is not saved because he has finally achieved union of the pagan and Christian, the sensual and the ideal, that had been symbolized in the romantic setting at the end of act 1, but because Elisabeth's sacrifice has made him acceptable to the Christian church. The conclusion of *Tannhäuser* betrays the drama's initial promise and Wagner is standing, however unwillingly, by the side of Meyerbeer, Scribe, and *Robert le diable*. It is not surprising he felt he owed the world another *Tannhäuser*.

LOHENGRIN: A GLIMPSE OF UTOPIA

The success of *Lohengrin* was crucial in Wagner's career, as through its widespread popularity in German opera houses during the 1850s he acquired a national reputation. While it is generally recognized as the crowning work of German romantic opera, it also represents Wagner's most finished exercise in the antithetical mode of historical realism associated with French grand opera.[28] There is little trace of the romantic dramaturgy of the earlier music-dramas. The setting is concrete and the period specific, Antwerp during the tenth century, and, even though the figure of Lohengrin has as much of the supernatural about him as the Dutchman, with the exception of the swan, Wagner makes no attempt to use either setting or staging to reflect this. Nor is the stage ever metaphorical for his inner life. *Lohengrin*, therefore, has all the appearance of grand opera, but unlike grand opera, where individuals are overwhelmed by the forces of history, here one individual prevails, and his heroic stature becomes the central issue of the drama.

Lohengrin's heroism is generically ambiguous. The fate of Tannhäuser suggests that Wagner had serious doubts about the viability of the romantic hero, and in Lohengrin he puts forward a seemingly more positive figure, held up as an ideal for the German people and an icon for German unity. This is not to say that Lohengrin does not share characteristics with the Dutchman and Tannhäuser; in fact, as we shall see, there is much in common between his predicament and theirs. But he has less in common with the romantic than the epic hero. Indeed, he is constantly on the verge of becoming the messianic hero glorified by Thomas Carlyle. Although at the time of composition, Carlyle can only have been known to Wagner, if at all, by reputation, *Lohengrin* intimates, as *Rienzi* before it, that his thought was tending toward the idea of the hero as the messiah of a divided society.

If there is one quality that has been universally attributed to *Lohengrin*, it is the compactness of its action. "Everything," as Liszt put it, "is combined, interlinked and intensified; everything has the tightest relationship to the theme and nothing can be separated from it."[29] As a drama, *Lohengrin* is Wagner's most accomplished exercise in the well-made play. There must have been a satisfying irony for him in this, because Wagner had applied to Scribe for help in having *Das Liebesverbot* accepted in Paris, but had been coldly rejected. *Lohengrin*, which is "well-made" to a degree that none of Scribe's grand opera libretti even approached, must surely be seen as his revenge upon the inhospitable French theatre. Its action is highly suspenseful and the entire plot centers on a secret, that of the hero's name. While the audience, by virtue of the music-drama's title, knows this, it does not detract from their involvement in the action. The first part of act 1 contains a double exposition, first an explanation of the political situation that has brought Henry the Fowler's troops to Brabant, then the narrative of the complex events surrounding Elsa and the disappearance of Gottfried. As the exposition unfolds, characters are introduced in order of rising importance, from the Herald through to Lohengrin, whose arrival in a swan-drawn boat provides the inciting moment. The first crisis is marked by the duel that ends act 1; act 2 is constructed on a series of rising crises that do not reach resolution until the carefully sculpted climax in act 3 scene 1, the *scène-à-faire* of the wedding night when, simultaneously, Elsa asks her bridegroom his name and he kills Telramund as he rushes in to slay him. In the denouement, Lohengrin reveals his name and parentage, and restores Gottfried to his rightful heritage. The unities are strictly observed, the whole action taking place in Antwerp over forty-eight hours.

The well-made play is an unromantic genre. It operates on a rigid concept of causality and rests on the assumption that the social world is a gigantic mechanism in which human action is determined solely by properties of the machine. As personality rarely if ever exercises an influence over action, the well-made play is not an appropriate form in which to enlarge upon the workings of heroism. It also shares with melodrama an uncomplicated moral vision in which good resides in compliance to social norms, while whatever is individual or aberrant lies outside the pale of the legitimate. Wagner's employment of the well-made play for an avowedly "romantic" purpose is therefore anomalous. Nevertheless, his recourse to dramatic configurations from German romantic opera, his adaptation of the "well-made" dramatic mechanism to explore the inner life of his characters, and his elevation of the hero to a height of eminence resulted in a poetically resonant action that has no parallel in the largely material ambience of Eugène Scribe's dramatic universe.

Although it is based mainly on the anonymous thirteenth-century epic poem, *Lohengrin*, Wagner's music-drama echoes situations from earlier romantic operas. The deliverance of Elsa by Lohengrin echoes a recurring situation in romantic fairy-tales, and Wagner's debt to Weber's *Euryanthe* (1823) has been widely discussed;[30] in particular, the pairing of the "light" and "dark" couples of Lohengrin and Elsa and Ortrud and Telramund was borrowed from a similar arrangement in Weber's opera where the "light" couple, Euryanthe and Adolar, are betrayed by the "dark" couple, Eglantine and Lysiart, in an intrigue centered on the conflict between trust and cynicism, which is also a feature of *Lohengrin*. But the opera in which the circumstances of *Lohengrin* are most clearly anticipated is Marschner's *Hans Heiling*. The formulation of character conflict and the use of a subterranean cavern as the realm of the earth spirits in this opera were models for both *Holländer* and *Tannhäuser*, but the story of Hans Heiling, a prince of the earth spirits who falls in love with a mortal woman only to be betrayed by her fickleness and rejected by humans because of his gloomy presence, foreshadows, in darker guise, the central situation of *Lohengrin*.

Reinhard Brinkmann has identified three planes of action in Wagner's music-drama, all of which are influenced by Lohengrin's advent: the military situation of King Henry's visitation on Brabant, the political intrigue of Ortrud and Telramund, and Elsa's emotional dilemma.[31] These might also be conceived as concentric circles with King Henry occupying the outermost circle, Ortrud and Telramund the intermediate, and Elsa the innermost, an arrangement reflected in the order in which respective characters are introduced in the exposition, the outermost coming first. Lohengrin's immediate mission is to save Elsa, so he begins by advancing at once into the inner circle, but by the time he has to leave, his influence has spread to all circles and participants in the drama.

As already noted, the conflict-ridden human world is represented with a concrete realism and an eye to spectacle characteristic of French grand opera. The opening and closing scenes, with their massive choruses, trumpet calls, and summonses to arms, provide a warlike frame for the action. This is a society threatened by both external invasion and internal dissension. The German lands are in danger of invasion by the Hungarians and the province of Brabant is in disarray as the succession to its dukedom is in dispute, Gottfried, the heir-apparent, having vanished when in the care of his sister Elsa. Although *Lohengrin* has been described as Wagner's "least political" work,[32] the presence of Henry the Fowler, a symbolic hero for the burgeoning German nationalism of the late Vormärz, suggests otherwise. Henry's appeal to the Brabantians, coupled with Telramund's accusation of Elsa, might well serve as a mirror for contemporary German society in which national union and the passage of legitimate authority were much in dispute.[33] When Wagner returns to the military sphere at the end of the opera, the authority that emanates from Lohengrin offers potential for social and national transformation.

The series of events that sets in when Lohengrin enters the action does not at first seem germane to the political concerns with which the music-drama opens. The action maintains strict causal unity, but with Lohengrin's entrance it undergoes a thematic shift not at all characteristic of the well-made play, which leads to a double conflict that complicates the action. The first conflict is between the "light" of Lohengrin and the "dark" of Ortrud, which is open to a broad range of interpretation. Wagner's association of Ortrud with Wodan and Freia indicates this as a confrontation between a triumphant Christianity and a paganism that was still powerfully residual in German lands. But the conflict means more. Anticipating the *Ring*, it dramatizes the friction between love as erotic desire and compassion against love used to achieve material gain. Also, as Wagner tells us in "Eine Mitteilung," it invokes the artist in conflict with a society that is indifferent to his plight and to the works of the imagination he produces. Ultimately the conflict resides in the tension between the ideal existence symbolized in Monsalvat and the reality of a world where survival is only possible through ruthless struggle.

The second conflict occurs within the two characters who are torn by the struggle between Lohengrin and Ortrud, Elsa and Telramund. Here the action penetrates to a level of personal turmoil that the well-made play never touched. Elsa is split between her love for Lohengrin and her need to know his name, a division that she feels with increasing intensity as the action progresses. Telramund's torment is no less severe than Elsa's. She has already rejected him as a suitor and now he is torn between his infatuation for Ortrud, his recognition of his own powerlessness, and an awareness that his ambitions fly in the face of a political order that his moral sense tells him is legitimate. Telramund, and Ortrud with him, are no conventional melodramatic villains. Wagner employs his most innovative and arresting musical idiom to depict their relationship at the start of act 2, when he abandons the periodically regular melody that characterizes most of *Lohengrin*'s music. Here melody is fragmented, following closely the sense of words, the tone is dark, and the guiding principle of the scene is not to produce beauty of sound, but to sculpt the contours of the struggle between a ruthless wife and her broken husband. It is music that is insinuating, hysterical, and arrhythmic, intensifying the emotional impact of the words. In this scene Wagner incorporates leitmotif as a structural principle, as phrases first introduced in the eerie conversation slide through the rest of the act "like a poisonous snake"[34] to undermine fatally Elsa's confidence in Lohengrin. But the most surprising effect of this music is its capacity to humanize figures whose interests in the moral spectrum of the well-made play had commonly been represented as lacking legitimacy. It arouses sympathy for the villains, so their needs are felt to be as germane as those associated with Elsa and Lohengrin. There is therefore an equality between the "light" and "dark" couples, which converts potential melodrama into tragedy.

The central issue of *Lohengrin* is, however, the love between Elsa and Lohengrin and the strange radiance diffused by the knight from Monsalvat, which, at the conclusion, holds the promise of transforming political and national affairs. Initially Wagner was ill at ease with his central figure. As he wrote in "Eine Mitteilung," "the medieval poem presented Lohengrin in a mystic twilight, that filled me with suspicion and that haunting feeling of repugnance with which we look upon the carved and painted saints and martyrs on the highways, or in the churches of Catholic lands."[35] Although he claimed later to warm to the figure and was even offended by audiences' coldness to it, it is questionable whether he ever really took to his creation.

In some regards Lohengrin is the antithesis of Tannhäuser. He is the first of Wagner's heroes to be hailed as "Held" and who is distinguished by conventional qualities of epic heroism. He comes accoutered with the glamorous mythological apparatus of the swan, he effortlessly saves a damsel in distress, he is prepared to lead German troops into war, and at the end he turns out to be from the mysterious brotherhood of the grail whose purpose it is to bring peace to a troubled world. Like the hero, he resists codification in the ranks of human society; he will accept no title – he insists on being designated "Protector" rather than "Duke" of Brabant – and he withstands all attempts by humans to impose identity upon him by telling them his name. But while he is more elevated than previous Wagnerian heroes, his trajectory in life resembles theirs and might even be paradigmatic. He comes from the realm of imagination and pure ideals, from a static condition of eternal recurrence, a brighter variant of the darker regions from which the Dutchman and Tannhäuser came. Like them he finds the human condition inadequate to his needs and is driven to return to the place from which he came. However, while the Dutchman and Tannhäuser are rescued from tragic defeat by a self-sacrificing and loving woman, Lohengrin is denied this salvation.

For the nominal protagonist of the action, Lohengrin is surprisingly absent from the stage, at least for the first two acts. After he has bidden farewell to the swan and betrothed himself to Elsa in act 1, he sings mostly in ensemble. He is on stage only for the last quarter of act 2 and here he is powerless against the stronger Ortrud. Only in act 3 does he come into his own and his extended solo passages, which include the Monsalvat narration, occur in the final scene as he is about to leave the world. Consequently, the aura he sheds and the values for which he stands seem more tangible than the man himself. The only opportunity we are given to feel with him is the love duet in the bridal chamber, but even here, despite the melting lyricism of the music, he remains restrained and distant. His desire for Elsa has none of the exaltation of Tannhäuser's love for Elisabeth or the urgency of Tristan's for Isolde. The leading melodies in the duet are introduced by Elsa, not Lohengrin, who thereby seems incapable of taking the initiative to forge a relationship that will make him human. Ultimately he can relate to Elsa and the world only as a superior to a less privileged being. So, while his departure is necessitated by Elsa asking the forbidden question, the predicament of loneliness in Monsalvat that he faces at the end is appropriate because, sanctified vacuum that he is, he could never adapt to human ways.

There are significant differences between Lohengrin and his supernatural predecessors in romantic opera. In Marschner, Hoffmann, Weber, and the early Wagner, the supernatural destroys human happiness. Hans Heiling, for example, wishes to exact a terrible revenge on those mortals who have frustrated his desires, while the supernatural powers in *Freischütz* are bent upon infecting all that brings human beings content or joy. While Wagner does not eschew the supernatural in *Lohengrin*, he avoids the Gothic apparatus of romantic opera and, even though the end involves a painful sundering, Lohengrin's desire to become human offers the possibility of a bridge between the human and the noumenal. Lohengrin, unlike his supernatural forebears in romantic opera, promises wholeness rather than division.

As we have seen, Wagner considered *Lohengrin* to be primarily an allegory of the artist in his troubled relationship with the modern world. In "Eine Mitteilung," Wagner describes the knight of the grail as the artist who dwells in the highest realms of consciousness, but wishes to be part of humanity through the love of a woman; that love, however, must be directed toward him as a human being, not toward his "higher nature," to those imaginative capacities which produce his art. If woman loves the artist rather than the man, her love is akin to worship and cannot therefore nourish the man. *Lohengrin*, therefore, is thematically closer to *Holländer* than to *Tannhäuser* because, as an allegory of the artist, it is concerned with the artist's predicament, not with the manner in which his art is created. Lohengrin's insistence on not revealing his name tells us much about the artist's nature. Among the distinctive features of romantic creativity are its unpredictability and its capacity to displace the artist's emotional life, which subverts his happiness. Although the urge to create arises from within the artist and is, particularly from the romantic viewpoint, self-expression, the artist can experience his creativity as an alien presence. The sources of romantic creativity are unknowable, and the ways in which the romantic artist comprehends the world and re-forms it in art are not subject to rational analysis. If they are, analysis will destroy them. The blind trust Lohengrin asks of others correlates to the uncritical acceptance of creativity that is required of the artist and those who experience his work. When that trust is broken, so too is the capacity of the artist to create and of his audience to accept that creation. So the secret that drives the well-made plot and eventually comes between Lohengrin and Elsa is no arbitrary imposition, as it initially appears to be, but a device that articulates precisely the symbolic plight of the drama's protagonist.

One quality that distinguishes *Lohengrin* from *Holländer* and *Tannhäuser* is the greater objectivity in the representation of the hero. Prior to *Lohengrin*, Wagner's discourse on the hero was not free of self-pity. The dark cogitation of the Dutchman implies an inordinate preoccupation with himself and the anguish of Tannhäuser's cry of "Erbarm dich mein" ("Have pity upon me") can easily embarrass because the situation, which Tannhäuser after all created for himself, hardly calls for so extreme a response. Even Wagner's retrospective analysis of *Lohengrin* in "Eine Mitteilung" has about it an air of naïve superiority that lacks credibility and smacks of special pleading. But in *Lohengrin* itself, this theme that had been of such pressing personal concern to Wagner has been objectified, so we can now examine it without any sense of being buttonholed by the composer. In this regard, *Lohengrin* represents a major step toward Wagner's maturation as a music-dramatist. The greater objectivity is due, in part, to the utilization of the realistic, historicist milieu of grand opera. Lohengrin comes from an ethereal domain known to us solely through the impression of unity conveyed by the sustained sublimity of the prelude and the serene image of the swan. It is a realm in which we sense the self and the objective world are one, a union that can never occur among humans, a contrast that is strikingly conveyed in the transition from the prelude to the opening of act 1, when the ecstatic music of Monsalvat is set off against the pronounced rhythms and vigorous melodies of the choruses and ensembles of Henry the Fowler's troops. Lohengrin might serve as a mediating influence in this harsh environment – the chorus that heralds his arrival and the choral passages in the extended bridal procession of act 2 are enveloped in an atmosphere of soft wonder that indicates his influence is palpable – but ultimately the distance between him and humanity is unbridgeable.

Wagner's objectivity in depicting the dilemma of the artist arises too from Lohengrin not being the only character to experience pain, or more correctly perhaps, not being the one who feels most pain. There is a symmetry between the "light" and "dark" couples. The two figures who embody the opposing forces of Christianity and paganism or of the artistic and material worlds, Lohengrin and Ortrud, are supremely confident characters; they know the powers behind them and they do not doubt them. As a result, they are two-dimensional figures, which results in a shift of dramatic interest to their partners, who suffer from their companions' insistent confidence. Telramund, in conflict with the world, his wife, and himself, is a more interesting and multi-dimensional figure than Ortrud. The same is true for Elsa. Vocally she has the longest role in the drama and she has more stage-time than other characters. Initially she is a nebulous figure. Throughout act 1, she refuses to answer all accusations made against her, only alludes to her dreams, and is abjectly submissive, first to the king, later to Lohengrin. As she sings to Lohengrin after he has defeated Telramund:

> Into you I must pass
> before you I vanish!
> if I am to be happy
> take everything that I am.[36]

But Elsa does not remain long in this mode of self-abasement. Her mis-guided compassion for Ortrud in act 2 scene 1, which she voices in the same ecstatic music that expresses her love for Lohengrin, arises from her naïvety, but the moment she is confronted by Ortrud's hostility during the bridal procession, her anger is aroused. This not only lends her strength, it leads her to become increasingly curious as to Lohengrin's identity, which goads her into an ever-increasing insistence on her own rights within the relationship. However, the attribute of silence that marked her first appearance never entirely leaves her, there is always a certain emptiness in her. This is no failing on Wagner's part, because the emptiness provides a space for the audience to occupy imaginatively. From this it can adopt Elsa's perspective on the action, which means that while it might acknowledge the legitimacy of Lohengrin's demands symbolically, it also understands through Elsa the human costs these demands entail. It realizes that the need for Elsa to know her husband's identity is crucial to her security. As Ortrud compellingly argues, in a society as subject to dynastic politics as Brabant, a woman's survival is dependent on the birth, rank, and lineage of her husband. Elsa is at a similar loss personally, as Lohengrin's refusal to identify himself by the accepted markers of society means she cannot wholly love him for she does not know who it is she loves. In the course of composition, Wagner found himself increasingly drawn to Elsa: "I grew to find her so justified in the final outburst of her jealousy, that from this very outburst I learnt first to thoroughly understand the purely human element of love; and I suffered deep and actual grief – often welling into bitter tears – as I saw the tragic necessity of the parting, the unavoidable undoing of this pair of lovers."[37] The legitimacy of Lohengrin and Elsa's needs and the impossibility of their reconciliation provides the most starkly tragic ending in Wagner, one that he rightly refused to alter. As Dahlhaus succinctly puts it, "the goal for which Lohengrin yearns is barred by the means whereby he seeks to reach it . . . In seeking to annul what sets him apart from others, Lohengrin only succeeds in reinforcing it."[38]

While the opera ends bleakly with the irreparable sundering of the lovers, the symbolic ramifications are touched with optimism, so the ending is not quite as closed as first appears. The symmetrical structure requires the action to return to where it began, to the gathering of troops and the site where Elsa was accused of the murder of her brother, which led to the breaking of the line of succession to the Dukedom of Brabant and to the potential for civil war, as distinct from war against the Hungarians. To move from the intimacy of the bridal chamber to the field of war, Wagner wrote one of his most thrilling orchestral interludes, built upon aggressive, militaristic themes and insistent trumpet fanfares that rise with formidable energy to a climax in which the massed troops welcome King Henry back to the banks of the Scheldt and herald the onset of stirring heroic deeds. The contrast is abrupt and in hindsight misleading, because no battle takes place, in fact, we might take the interlude itself as being in lieu of battle. Instead, we witness the less stirring dissolution of Lohengrin and Elsa's marriage. However, in the process, Lohengrin asserts his heroic stature, not by assuming military leadership, but by revealing the extra-human realm from which he comes. As he describes the ceremonies of the grail in his solo "In fernem Land" ("In a distant land"), he depicts a landscape of light and a brotherhood of knights who spread virtue through the world not as a defined mission, but by the power of personality that can only be effective when it is not recognized, but only trusted.

> Whoever is sent by it into a distant land
> appointed as champion of virtue
> will not have its holy power stolen
> so long as no one there recognize him as a knight.[39]

It is a heroic dispensation Lohengrin summons up and perhaps it is not surprising that autocratic rulers from Ludwig II to Adolf Hitler have identified with him. But if they saw reflected in him their own glory as leaders, they misread him. Lohengrin, like both the epic and romantic hero, eschews earthly authority. In his narration, the grail stands at the apex of a rigidly hierarchical order that is not open to question, the crowning symbol of a universe in which motive force comes not from below – the massive choruses in *Lohengrin*, in contrast to those in Wagner's earlier music-dramas, are dramatically supine – but above. Lohengrin as epic hero announces that the future prosperity of Brabant will be guaranteed by the restoration of its leader, and he strengthens King Henry's authority over Germany by his prophecy that Germany will never be invaded by hordes from the east. But he denies himself a messianic role: he is only the messenger, not the ruler. This is all the hero can be as his strength, as Raglan observed, declines the moment he takes on the responsibility of ruling. Ruling requires compromise and accommodation, attributes that do not fit the hero well. It is only by leaving the world and becoming an inspiration, not a leader, that Lohengrin remains a hero.

When *Lohengrin* is viewed as an allegory of the loneliness of the artist, the grail stands as a symbol of romantic creativity, which, once it is named and understood, will disappear, and as an image for the absolute value of beauty released through the work of art. But it also has a more egalitarian dimension, for it states the need for trust among human beings. Through the grail, one can understand that the binding force between people need not be loyalty to political or military authority but its opposite, an unspoken recognition of a common identity. Redemption in *Lohengrin* comes not through the self-sacrifice of the loving woman, but through the vision of a utopia where human difference is cancelled and the conflicts of action nullified. Utopia is impossible, but the desire for it provides a motive force in human affairs. Lohengrin's last act is to revive the young Gottfried, so restoring to Brabant an icon of authority that has grown from its past and is not an alien imposition, as Telramund's rule would have been. He endows the young Duke with the insignia of the grail, a horn, a sword, and a ring. These will protect him in battle and remind him of the values of trust embedded in the grail. But these talismans serve too as signs that, while the utopia of an artist living at one with the world will never be achieved, the instinct for beauty and the power of the imagination for which Monsalvat stands will reside in collective memory. Through the energies released by the aesthetic sense, society will attain a wholeness that will guarantee its survival. In *Lohengrin* Wagner first posits the argument that salvation lies in love as trust and in devotion to the beautiful as revealed in art. Without them society cannot survive because it lacks wholeness and any sense of continuity. As a result, coherence disappears and chaos will come. It is through the workings of the aesthetic sense that social community, harmony, and equality will be achieved. This was a theme Wagner would next take up in *Die Meistersinger*. Meanwhile, although the desolate conclusion of *Lohengrin* offers a firm sense of closure, the future entrusted to Gottfried is open. As the latest emissary of the grail he may bring national unity and the victory of Germany over its enemies, but if he is not recognized as a knight of the grail, if he denies himself the power of the ruler, he may serve as a conduit for those powers of the grail that can bring peace. In him the contradictory powers and purposes of the hero are concentrated.

4

Heroism, tragedy, and the Ring

THE *RING* AND TRAGEDY

There was no doubt in Wagner's mind that the *Ring* was a tragedy. While he was writing the poem, he described it as "a tragedy of the most shattering effectiveness."[1] There is abundant evidence that he thought of the Festival of Dionysus as a model, and both the Oedipus myth[2] and the *Oresteia*[3] have been mined for parallels. More generally, his correspondence and Cosima's diaries are packed with references to the Greek tragedians, Shakespeare, Calderón, Schiller, and other tragic writers, in contexts indicating that he considered himself to be among their company. Modern critics have been less certain. George Steiner, in his search for symptoms of the "death of tragedy," fastens on *Götterdämmerung* as one of those dramas in which the uncompromising forces that destroy human freedom are palliated by "the apotheosis of redemption,"[4] while Lloyd-Jones, influenced by Steiner, argues that "in the *Ring* in general we find something profoundly alien to the spirit of an ancient tragedy," citing Wagner's belief in the essential goodness of humanity as the source of this.[5] Whether belief in human goodness and the powers of redemption preclude tragedy is a matter for debate – after all, the *Oresteia*, that touchstone of Greek tragedy, finishes with a more explicitly redemptive end than the *Ring* – but the precise nature of the tragedy of the *Ring* does remain in doubt. This is because in it different modes of tragedy that imply differing and potentially incompatible views of the human condition are fused. Action in the first two music-dramas, *Das Rheingold* and *Die Walküre*, is driven by a determinist force that deprives all agents of free will. *Siegfried*, however, is dominated by a romantic optimism, and *Götterdämmerung*, for all the grimness of its plot and score, concludes with a utopian vision that gives rise to Steiner's and Lloyd-Jones' reservations. The *Ring*, it seems, is both deterministic tragedy and a drama of romantic salvation.

68

Tragedy most frequently involves catastrophic events that lead to the death of the hero and many associated with him. These deaths seem not to occur in the natural course of things. Death from old age is not tragic because it is expected and natural, but tragedy cuts off people in their prime and arouses an acute sense of promise destroyed. Ideally the action leading to that death points to a fundamental contradiction in the constitution of things, an existential condition that allows for no remedy. "All tragedy depends on an insoluble conflict," Goethe wrote. "As soon as harmony is obtained, or becomes a possibility, tragedy vanishes."[6] Tragedy focuses on what cannot be altered. Hence, while tragic characters bear moral responsibility for their actions, the catastrophe that destroys them is larger than they are. Because of this, there is an element of innocence about them, so that even those whose deeds are criminal still seem to display qualities of courage and nobility of soul,[7] while the energy that they summon to defeat the forces that oppose them testifies to the strength and depth of their character and their commitment to deep suffering. As the predicament of the tragic hero points beyond the pale of individual experience to social, political, or metaphysical realms, the fall of the hero can arouse a sense of community among members of the audience, as through it, they recognize a predicament in which all participate. Crucial to much tragic conflict is the ironic perspective through which it is clear that whatever tragic heroes do to escape from the consequences of their action brings them closer to the disaster they have been trying to avoid. In tragedy, we face up to the elemental harshness of life, which we view without compromise. As I. A. Richards put it, "the mind does not shy away from anything, it does not protect itself with any illusion, it stands uncomforted, unintimidated, alone and self-reliant." We must not resort to "suppressions and sublimations" to mitigate the cruel impact of tragedy upon us.[8]

While Richards' stern view identifies the rigors of tragedy, it is striking how rarely the mind does stand "uncomforted" in the tragic theatre. Richards himself admitted that his demands for tragedy were only fulfilled in six of Shakespeare's tragedies and a handful of Greek dramas. Other scholars might add to this a few tragedies by Racine, a handful of works from the Spanish Golden Age, and some of the realistic tragedies contemporary with and after Wagner, but one rarely encounters tragedy that unfailingly sustains the spectacle of individuals up against unrelenting forces that they heroically oppose and then die in the face of an incomprehensible void. Steiner has argued that ever since Rousseau convinced the world that humans are perfectible this unrelenting vision has been impossible. Once we think humans are perfectible, we can no longer conceive of a universe in which there is no justice, where humans are punished for their actions far in excess of their guilt. After Rousseau, he argues, we no longer acknowledge that conflicts can be irresolvable or generated by forces beyond our comprehension. Misery no longer comes about by a fall from grace, or even through fissures in character because humans are fundamentally good. Any deviation from the norm can be imputed not to fatal defects in character, but to social failings to which they are victim, such as inadequate education or political corruption. Once these problems have been solved, so too will be the troubles of humanity. The romantic view of life, which incorporates these ideas, is essentially optimistic and therefore anti-tragic.[9] Many of Steiner's assumptions are open to argument. For a start, while Rousseau believed that humans were inherently good, he insisted that this goodness could only survive in those natural communities that he carefully outlined. Once original goodness was lost, it was gone for ever. This in itself is tragic, because as such loss is inevitable, all we can do is construct a society in which the individual is protected by social bonds and justice that preserve some vestige of goodness or return to nature and solitude.

Steiner was, however, right to perceive a historic shift in tragic sensibility around the end of the eighteenth century. August Wilhelm Schlegel, writing in 1807, argued that we watch tragedy for one of two reasons: either to admire the dignity of heroic humanity in its struggle against overwhelming odds, or to acquire an understanding of realms of experience beyond the purely human, through which we gather "the intimation of an order of things which is supernatural, imprinted and . . . mysteriously revealed."[10] Neither the ancients nor the moderns, he pointed out, restrict themselves exclusively to these understandings of tragedy, and often one subsumes the other. Some plays from the past face up to the hard facts of a tragic universe – *Oedipus the King*, for example, or *King Lear* – while others, such as the *Oresteia*, represent the workings of a benign order. Yet others, like *Hamlet*, at least end with a hint of reconciliation to the universal order. But his own time, Schlegel claimed, clearly preferred the second mode of tragedy over the first, favoring works that gave intimations or even visions of a condition of ameliorating harmony beyond life, though he felt that modern playwrights did not have a very clear idea of the direction in which they were moving, because they did not fully understand it.

One who did understand it was the German tragedian Johann Friedrich Schiller, who, in a series of influential essays written in the final decades of the eighteenth century, saw the main purpose of tragedy to be the freeing of human will from the sensuous domain of the body so that it can "look upon the fearful without fear." As the will attains this supernal state through tragic action, it assumes the condition of the "sublime," a state of mind that the tragic hero achieves close to the point of death, so that death comes not as a defeat but as the consummation of a life. Tragic action explores irreconcilable conflicts in human affairs and represents them as insoluble within the purely human sphere, but as death approaches, there arises in the mind of the hero and, by implication, of the audience, "a distinct consciousness of a teleological connection among things, a sublime order, a benevolent will." By this consciousness we come to realize how "the isolated dissonance [is resolved] within the greater harmony."[11] Tragic heroes who reach this sublime state are no longer encumbered by human affairs, nor are their actions determined by them. This does not imply they are indifferent, but they have achieved the only true freedom, they have accepted their death. As death is the only force that limits human action and aspiration, full freedom can only be achieved when fear of it has been annulled, which can only be done by willingly accepting it. The consequence is a sublime understanding of the world.

The sublime as the end of tragedy exercised the mind of the thinker who had more of an impact on Wagner than any other, Arthur Schopenhauer. He too looked on tragedy as a species of the sublime, though with less optimism than Schiller, because while Schiller did not see the sublime as a turning away from life, Schopenhauer did. For him tragedy awakens in us "the knowledge that the world, life, can afford us no true pleasure."[12] The pain aroused by tragic action cannot lead us toward a love of life; rather it reveals an existence beyond life which, had we not experienced the tragedy, would have been "quite inconceivable." Tragedy opens up a numinous realm as a desired alternative to life on earth; Schiller understood it as deepening our knowledge of life on earth.

German writings on tragedy over the romantic period emphasize consciousness of harmony as an ultimate goal. But this is a state more easily defined in theory than realized on stage. In the spoken theatre, extended passages representing the achievement of a sublime point of view can lack credibility. The passage of the Eumenides into the caverns beneath the Acropolis at the end of Aeschylus' *Oresteia* or the vision of Goethe's Faust creating a more productive world at the end of *Part II* can easily devolve into cloudy abstraction or reach bathos by becoming mired in commonplace detail. The irredeemably physical presence of the actor and, in the early nineteenth century, prosaically realistic stage settings made it difficult to actualize sublime experience. So sublimity only appeared fleetingly on stage, in Hamlet recognizing "the readiness is all" or Mary Stuart silently casting off all ties that bind her to the physical world. It was, however, more possible to give a credible, extended representation of the sublime in the operatic theatre than in the spoken. Schopenhauer, searching for an example of a "genuine tragic effect of the catastrophe" which leads to "the resignation and exaltation of the mind of the hero," found it in Bellini's *Norma* where, as Norma and Pollione prepare for death, "the change of will is distinctly indicated by the quietness that is suddenly introduced into the music."[13] Schopenhauer regarded music as the only means by which humanity could understand the workings of the world's will. Through it, we come to apprehend the "inconceivable existence" that tragedy points toward. However, his citation of *Norma* also suggests another dimension of music as a dramatic language, which is its capacity to suspend the onward movement of dramatic action without any strain on audience credibility. In these moments of suspension, which can last for extended periods of time, we gain access to the characters' emotional lives and, importantly for the purpose of tragedy, to the extra-human destination toward which those lives are tending. Music as a dramatic language realizes, tangibly and precisely, emotional and symbolic worlds important to tragedy that words alone are inadequate to express.

Heroism and tragedy have always been closely related. While heroes glorify human strength and aspiration, tragedy displays whatever limits them. It "stresses," as Terry Eagleton has observed, "how we are acted upon rather than robustly enterprising, as well as what meagre space for manoeuvre we often have available."[14] Nevertheless, tragedy does not degrade the hero; on the contrary, the hero's true courage may become apparent only at the moment of defeat. The nature of the tragedy, and the role of the hero in it, can be determined by where the emphasis lies in the representation of this courage. If it is on those forces that have led to the destruction of the hero, then whatever glory the hero reaps from defeat is testimony to human stoicism and obduracy in the face of an unknowable universe. But if emphasis is placed on potentially auspicious consequences or on the hero's admirable qualities, even though the action ends in defeat, the hero's final state can arouse optimism rather than despair. The *Ring* displays a plenitude of heroes, all with different tragic destinies. Siegmund and Siegfried, romantic and epic heroes respectively, both die violently, but while Siegmund's death reveals nothing but the senseless cruelty of the universe, some hope for a better world follows from Siegfried's. The most thoroughly defeated of the heroic figures is Wotan, the main tragic hero of the first two dramas, a romantic hero in the third, and an absent victim dying in abject fear in the fourth. Meanwhile, as the full depth of his fall becomes apparent, heroic agency passes to Brünnhilde, who achieves a level of sublime understanding denied to any other character. The *Ring*, therefore, displays more than one tragic model and one tragic hero. While Steiner may be right in seeing its ending as a mitigation of the harsh imperatives of tragic determination, this does not remove it from consideration as a tragic work.

In the *Ring* tragedy both represents humans as determined beings and follows a path toward the sublime. While Schopenhauer was the single most important influence over Wagner's mature intellectual development, his ideas about tragedy were not the only ones to affect his growth as a tragic dramatist. Wagner was working in a theatrical environment where audiences, when they attended tragedies, had a variety of expectations, none of which was fully formulated. No doubt it was this vagueness in the conception of tragedy that caused that lack of direction among tragic writers identified by Schlegel. Forty years after Schlegel's lectures, when Wagner's music-dramas were making their way to the German operatic stage, not much had changed. By this time Shakespeare had become the most widely performed of classic dramatists in the German theatre. Although the only versions then in use were the Schlegel/Tieck translations, which have a fullness of expression and resonance lacking in the terser English, audiences were familiar with their bleak endings. They would have known Greek tragedy more through reading than performance, and from this they would have learnt that tragic action can either be constrained by the harshest determinism or resolved by the intervention of benign gods. Other tragedies that were finding their way into the German repertoire would have encouraged a more catholic understanding of the nature of tragic action. While Racine's plays, very occasionally performed, operated on rigorously deterministic principles, Calderón's dramas, which found sympathetic audiences in Germany, set up continuities between human action and divine grace. Within the contemporary German repertoire, similar contrasts were apparent. While Schiller's early tragedies concluded against a blank wall of incomprehensible pain, his later work, from *Wallenstein* on, was influenced by his own theories of the sublime. Meanwhile, the *Schicksalstragödie* or "tragedy of fate" that was the most distinctive contribution of romanticism to the popular theatre disclosed a radical view of human action determined by a fathomless fate in which salvation has no part. As Wagner's own work attests, his view of tragedy was as catholic as any of his contemporaries and his knowledge greater than most.

THE *RING* AS HEROIC DEED

In several regards, *Der Ring des Nibelungen* (*The Ring of the Nibelung*) was the most heroic enterprise of Wagner's life. The twenty-eight-year span of its composition, from the initial draft of the plot, published in 1848, to the first complete production of the cycle at Bayreuth in 1876, represents one of the most impressive feats of sustained concentration in the history of music and the theatre, one that is made more, not less remarkable by Wagner suspending composition for twelve years in the middle of the project. When we attend performances of the *Ring*, the heroic will of the composer seems matched by the equally heroic efforts of the singers, whose roles over the complete cycle are the longest in opera. As their voices must be heard over one of the largest orchestras ever employed in the opera house, the act of singing also takes on heroic dimensions.

The process of composition had an aura of the heroic about it as well. As he wrote the poem, Wagner, like the hero, seems to have been engaged on a quest into the past to find sources of primal energy. The first poem, *Siegfrieds Tod* (*Siegfried's Death*), which would eventually become *Götterdämmerung* (*Twilight of the Gods*), depended so heavily on exposition that he needed to write *Der junge Siegfried* (*The Young Siegfried*), ultimately *Siegfried*, to make the action clear. But the significance of this drama could not be fully grasped without further exposition, whereupon Wagner traveled back into mythology, through the poem of *Die Walküre* (*The Valkyrie*) to the origin of all things in *Das Rheingold* (*The Rhinegold*). As audience members we can still recapture some of the quest-like nature of the composition, because while the action of the *Ring* begins with Creation and presses forward through successive generations of giants, gods, and humans to Doomsday, our awareness of what happened in the past grows exponentially with this progress. Only in *Götterdämmerung* do we learn about the root cause of all evil, Wotan's striking a limb off the world's ash-tree, an event that sounds, in the narration of the Norns, as if it had occurred aeons prior to Alberich's theft of the Rhinegold. Then, only in the final moments of the cycle, as flames from the burning ash-tree set fire to Valhalla, do we understand the full consequences of Wotan's violation of nature. As the action advances toward a utopia, the audience's consciousness of its origins in the distant past grows. "The future is prefigured in an image of the past."[15]

The action of the *Ring* takes place consistently on the plane of the heroic, which Wagner discovered by reaching beyond the literary sources most readily to hand, the chivalric poem *Nibelungenlied* and Germanic works based on related material, to the Scandinavian sagas. Here, divested of their medieval accoutrements, Wagner discovered the figures of Germanic legend in atavistic form. This gave impetus to the turn away from historicism toward myth that was already potential in *Lohengrin* and encouraged him to develop an essentialist view of his material. In the sagas he found "no longer the figure of conventional history . . . but the real naked man, in whom I might spy each throbbing of his pulses . . . in uncramped, freest motion." It was in the sagas that he found Siegfried "in his purest human form."[16] As the concept for the *Ring* grew in his imagination, he came to see the myths disclosed by the sagas as revelations of a truth existing outside time.

Wagner therefore conceived of the *Ring* as exercising a function in the society of his time, similar to that of the hero toward society. The theme that unites the series of polemical and theoretical essays that he wrote while the *Ring* was germinating in his imagination is the need for an art that will cleanse that "efflorescence of corruption, of a hollow, soulless and unnatural condition of human affairs and human relations"[17] created by the commercial exploitation of art. In place of enervating grand opera, his music-drama would renew the energies of his audiences by reconnecting them with primeval myths. Like the tragedies at the Festival of Dionysus, it would instill them with confidence in who they are by helping them understand who they had been. The exalted aspirations Wagner fostered for the *Ring* are reflected in the hyperbolic atmosphere of the work, the elaborate natural settings, the lush grandeur and virtually unremitting energy of the music, the relentless alliteration, the inflated diction in which characters address each other, and the carefully wrought, massive dramatic climaxes. For those who resist this overstated ambience and atmosphere, this "world dominated by heroes and hero worship"[18] should be placed at arm's length, but for those amenable to the vast range and size of Wagner's vision, the *Ring* is, in the words of Thomas Mann, "the most sublime, the most compelling work the [nineteenth] century has to offer."[19]

But while the *Ring* has the trappings of heroic art, the heroism that unfolds in the course of its action hardly complements its grandiose ambience. For a start, the most widespread concept of heroism among Wagner's contemporaries, which Wagner himself inherited from the Scandinavian sagas and which his music seems frequently to endorse, is not only at odds with the models of heroism that impel the action of the *Ring*, but actively hostile to them. This is what we might call a "tribal" heroism, represented by Hunding, by the heroes whom the Valkyries gather to defend Valhalla, and by Hagen. Although Hunding himself is no hero, he is, as Anthony Winterbourne points out, champion of a heroic society as he scrupulously

follows the warrior's code of honor and dies fighting for it, thereby display-
ing the selflessness expected of the hero.[20] He dies too for Fricka, whose
understanding of the rigorous obligations imposed by marriage and family
ordains her guardian of the values of a tribal, heroic society, which is what
Valhalla is too. It is not always easy to gauge Wagner's attitude toward these
values and interests. For example, as the gods enter their new home at the
end of *Das Rheingold*, the grandeur of the music suggests this is a mighty
achievement, while the dramatic context tells us the opposite. Similarly,
as the Valkyries gather slain warriors from the battlefield to strengthen
Wotan's power, the stirring Ride of the Valkyries suggests Wagner sanctions this custom, but the drama makes clear that these heroes and the
warrior maidens serve only what is corrupt, oppressive, and impermanent.
Whatever lasting heroism the *Ring* possesses must be found elsewhere.

THE DESTRUCTION OF NATURE AND THE COMING OF FEAR

The late romantic hero was at the center of Wagner's early music-dramas
and he is not, as we shall see, absent from the *Ring*. But to create a hero who
would defy the deadening forces of materialism, lovelessness, and violence,
Wagner had to look beyond the iconic figures of late romanticism. The
primal energy that the hero is to recapture and preserve is present at the
beginning of *Das Rheingold*, in the Rhinegold itself. It recalls Rousseau's naturalistic paradise, but unlike Rousseau Wagner did not conceive of nature
as a pure and benign realm in which humans and nature live in harmony;
on the contrary, as the Rhine daughters' taunting of Alberich demonstrates,
nature generates its own divisions. But it can provide a vision of elemental
beauty, the radiant spectacle of the Rhinegold, in which Rousseau's union
of humanity and nature seems possible. If the Rhinegold is not the source
of life itself, it stands for whatever makes life worth living and gives it
energy and vitality. As the sun strikes the Rhinegold through the water, the
shimmering strings stir associations of constant movement, the trumpet
announces the awakening of life, and the quiet horn-calls kindle a sense of
wonder. The pleasurable associations aroused by the music include delight
in physical being, the phenomenon of perpetual change, and love and sexual
desire, all of which we sense as ultimately good. The Rhinegold can also be
read as an embodiment of Wagner's concept of art as nothing but "pleasure
in itself,"[21] while the Rhine daughters' playful adoration of the gold evokes
the mental freedom that we experience in contemplating a work of art. The
Rhinegold embodies energy beyond the immediacy of the sensate world,
which, while giving humans a sense of purpose and joy, is not bound to

any utilitarian purpose. It is, nonetheless, vital to the survival of the human race. There has been no precise parallel to the Rhinegold in the earlier music-dramas. The Dutchman drew strength from the deep past out of which his memory of Senta came and the unearthly beauty of Lohengrin's Monsalvat filled those who understood it with awe, but neither has the natural allure of the Rhinegold. It celebrates the bonds between humans and nature and comprises a beauty that can defuse violence in both.

The mission of the hero in the *Ring* will be the preservation, restoration, and perpetuation of the energies that radiate from the Rhinegold, thereby guaranteeing the continuation of the human race. Therefore, the hero, acting in the service of the Rhinegold, will not strengthen those tribal bonds that force humans to live in subservience to each other, but will spark a natural vigor in people that will generate personal happiness and a capacity to live in harmony with each other. Such impulses arise from the self in conversation with nature and are realized primarily through sensual pleasure and aesthetic delight. The action of the *Ring* is devoted to representing the consequences of the fall of nature and its creatures – magical, divine, and human – from the state of grace embodied by the Rhinegold and the endeavors of the hero to restore them. It also sets out the consequences to humanity when the goodness of nature is vitiated. There are two ways by which this tainting occurs. The first is Alberich's theft of the Rhinegold, which triggers the action of the entire cycle. The other signifies a permanent condition rather than a series of actions: Wotan's cutting a branch off the tree of life to craft the spear with which he will rule the world, which leads to the withering of the tree and the drying up of the spring at its roots. The consequence of this violation of nature is only fully understood in the closing moments of the cycle.

Alberich achieves power and wealth by forcing the energies of the Rhine-gold into forms that are alien to them and imposing upon them a stasis that will sicken them and lead to their annihilation and the death of humanity. His path can only be pursued by one who has renounced love and can-not, therefore, feel the life-enhancing powers of nature. When he turns the Rhinegold into wealth, he instigates conflicts which impel the action of the entire *Ring*, between nature and humans' self-destructive exploitation of it and between the natural emotion of love and the unnatural ambition to achieve wealth and power. But Alberich is aided and abetted by Wotan, who, though nominally his enemy, is driven by seemingly identical motives. Initially, Wotan's path is the same as Alberich's. He is ready to give Freia to the giants in payment for the building of Valhalla, which indicates that he, like Alberich, is prepared to sacrifice love, eternal youth, and the beneficent forces of nature for his own political power and security. He is prevented from doing this only by his more capacious mind and imagination, which lead him to accept the mutability of all things, an insight reached in his colloquy with Erda. His susceptibility to Erda's arguments makes him a more vulnerable and complex character than Alberich, and the path through the *Ring*, by which he comes to terms with his crime against nature and his sense of his own mortality, is dramatically richer. The character of his crime against nature is also more complex and elusive than Alberich's.

In a famous letter to August Röckel, written while he was still composing the poem to the *Ring*, Wagner argues that the gods would not have been open to harm by Alberich had they not already been "susceptible to evil."[22] This weakness, Wagner observes, stems from the relationship between Wotan and Fricka. Their love has died and yet they are forced to stay together because they are married; marriage, therefore, is a prison, which prevents them from acting according to their changing feelings. Although their marriage does not literally despoil nature, it is cognate to Alberich's violation of the Rhinegold and Wotan's sacrifice of Freia. The decline of their love is natural and to deny this by pretending it is still whole denies the phenomenon of transformation, as symbolized in the Rhinegold. As Rousseau observed, "everything is in constant flux on this earth. Nothing keeps the same unchanging shape, and our affections, being attached to things outside us, necessarily change and pass away as they do."[23] The tragedy of the *Ring* arises as much from Wotan's fear and incapacity to live with nature as from Alberich's theft.

But Wotan is not Alberich. Alberich is a melodramatic villain, with no doubts about himself. Wotan, however, faces a tragic dilemma. He wishes to live in the natural freedom signified by the Rhinegold, but cannot because, if he does, his power as a ruler will be destroyed along with the order on which his authority is based. He has ideals, he is not just a harsh oppressor, but he is divided between his dependence on power and his desire to create a world free of the evil brought about by power. He has no choice but to submit to the obligations incurred through his exercise of power, though his desire to substantiate the ideal that will annul power grows correlative to his intensifying awareness of the trap in which he has caught himself. The action of the *Ring* is a working out of that dilemma and Wotan, in the first two music-dramas, serves as its tragic hero, though his status as hero, in *Das Rheingold* especially, depends more upon the technical function he fulfils in the drama than upon possession of heroic qualities.

Wotan's dilemma as it unfolds in *Das Rheingold* and *Die Walküre* has all the marks of Goethe's description of tragedy as an action arising from the nature of things. Although the two later dramas of the *Ring* are less rigorous in vision as they posit solutions to an insoluble problem, their themes are the same as those of the earlier dramas, so that while the *Ring* is generically mixed, the action is coherent. It is fuelled by the conflict between power and love, and from this comes the cycle's most persistent theme, the death of love and the consequent fear of death. "We must learn *to die*, and to die in the fullest sense of the word," Wagner wrote memorably to Röckel. "The fear of the end is the source of all lovelessness, and this fear is only generated when love itself begins to wane."[24] Fear arising from lovelessness, as revealed in Wotan and Fricka's marriage and the bargaining over Freia in *Das Rheingold*, and fearlessness, which will be embodied in Siegfried, has even been seen as the unifying dialectic of the cycle.[25] It appears at its most devastating in Alberich's curse, which ensures that whoever possesses the ring will never enjoy the limitless power Wellgunde claimed for it when Alberich first set eyes on the Rhinegold. Quite the opposite in fact. Whoever possesses the ring will live in terror at losing it and whoever desires it will live in torment at not having it:

> may he who owns it
> be wracked by care,
> and he who does not
> be ravaged by greed!
> . . .
> Doomed to die,
> may the coward be fettered by fear;
> as long as he lives,
> let him pine away, languishing,
> lord of the ring
> as the slave of the ring.[26]

As Alberich delivers his curse, the stage directions indicate that Wotan "is lost in contemplation of the ring on his finger." Although he gives it up to the giants after Erda has made him aware of his mortality, the effects of the curse will never leave him. While he is never lord of the ring, to the end of *Götterdämmerung* he remains its slave.

Of the four dramas of the *Ring*, *Rheingold* comes closest to the "tragedy of fate" that had enjoyed a vogue in the early nineteenth-century German theatre. An austere abstract of classical tragedy, the tragedy of fate represented human destiny as subject to the rigorous laws of causality and prey to a dreadful preordained fate. Although Wotan is responsible for the dilemma raised by his refusal to honor his contract with the giants and to acknowledge his failing marriage, the consequences of these errors are unfolded with such clarity that we understand them as universal issues, not purely personal problems. By the time Fafner bludgeons Fasolt to death, responsibility resides both in individual action and in causality itself.

The function of *Das Rheingold* in the cycle is ambiguous. The order in which Wagner wrote the poems suggests its purpose is chiefly to account for events prior to the action of the three main dramas of the cycle. But a cursory analysis of the plots and expository passages in the main dramas indicates a prologue is unnecessary, as they provide enough retrospective narrative to allow the audience to comprehend the story without the events of *Das Rheingold* being enacted for them. It has been suggested we view *Das Rheingold* as equivalent to a satyr play in the Festival of Dionysus, a work usually performed after the tragic trilogy, in which the theme of the tragedy received ironic treatment.[27] If we do see it as an introductory satyr play, it appears to be less exposition than an epitome of the three later dramas, a representation *in nuce* of the total action of the *Ring*. Even though the plot of *Das Rheingold* is unremittingly fatalistic, the murder of Fasolt being a direct consequence of Alberich and Wotan's violation of the Rhinegold, the grim action is leavened, especially through Loge, by an irony reminiscent of the satyr play. Action is headlong with few pauses for passages of lyrical meditation. It covers, in a breathtaking two and a half hours, the passage of the world from a state of nature to an advanced condition of economic repression and political tyranny, from "natural man" to humanity in chains. The downward pattern of *Das Rheingold* prefigures the action of the *Ring* as a whole, though the longer action is not as relentless as in *Das Rheingold*, but proceeds in a more leisurely manner, so that between dramatic climaxes we relish poetic landscapes of nature and the emotional depths of the characters. In *Das Rheingold* there is no respite to the fall, but in the main body of the cycle, the powers of love and desire for freedom resist the relentless degradation of the human condition brought about by the obsession with wealth and power, a resistance embodied in the concept of heroic action.

THE PRISON OF THE PAST

Despite its pessimism, *Rheingold* ends, as will the whole cycle, with the prospect of a more hopeful world. As Wotan, shaken by the murder of Fasolt, contemplates Valhalla, a thought occurs to him, designated by Wagner as "a great idea," expressed in one of the most stirring of all leit-motifs, a striding upward phrase on the high brass, often referred to as the "sword" motif. It represents Wotan's greeting to Valhalla as "a stronghold" he wishes to keep "safe from terror and dread,"[28] but it is obvious his new castle will offer him no such security. Nevertheless, his declaration is so powerful that the leitmotif has a warming effect upon the gloomy culmination of the action, allowing *Das Rheingold* to end on a note of optimism. Wotan appears to have conceived how to reverse the tragic chain of events that has set in as a result of his and Alberich's rape of the Rhinegold. Equally to the point, the "great idea" offers the possibility of canceling the crippling fear that came upon Wotan as he witnessed the death of Fasolt.

The optimism that ends *Das Rheingold* carries over into *Die Walküre* and even seems to affect the structure of the second drama. The actions of both *Das Rheingold* and *Die Walküre* are built on four events or confrontations that further the dialectic of love and nature with power and wealth. At each of these points in *Das Rheingold*, power wins out over love; at the corresponding points in *Die Walküre*, while love does not always win out over power, it displays the potential to reverse the destruction caused by power or at least arrest the rush of humanity toward self-destruction. In the first parallel, in *Das Rheingold* Alberich steals the Rhinegold, and power wins out over love; in *Die Walküre* Siegmund "steals" Sieglinde, and love wins over power. The second parallel, pointed out by Wagner himself,[29] is in the confrontations between Wotan and Fricka. In *Das Rheingold* Wotan quarrels with Fricka and realizes the limitations of his power, in *Die Walküre* they quarrel again, but Wotan understands more clearly his tragic dilemma and begins to think of abandoning power. Thirdly, Wotan and Loge plunder Alberich's hoard and show themselves to be in thrall to their obsession with wealth and power; in contrast, Siegmund, offered the chance of eternal bliss in Valhalla, the citadel of wealth and power, refuses it out of love for Sieglinde. Finally, when Fafner murders Fasolt, power wins out over love; in contrast, at the end of *Die Walküre*, as Wotan bids farewell to Brünnhilde, he is overwhelmed by his love for his daughter, which starts him on the road toward the abandonment of power he had first thought of in act 2.

For most of *Das Rheingold*, Wotan is too determined by events to qualify as any sort of hero. There are moments when he stands outside himself – the appearance of Erda being the first instance, the "great idea" the second – but mostly he is unable to attain the detachment from others that is a prerequisite of any hero. In *Die Walküre* we encounter a very different figure. In his majesty and wrath, he reminds us of the Odin described by Thomas Carlyle, "a hero . . . in his own rude manner; a wise, gifted, noble-hearted man . . . Hero, Prophet, God; Wuotan [sic], the greatest of all." Odin is an embodiment of nature in turmoil, and Carlyle insisted that "recognition of the divineness of Nature" was the essence of Scandinavian mythology. Wagner's Wotan and his warrior Valkyrie daughters seem to keep constantly to the forefront of their minds what Carlyle described as an awareness

of an inflexible *Destiny*; and that the one thing needful for a man was *to be brave*. The *Valkyrs* are Choosers of the Slain: a Destiny inexorable, which it is useless trying to bend or soften, has appointed who is to be slain . . . It is an everlasting duty, valid in our day as in that, the duty of being brave. *Valour* is still *value*. The first duty for a man is still that of subduing *Fear*. We must get rid of Fear: we cannot act at all until then.[30]

But while Wotan might aspire toward the messianic role similar to that ascribed to the "Hero as God" by Carlyle, his career in the *Ring* takes him in the opposite direction. He begins the first two music-dramas a supremely self-confident figure, in *Das Rheingold* dreaming of the permanent security he imagines Valhalla offers him, in *Die Walküre* anticipating the victory of Siegmund, which will win him the security that has so far eluded him. He ends both dramas confounded with doubt and fear, faced with the reality of things as they are. He ends up the opposite of Carlyle's heroic Odin.

But while we regard Wotan in *Das Rheingold* with suspicion and perhaps even dislike, in *Die Walküre*, as the principles on which his putative messianic power is based are revealed to be false, he starts calling on our sympathy and admiration. Now he becomes a tragic hero, an epic hero in the final stage of his power, but his downfall suggests the futility rather than the potency of heroism. Nevertheless, it does prepare him for his later role as romantic hero. His precipitate rush for power is balanced in *Die Walküre* by a growing awareness of the sacrifices power entails and, crucially, by the growth of the "great idea," born at the end of *Das Rheingold*, of the practical project of creating a new hero who will restore the damage that the unchecked drive for wealth and power has wreaked on the world. Even as *Die Walküre* begins, we hear of Wotan wandering through the world, as if he is preparing to withdraw from active participation in it, so our attention is directed less toward his complicity in evil than to how he is caught in the toils of a situation that, by the nature of things, cannot be solved. This tragic perspective makes his scene with Fricka one of the most compelling in the *Ring*. Fricka is not only a mouthpiece for conventional morality and the honor of the tribal system, but for the force of necessity that confines achievement and marks the fortune of humans and gods as tragic. The necessities that bind Wotan are the treaties and customs by which his power is maintained, acts committed in the past, now exercising inescapable consequences. Rarely in Western drama have the contradictions which construct the trap of tragedy been explicated with such clarity. If Wotan allows Siegmund to live, he will destroy the principles on which his power is based, and if he allows him to die, he will be denying nature, just as he did when he was prepared to abandon Freia in *Das Rheingold*. The predicament is presented with such lucidity that we recognize it as existing within and outside him, so that he and the order of things must bear responsibility, but the concrete reality of a divided husband and wife in whom love has died makes the tragic pattern that emerges from their confrontation quite excruciatingly painful. As Fricka leaves the stage, her majesty dwarfs Wotan and the curse motif in the trombones heralds the return of the fear and uncertainty born in Wotan as he witnessed Fasolt's murder.

A distinctive feature of the *Ring* is the extended passages of exposition, originating from Wagner's retrogressive method in writing the poem. The effect of these excursions into the past is to place an emphasis on how the past determines the present and cripples freedom of action. The immense length of Wotan's monologue displays how he is enslaved by the past, and the tale he tells confirms his fear. After Alberich's curse, he lost all "lightness of heart" and his subsequent actions – his coupling with Erda, the consequent birth of Brünnhilde, and the siring of his Valkyrie daughters to defend Valhalla – are nothing but a denial of his knowledge that Alberich, if he regains the ring, will destroy him. The only defence against this hideous demise is to create a hero who will act free of any coercion, obligation, or motive to acquire power or wealth. It is a noble concept, but as Fricka has pointed out with devastating logic, an impossible one, as everything Wotan creates has within it the substance of his self. The woman to whom Wotan is bound in a loveless relationship demonstrates the vanity of his ambitions and the necessity for him to continue to live in fear. But his moment of self-recognition is not followed by resigned acceptance of his fate. As he nears the end of his monologue and orders Brünnhilde to slay Siegmund, thereby perpetuating the conditions of fear under which he must live, his music rises to new heights of fury, and in the grandeur of his exit from the stage for the first time we hear the harsh tones of the primitive Odin. But the elemental wrath is nothing but a mask for his profound uncertainty.

THE FAILED ROMANTIC HERO

Wotan's diminished stature is apparent in the ease with which he capitulates to Fricka. While this is dictated by the logic of the situation, it also suggests that the heroic ideal that Wotan came upon at the end of *Das Rheingold* is lacking. In *Die Walküre*, the ideal is embodied in the figure of Siegmund and given expression mainly through Siegmund's love for his sister, Sieglinde. If Siegmund stands for the "free hero" who will save the world from destruction by human greed, the qualities of his character must define what that heroism is. In the course of act 1, they are centered almost exclusively on sexual desire. If fear arises from love-lessness, its opposite, confidence in the free activity of human beings, is rooted in love, specifically the sexual love of man and woman which Wagner considered fundamental to all other forms of love.[31] Sexual love signifies that the benign forces of the Rhinegold are still alive in humans. Until the end of act 2 of *Siegfried*, the Rousseauist ideal of humans living in harmony with nature and themselves remains the most desirable of conditions. As the Volsung twins' attraction to each other grows, erotic love and oneness with nature are elided to the point where they are identical. When the door of Hunding's hut opens to the spring, the tremolo in the orchestra, suggestive of leaves in the wind, recalls the sonic ambience of the Rhinegold and brother and sister feel their rising emotions as phenomena of nature. Siegmund describes his love for Sieglinde as the rebirth of spring, while Sieglinde responds by imagining their love as born in the natural element of the Rhinegold, water.

> My own likeness
> I glimpsed in the brook –
> and now I see it again:
> as once it rose from the pool,
> to me now you show that likeness.[32]

But their love is not kindled by nature alone. Throughout the act, much play is made with the gleam that shines from the twins' eyes. It seems literally to fire their love for each other, while Hunding, incapable of love, can see in it only a cause for suspicion. For him "the selfsame glittering serpent," in Siegmund's as in Sieglinde's eyes, is a covert bond between the two. Their eyes also connect them to a common past. Sieglinde describes how the wandering Wotan who thrust the sword into the tree at her wedding cowed all with the flash of his eye. As themes of freedom through love fasten themselves to the sword, the glow that radiates from its hilt seems to emit a similar energy and the twins' sexual delirium intensifies, until Sieglinde cries that Siegmund's glance is the same as that of the old man:

> Your eye's smouldering glance
> glinted upon me ere now: –
> so the greybeard looked
> as he greeted me once
> and brought comfort to me in my sadness.[33]

This leads them to acknowledge their kinship and, as Siegmund withdraws the sword from the tree and they rush out to consummate their love, the past arises not as a tragic force that cripples present action, but as a source of energy that vitalizes the present. Siegmund and Sieglinde are in touch with their heroic origins. Before withdrawing the sword, Siegmund sings the motif that accompanied Woglinde's warning about the renunciation of love in *Das Rheingold* and so proclaims that the baleful effects of the renunciation will be annulled. The romantic exaltation that ends act 1 is one of two moments in the *Ring* when Wotan's desire to achieve a world "safe from terror and dread" seems to have reached fulfillment in a union of nature and Eros.

But it is a moment only. Siegmund turns out a failure, incapable of fulfilling Wotan's ambitions. Admittedly he is destroyed by circumstances beyond his control, a victim of Wotan's need to maintain his authority. However, his grim end does not seem inappropriate, but warranted by his character. Siegmund has always been a fugitive. When we first see him he does not know where he is, all we know is that he is on the run. When he speaks of his heroic deeds, they are in the past. Furthermore, they never had that galvanizing impact on society that is the basic effect of all heroic action. Rather, he is the opposite of a hero, constantly rejected by a world that considers him nothing more than a threat to its own stability. He has magnificent moments. Deryck Cooke is right to see his renunciation of Valhalla for Sieglinde as the most decisive moment in the *Ring*,[34] as it is the first act of free will in the cycle, the first manifestation of Wotan's ideal. But there is much in Siegmund that prevents him from living up to his newly gained moral stature. He reacts more than he acts and the moment he engages in action instead of recounting it, he is defeated. While Wotan puts up considerable defence against Fricka in justifying the principle of the free hero, he capitulates to her instantly when it comes to the specifics of Siegmund's fate. Siegmund is not, ultimately, worth fighting for. Despite the exhilaration we feel at his sexual prowess and the splendor of his denial of Valhalla, he remains in our imagination as a weak figure, driven more by fear than hope, not equipped to lead the human race into a utopia of secure life. In the end he is defeated by the forces of the past and is quickly forgotten when more powerful struggles between love and necessity occupy the last act of *Die Walküre*. Are, therefore, the values that he stands for inadequate? Are the powers that emanated from the Rhinegold at the start of the *Ring* lacking?

THE NEW HERO

Whatever answers Wagner has to these questions lie in the second half of the *Ring*. Throughout *Siegfried* and at the start of *Götterdämmerung*, Siegfried seems to be the figure to dispel the doubts cast upon the viability of free heroism by his father Siegmund. No character in Wagner enters a drama with such expectations as Siegfried and none seems to have engaged the feelings of his creator so warmly. Siegfried for Wagner was a paragon of self-confidence, an "inwardly secure being" living "for his own calling."[35] Ever since, Siegfried has found his champions among Wagner's critics. In his own time, for those familiar with *Nibelungenlied*, he was the acme of the epic hero, a paragon of courage and strength, whose exploits strengthened the bonds of a chivalric society. His blond hair, rubicund complexion, and imposing stature, as well as his centrality to a work that was acquiring the status of a national poem, made Siegfried into a German national hero. He could dissolve the uncertainties arising from modern civilization. Siegfried was an embodiment of Feuerbach's idea of man's self-projection as god, Friedrich Engels saw him as "the crown of life" for German youth, while George Bernard Shaw considered him a born anarchist, a Bakunin, or a foreshadowing of the Nietzschean "overman." Siegfried also parallels figures in world mythology, resembling gods of light such as Swipdag from the Eddas, the Norse god Baldur, and the Egyptian Osiris. His bravery recalls Heracles and Achilles, while his divine ancestry places him, like Prometheus, halfway between the gods and humanity.[36]

But Siegfried fulfills neither the nationalist ambitions nor the high ideals that are placed in him. He does not become the "free hero" Wotan had imagined, nor, when he fails to live up to expectations, is he a particularly compelling tragic hero. He begins his career in the *Ring* as the most complete incarnation of early romantic naturalism. He grows up in the forest, in the company of animals, he understands parental love through watching the birds, and he knows himself through seeing his reflection in water. He is boisterous and full of energy, akin to several of the fictional manifestations of Rousseau's "natural man."[37] Bound by nothing, he has neither knowledge of the past nor fear of the future: "he knows neither his father nor mother, knows no order nor custom, knows no law nor measure."[38] He has grown up under the tutelage of Mime, who is the last person one can imagine nurturing the feelings of the young, but he has come through this unscathed, with no respect for the systematic learning that the Nibelung dwarf tried to din into him. In contrast to his father, his life follows a pattern characteristic of the epic hero. He is by birth semi-divine, he grows up in the wilderness, close to nature, under the nominal care of a guardian, who parallels the figure of a shepherd who often discovers the infant hero. When young he reveals both strength and courage, his advance into the world of adulthood is symbolized by the slaying of a dragon, and, as a result of this deed, he wins the hand of a maiden and so achieves sexual maturity.[39] His advance indicates he might successfully embody Wotan's ideal of the free hero.

But even in act 1 of *Siegfried* doubts arise about the integrity of his mission. The essence of free heroism is the capacity to act without regard for the past or fear of the future, but as soon as Siegfried commits himself to action by the forging of Nothung, he is, unknowingly, tying himself to the past. His refusal to follow the methods of forging relayed to him by Mime exemplifies the elevation of instinctual over acquired knowledge and the natural over the technological, but the act of forging parallels Wotan's original destruction of nature, as Nothung is fabricated on the charcoal from a felled ash-tree. The clang of Siegfried's hammer on the sword insistently reminds us of the anvils of Nibelheim, that nightmare site of blighted nature. Is Siegfried really setting out on new paths or will he repeat the patterns of the past? Within the scene itself it is difficult to tell, as Wagner's exuberance as a composer undermines the ironic insight granted by the action. The insistent, pounding rhythms fill the scene with an exhilarating energy, and as they rise to the climax of Siegfried splitting the anvil in two, give every indication that the young hero rushing off into the forest will indeed create a new world of free heroism.

Once we see him in the forest, however, it seems at first that his heroism will be a repetition of his father's. In the enchanting and sensuous "Forest Murmurs" that accompany his reverie beneath the trees, Siegfried meditates rhapsodically on the mother he has never known. The strings recall the sunshine striking the Rhinegold through the pellucid waters of the Rhine, so that the forest becomes a symbolic area in which the bond between humans and nature is realized. Siegfried's subsequent killing of Fafner ties him even more closely to nature as symbolically it indicates he can overcome the deadening force of sheer matter that is the antithesis of the constant change that is nature. Therefore, after his victory he more readily understands the language of nature. It is also nature in the guise of the Woodbird and not Wotan that leads him toward Brünnhilde on the rock.

A CRISIS IN COMPOSITION: WHO IS THE HERO?

At this point, Wagner encountered an impasse. After finishing the composition of act 2, he laid down his pen for twelve years, at precisely the point where the promise of all that had occurred was on the verge of fulfillment. He abandoned the _Ring_ partly for financial reasons, as he needed to write a music-drama that stood a chance of being widely performed in German opera-houses, partly for personal reasons, when developments in his emotional life prompted him to turn his attention to the myth of Tristan and Isolde. But his energies were also flagging. For all its beguiling nature music and the excitement of Siegfried's fight with Fafner, act 2 of _Siegfried_ has less momentum than any other act in the cycle. The drama seems to be running out of steam. Might this also indicate that Wagner was questioning the romantic value of oneness with nature that, until this point, had been assumed as the condition within which humans can most happily live? Is living in nature, which involves mainly a passive surrender to the senses, the solution to the world's ills? Is it strong enough to counter the onrush of power from those who renounce love and nature? Even though Siegfried kills Fafner and challenges the oppressive world of wealth, is the boy of "Forest Murmurs" sufficient to the task of saving the world? Or will he be like his father, a fugitive when faced with continuous opposition? It is much to the point that though Wagner completed act 2, he decided to give up composition at an earlier point, when Siegfried was daydreaming about his mother. "I have led my young Siegfried to a beautiful forest solitude," he wrote to Liszt, "and there have left him under a linden tree, and taken leave of him with heartfelt tears. He will be better off there than elsewhere."[40] In Wagner's imagination, Siegfried was still a passive figure, living without will in a natural world.

In fact Wagner had been having doubts about the viability of the _Ring_ some several months before breaking off composition. Nine months before, he had written to Röckel that when he embarked upon the cycle he "had built up an optimistic world, on Hellenic principles; believing that in order to realize such a world, it was only necessary for man to wish it." Later, however, he claimed to have been "unconsciously guided by a wholly different, infinitely more profound intuition . . . I had grasped the very essence and meaning of the world itself in all its possible phases, and had realized its nothingness."[41] Consequently, the mission that Siegfried is embarked on by the end of act 2 had, in Wagner's mind, no authenticity. The crisis of Siegfried's heroism brought to the surface a deeper tension within the _Ring_. The poem had been written largely under the influence of Feuerbach's secular humanism, which championed the capacity of human beings to achieve a free society once they had recognized that all concepts of the divine are merely projections of their own idealism. But the majority of the score was written after Wagner had read Schopenhauer, who negated any possibility of humans achieving freedom and happiness by actively striving toward them. Wagner interpreted Schopenhauer's principal idea to be "the final denial of the desire to live" and claimed that he found salvation in it. If salvation is not a goal that can be consciously attained and lies instead in "the end of all dreams,"[42] then the central figure of the *Ring* might not be Siegfried, but Wotan. By the end of act 2 of *Siegfried*, Wagner seemed to have misidentified his hero and the nature of the tragedy he was writing.

A remarkable feature of *Siegfried* is the way in which it combines the contrasting trajectories of comedy and tragedy, Siegfried's rise and the Wanderer/Wotan's fall, with neither modifying nor trivializing the other. Wotan is no longer central to the action, but occupies one part of a double drama. He is no longer the tragic hero of *Die Walküre*, and he has given up any messianic ambitions he had. Instead, he carries the resignation that Wagner had acquired from his reading of Schopenhauer. The result is a reconstitution of the romantic hero of the earlier music-dramas; as Winterbourne observes, the Wanderer is a complete realization of the romantic hero because of his profound sense of irony and his "incessant brooding on his state of mind."[43] The figure in the early music-dramas he most readily recalls is the Flying Dutchman. Initially, the Wanderer seems less engaged than the Dutchman, because while the Dutchman longs for a human community he has never experienced, the Wanderer has willingly abandoned one to wander through the world with no desire to be a participant in it. But the detachment is a façade. As Wotan had fallen from a state of confidence to fear and uncertainty in *Das Rheingold* and *Die Walküre*, so does he as the Wanderer. The supernal gravity of his music during the battle of questions in act 1 implies limitless wisdom in face of the uncertainties of the future. He seems to have transcended the crippling fear of all who are touched by the curse on the ring. Mime, in contrast, is driven solely by terror, which never allows him to escape from the prison of his own self and prevents him from learning anything from the Wanderer. But despite the guise of the detached romantic hero, the Wanderer is pursued by fear. Alberich recognizes this in their nocturnal meeting outside Fafner's lair.

> How proudly you threaten
> with insolent strength,
> yet how fearful you are at heart.[44]

The Wanderer denies this, claiming that "heroes alone can help me," but he is quick to waken Fafner and offers to save his life if he will give the ring to him and not the approaching Siegfried. He is not the observer his demeanor suggests, and Alberich's insistence on his fear suggests that he is closer to Mime than he appeared to be in the battle of questions in act 1.

COMPASSION AS A HEROIC FORCE

At the end of act 2 of *Siegfried*, there is no viable character to propel the drama through to its utopian conclusion in which the determining force of causality will be effectively resisted and the fear of death overcome. Siegfried is still passive and the Wanderer disillusioned and frightened. Both are lacking in love, the only force capable of instilling individuals with the strength to withstand the claims of power. But though love has hardly figured in the first two acts of *Siegfried*, it is only in abeyance, not dead. Furthermore, although sexual love was, for Wagner, the most fundamental form of love, it is more complex than pure physical desire, as it includes compassion. To determine how, we must return briefly to *Die Walküre*.

Although Siegmund and Sieglinde's love had been intensely sexual, compassion rather than Eros first drew them to each other. The lingering, attenuated melodies when they first meet speak more of compassion than desire, Siegmund feels Sieglinde's initial influence on him as soothing not physically arousing, and when he is about to leave, refreshed by her care, he stays only because she begs him to remain to comfort her. Only when spring bursts into the hut do they declare passionate love. Then in the desolate scene where they are pursued by the vengeful Hunding, compassion rather than desire keeps them together. Siegmund denies the conventional attributes of heroism by refusing to enter Valhalla, in the name of a love that transcends desire, which is motivated not by desire but by concern for the happiness of someone other than himself. It is a priority Wotan could never achieve because, as he had complained in his monologue, he is unable to distinguish between the world and himself, because he is in all things. Accordingly he called out for

> that other self for which I yearn,
> that other self I never see.[45]

But he remains caught in a state close to adolescence, in which there is no sense of difference between himself and the world. Siegmund, however, has moved on to maturity by recognizing that the claims of others have as much legitimacy as, if not more than, his own. He has never been an epic hero, having never found an admiring society for which he might sacrifice himself, and as a romantic hero he has been ineffective, because he remains caught in the projection of his own ego onto the world. But as one who feels compassion, a selfless interest in another individual, he acquires new stature. The most basic quality of all heroism has been the willingness to sacrifice oneself for others. In compassion, heroism appears once again, in rarefied form.

The compassion born in Siegmund and Sieglinde finds fuller realization in Brünnhilde. While Siegmund's love for Sieglinde transforms him morally, he is killed before he has the opportunity to act upon it. Brünnhilde, however, undergoes a more extended and consequential change. When she first appears, she is nothing but "the blindly elective tool of [Wotan's] will,"[46] but she finds herself forced to disengage from her father when she becomes involved in the events of the drama. When Wotan divulges his fear and pain to her through his monologue, she is at one with him, but she realizes she must struggle for freedom when she witnesses him turning against Siegmund. When she hears Siegmund renounce Valhalla for Sieglinde, she understands that freedom is not an inherent state, but something to be achieved by choice alone. In deciding to protect Siegmund in his battle with Hunding, she makes the same choice that Siegmund did with regard to Sieglinde: she denies herself the glories of Valhalla in the interests of another. This love, based more on compassion than desire, becomes a dominant motive in the final act. Brünnhilde sacrifices herself to ensure that Sieglinde escapes with Siegfried in her womb. After that, the condition of knowingly being separate from others, a precondition of compassion, is forced upon Brünnhilde by Wotan. He drives her from him because she acted separately from his will, but as she insistently points out, she did this to preserve his better self and to protect Siegmund in whom his ambitions were to be fulfilled. Once again, Wotan's tragic dilemma is emphasized. But even he breaks out of it temporarily when he lets his overwhelming love for his daughter break down his reserve. As his feelings for Brünnhilde hover between paternal solicitude and scarcely veiled sexual desire, he too comes to realize that the happiness of another person is of greater importance than his own, the sign of which is the wall of flame with which he surrounds her. As this can be pierced only by a man who knows no fear, the ideal of heroism that he had first conceived before crossing to Valhalla remains alive through his compassion. It is, therefore, in compassion that Wotan's concept of the free hero really lies. It is compassion that both imbues *Die Walküre* with an atmosphere of hope and provides the overwhelming pathos of its ending. It does not, however, permanently change Wotan. He returns at the end of *Die Walküre* to a loveless world.

RETURN TO THE *RING*

With the exception of Siegfried's tentatively articulated longings for his mother, the first two acts of *Siegfried* are largely lacking in love and compassion. When Wagner resumed composition on act 3, he was faced by the challenge to find a credible representation for compassionate love on stage. The legacy of romanticism offered him little help. Rousseauian naturalism was inadequate, as it was passive and provided no means of escape from eternally repeating the conditions of one's origin. The iconic figures of late romanticism, including the Wanderer, were alienated and disaffected, offering no foundation for a compassionate hero. The thought of Feuerbach and Schopenhauer undoubtedly aided Wagner in conceiving the dynamics of compassionate love, because both saw it as a binding power in the human community, but only after one had renounced all striving for oneself. But these concepts of compassion were not viable as models that would work effectively on stage.

When Wagner returned to the *Ring*, he did so with renewed vigor. The opening of act 3 of *Siegfried* is a moment of great exhilaration: the dynamics of the drama have changed and the score has a vast, restless energy that rarely lets up. This is a domain at once troubled and sublime, wracked with anxiety and touching the peaks of ecstasy. The act begins with Wotan's second encounter with Erda. In *Das Rheingold* Erda had foretold the end of all things with a choric solemnity that seemed to foreshadow the serene acceptance of death that Wagner would later recognize in his reading of Schopenhauer. But her reappearance in *Siegfried* is more disturbing. Erda is the source of all knowledge from whom the Wanderer wishes to learn, but she offers no solace. The tragic dilemma that made him a scourge of all he prized and yet destroyed the power he wished to maintain has created a universe of no value, direction, or control:

> wild and awry
> the world revolves.[47]

Erda cannot even offer the Wanderer the comfort of death in a universe of inevitable decline. Instead, she wishes only to sleep. The deepest realms of nature have abandoned Wotan. From the wildness of the music it is clear he is driven to the verge of despair, but as Erda is about to sink into the earth, he responds aggressively that a new world will be realized in Siegfried and Brünnhilde's love, an idea announced by one of the most generous, passionate themes in the whole cycle, a leitmotif described by Newman as "the World Inheritance motive, because it is associated later with the coming of the new and better world symbolised by Brynhilde [sic] and Siegfried."[48]

The advent of this theme represents a turning point, similar to Wotan's "great idea" at the end of *Das Rheingold* and Siegmund's rejection of Valhalla in *Die Walküre*, as it offers renewed hope that fear might be overcome. But this time love is not to be just an easy surrender to the sensuous delights of nature, but a denial of meaninglessness, "the deed that redeems the world."[49] In his exaltation, the Wanderer envisions humans determining their own future, a visionary idea that turns from the naturalism of Rousseau, the utopianism of Feuerbach, and even the resigned pessimism of Schopenhauer, toward the existentialism of Nietzsche and modern philosophy, where the only choice open to humans is to create, by their own volition, a world where they can live in freedom. But the Wanderer cannot live his ideal. In his confrontation with Siegfried several paths meet – tragedy and comedy, late and early romanticism, age and youth, the divine and the human. At this momentous point, the Wanderer finds he cannot face his own defeat, and his resistance to Siegfried's ascent of the mountain toward Brünnhilde is far from token. He fights his grandson with all his strength, but that strength is lacking, and he leaves the stage not as a nobly resigned hero, but a defeated, frightened man, a predicament from which he will never escape.

It is also possible that Siegfried may never escape from the childlike condition portrayed in "Forest Murmurs," where his sensuous enjoyment of nature intertwined with the longing for his unknown mother. Much has been written on incest in the *Ring*. One can interpret the coupling of Siegmund and Sieglinde in *Die Walküre* as nothing other than what Wotan claims it to be, an example of unconventional love, but it is difficult to avoid the implication that to be the new hero, one must come from pure, untainted blood, a circumstance triumphantly celebrated when the siblings rush into each others' arms and Siegmund sings of the triumph of Wälsung blood. Incest has, as a consequence, even been referred to as a "privilege" in the *Ring*.[50] Siegfried and Brünnhilde are scarcely less closely related than Siegmund and Sieglinde, and Siegfried calls twice on his mother when he first sees Brünnhilde, then he actually mistakes the Valkyrie for her:

> So my mother did not die?
> Was the lovely woman merely asleep?[51]

Brünnhilde is, of course, his aunt. But Wagner does not dwell on this consanguinity as he does with Siegmund and Sieglinde, though it is impossible to ignore the narrow latitude within which Siegfried is maturing. As a free hero, his sexual prowess should emancipate him from his family, but it does the opposite, it draws him back. Wotan, of course, has arranged things this way, a further circumstance that subverts Siegfried's freedom and points to a condition underlying all sexual congress, that it places the male in a state of dependence, which returns him to the condition of childhood. Siegfried, therefore, is as subject as Wagner's earlier heroes had been to the cycle of repetition.

Whether Wagner celebrated or deplored incest is difficult to judge. Once again, his proclivity to craft powerful dramatic climaxes did not allow him to cast an ironic light on the endings of either act 1 of *Die Walküre* or act 3 of *Siegfried*. But there is a fundamental difference in mood between the two love duets. Although Siegfried and Brünnhilde are mutually attracted, their wooing has none of the erotic animation that kindled Siegmund and Sieglinde. Once they have overcome their initial reserve, their love grows as a universal force, and they seem driven not so much by the immediacy of physical desire as by a consciousness of the ends that the consummation of desire will achieve, which are the breaking of bonds with the past and the discovery of a power that will defeat death. Compassion has little place. Dramatically the duet is the most dangerous moment in the *Ring* as, for the first time in the cycle, Wagner abandons the detailed attention to his characters' emotional lives, which had made them dramatically credible even when symbolic dimensions of the action were uppermost. Brünnhilde and Siegfried do not so much celebrate their love, as sing of the ultimate values to which that love points. They become all symbol. The alluring ideal of humans living at one with nature has been forgotten; instead, they strive to dominate nature, even to reverse it. In this new, rhetorical mode of love, compassion seems to have no part. Effective realization of a new heroism through compassionate love seems, in the clamorous ending of *Siegfried*, to have disappeared.

SIEGFRIED, THE SON OF HIS FATHER

With *Götterdämmerung* the *Ring*, it has sometimes been claimed, appears to lose coherence. Shaw famously attributed this to the conditions of Bismarck's Germany, which were different from those following the revolution of 1848–49. In the life of Germany, the forces of matter, which Wotan and Alberich released in *Das Rheingold*, had not been defeated as Wagner had hoped they would be; hence, when he came to compose the score of *Götterdämmerung*, the allegory he had created in the *Ring* no longer meant anything to him, so he finished the whole thing off as a glorified grand opera.[52] But this is an inadequate explanation. Wagner was never a man to waste his energies on a project he considered worthless. If he had done so, the ending of the *Ring* project would have smacked of cynicism, and, whatever his failings, cynicism was never one of them. If there is any loss of coherence, it is not in the plot, which is as clear-cut as *Das Rheingold*, while the music of *Götterdämmerung* is the mightiest he wrote and the stage-spectacle the grandest he devised. The problem, if there is one, lies mainly with Siegfried. He never becomes what he promised to be, the lover who defeats death and the hero who fulfills Wotan's "great idea" by acting out of free will so as to ensure the freedom of others and bring reconciliation among them, thereby defeating the baleful forces of Alberich. Siegfried's potential to be the new hero hinges upon two factors. First, he knows no fear, and although he felt it when he first saw the sleeping Brünnhilde, it soon disappeared. Secondly, he has no regard for the past. Although he occasionally refers to past events, for the whole of *Siegfried* and most of *Götterdämmerung*, he never engages in the extended retrospection that other characters do. Instead, he looks to the future, so remains unscathed by forces that motivate and determine the actions of others.

Siegfried's heroism is fine when it is a question of dealing with a world where appearances do not deceive and evil declares itself in the form of a hideous dragon, but it is poor preparation for the social and political world, which is constructed upon the very fear that Alberich invested in the ring through his curse. The first words Gunther sings are about his fear that he does not have the authority that his role as chief of the Gibichungs requires, and much of the drama, including the intrigue that ensnares Siegfried, is devoted to establishing a façade of power to mask that fear. Siegfried's incapacity to live in this world is exemplified by the drink that Hagen gives him, which is no love potion, but a drink of forgetfulness. This does nothing more than indicate Siegfried's present state of mind when he meets Gutrune. His surrender to her charms displays an inner lack of resilience and shows him an instant victim of society rather than a hero who will transform it. He even becomes the antithesis of a hero as the one nominal act of heroism he commits, crossing the wall of fire that surrounds Brünnhilde's rock, leads to the subjugation of Brünnhilde in a marriage where love is used in the interests of power. The forces of Alberich, under the guidance of Hagen, have won.

Siegfried's shameful career of betrayal, lying, womanizing, and indolence can quite credibly be read as evidence that the ideal Wotan intended to realize could never have been achieved in the first place and is therefore worthless. This may be the tragedy, human nature is too frail to live up to the high expectations of free heroism. But if that is the resolution of the drama, it is unsatisfactory and smacks, once again, of cynicism. Wagner always maintained a fundamental confidence in his protagonists, and he seems in particular to have wanted to keep faith with Siegfried. He was perfectly capable of musically indicating changes in the personalities and predicaments of his characters, but Siegfried never changes. He is as buoyant and optimistic in the minutes before his death as he was as a youth in the forest. But he acquires an added gravity when he dies, a moment of high pathos that invests him with the nobility he so lacked among the Gibichungs.

This pathos arises from the illusion of Siegfried falling prey to the structure of the *Ring* cycle itself. As already noted, he does not engage in those long passages of recollection that are among the most distinctive features of the *Ring* and always show how the present is determined by the past. His lack of concern for the past is an aspect of his fearlessness; he can be free because he is not crippled by guilt from the past, nor is he hampered by any awareness of the consequences of his action. As Wagner wrote to Röckel, Siegfried was "my ideal of the perfect human being, whose highest consciousness manifests itself in the acknowledgement that all consciousness must find expression in present life and action."[53] This means he can never tell stories, as stories tie him to the past. But as *Götterdämmerung* proceeds, memory begins to plague him. When Brünnhilde, hostage in the halls of the Gibichungs, accuses him of treachery and he falls victim to intrigue, he starts looking back to defend himself and remembers that the ring he wears on his finger came from the hoard at Neidhöhle. Memory becomes a permanent attribute in the final act when, for the first time, he volunteers to tell the tale of his boyhood days. By telling a story he shows himself to be part of society rather than outside it, and society always legitimates the present by the sanction of the past. The act of telling the story therefore betrays those qualities that made him a hero, so when Hagen plunges the spear into his back, it is no arbitrary act, but congruous with the action as it marks the death of heroism within Siegfried. As he dies, memories flood back in luminous and intense nostalgia. He recalls the moment when free heroism was fulfilled, in his and Brünnhilde's love. But nothing came from it. He dies as the son of his father, glimpsing the new world, but unable to achieve it. The *Trauermusik* that follows, misleadingly referred to

as "Siegfried's Funeral March," does not celebrate the individual hero who
has died, but the passing of Wotan's grand idea itself.[54] At this point, the
Ring bears all the marks of a tragedy without a hero.

The most confusing aspect of *Götterdämmerung* is Wagner's apparent
insistence that Siegfried actually was the hero he had never been. As
Brünnhilde embarks upon the great peroration that brings the *Ring* to
a close, she claims him to have been the most honest of men, a great maker
of treaties, a paragon of loyalty; in short, the purest of heroes.

> Never were oaths
> more nobly sworn;
> never were treaties
> kept more truly;
> never did any man
> love more loyally.[55]

But this is a Siegfried we have never seen. The tight structure of the cycle
has never even allowed for such a man, who easily and nobly engages in
the political world of oaths and treaties, to reveal himself. In fact, had he
done so, he would never have fallen prey to the intrigue of Hagen and the
Gibichungs. In that realm of action where Brünnhilde considers Siegfried
to have been most heroic, he has been an utter failure.

The reason for this puzzling gap, between Siegfried's character and
Brünnhilde's praise of it, may be due to the immense time-lag between
the composition of the poem and the music of *Götterdämmerung*. While
the poem and music of *Rheingold* were written within two years of each
other, about twenty-six years separate Wagner's writing of the first draft
of *Siegfrieds Tod* and the composition of the music of the final act of
Götterdämmerung. As the long hiatus in composition testified, Wagner's
understanding of the *Ring*, which included his ideas as to what constituted
a hero, had changed and, after his reading of Schopenhauer especially, his
priorities had shifted. Perhaps he should have altered his plot and dialogue
to reflect this, but he did not and for good reason. If he altered parts of
the poem this late in the game, he would have had to change much else
in the cycle that had already been composed, leading to a compositional
nightmare and, almost certainly, failure to complete the score. The Siegfried
that Brünnhilde describes belongs to the earlier years of composition, when
Wagner was more confident of the values attached to epic heroism.

Does this mean, therefore, that the resolution of Siegfried's career is an
artistic failure, which, coming as it does at the end of such an immense
and pivotal work, must stand as the most significant in Wagner's career?

Probably not, because Brünnhilde's solo underscores the most essential feature of heroism, that it is an idea only and must remain as such. Heroism ultimately resides not in the deeds of the hero, but in the memory of them after his death. Only in memory, not in action, can a hero be a hero. An unvarying mark of all the heroic lives tabulated by Raglan had been the decline of the hero after he acquires power. Heroism is a quality that flourishes outside society and can only be properly laid claim to after one's death. Wagner's Siegfried goes the necessary way of all heroes, because if the hero acquires power in life and uses it to legitimate his heroic status, he would deny human freedom. Heroism can only be itself when it does not touch us directly, is not part of our daily life. If it does, it assumes totalitarian authority and becomes that literal heroism with which the twentieth century in particular was cursed. Wagner, in killing Siegfried, seems to have turned from rather than anticipated that mode of heroism.

BRÜNNHILDE

Nevertheless, the conclusion to the *Ring*, aurally and visually one of Wagner's most spectacular achievements, is suffused with the ambience of the heroic. It is, however, heroism of a different constitution, a heroism with which we may live, rather than an epic heroism by which we would probably die. In *Die Walküre*, Brünnhilde was alienated from Wotan because she paid more attention to Siegmund's needs than her own. Her choice did not cater to desire, but expressed compassion and an acknowledgement that the world is different from oneself, a state of mind achieved by neither the epic nor the romantic hero. Siegmund's denial of Valhalla taught her independence of will and while her will did not emancipate her from her father, it saves "vital aspects of her father's nature from annihilation," because, other than Siegmund, she is the only individual in the *Ring* who acts free of coercion, fear, or self-interest. Even before Siegfried is born, she displays the new heroic qualities that will save the world from destruction by human greed.[56]

While Brünnhilde emerges as a compassionate individual of moral integrity who has the potential to bring about social cohesion, she is still a scion of the natural world, though the realm of nature she occupies is different from the young Siegfried's. She is the daughter of Erda, the goddess who sees all things, who recognizes necessity. When Erda and Wotan leave the stage in the last act of *Siegfried*, Brünnhilde effectively takes over from them. She acts out of her understanding of necessity, but while Erda had encouraged fatalistic acceptance in Wotan, inducing him to contemplate his end with serenity, Brünnhilde adopts a less passive attitude and heralds the utopia that Wotan had once envisaged in Valhalla, a state where people would live "safe from dread and dismay."

This new dispensation is first glimpsed in the union of Siegfried and Brünnhilde, when they are seized by the illusion that through their love they can laugh at death. The transformation caused by their love still possesses them at the start of *Götterdämmerung*. Brünnhilde here becomes the fully compassionate figure she has always potentially been: she grants Siegfried the freedom to go out into the world – a freedom not available to her – and Siegfried insists that in all his actions he will be inspired solely by the thought of her. In their last duet, the other is more important than the self, and the condition that appalled Wotan, his incapacity to find anything other than himself in whatever he saw around him, has been dissolved. If this moment in the love of Brünnhilde and Siegfried were to become permanent, utopia would have arrived. But *Götterdämmerung* reminds us that utopias are not possible.

Brünnhilde was born to help Wotan defend Valhalla, meaning she warded off his awareness of death by deflecting the fear and uncertainty it aroused in him. Once she has left, he is again vulnerable to that fear. Whether Wotan ever calmly contemplates his inevitable demise is questionable. In *Siegfried*, the Wanderer's anxiety over Alberich regaining power intensifies, as does his exaltation at the prospect of Siegfried and Brünnhilde's victory. He does not surrender to Siegfried happily, and in *Götterdämmerung* we no longer see him, but when Waltraute visits Brünnhilde to beg her to return the ring to the Rhine daughters, we learn that he has not accepted his decline philosophically. On the contrary, he is filled with terror of the end. He returned home from his defeat by Siegfried cowed and depressed, not serene and accepting his fate. Waltraute describes a Valhalla bereft of energy, transfixed by fear. Wotan is still haunted by Alberich's curse, as evidenced in his words whispered to Waltraute.

> If she gave back the ring
> to the deep Rhine's daughters,
> from the weight of the curse
> both god and world would be freed.[57]

He is still possessed by the fear that came upon him at the end of *Rheingold*, and the hushed horror of the music indicates that he has failed to accept "what necessity imposes," as Wagner, in the earlier stages of composing the *Ring*, claimed he did.[58] Brünnhilde's dismissal of Waltraute signifies her final emancipation from Wotan and the primacy of her love for Siegfried over any concern for Wotan's fear.

Brünnhilde, though devastated by Siegfried's betrayal and driven to disclose to Hagen the secret that will lead to his death, ultimately remains untouched by the tragic events. As she enters the Gibichung Hall to gaze on Siegfried's body on his bier, she does so with supreme detachment, dismissing the argument over his corpse as the squabbling of children. She has reached the state of the sublime central to Schiller's understanding of tragedy. She is now able to act without fear of personal consequences and with a knowledge of ultimate truth. After her eulogy to Siegfried, she claims he was not responsible for his own fall, as he was a victim of Wotan; he fell as a sacrifice to the curse the gods wished to avoid, which makes a mockery of the "great idea" it was his mission to embody. She then puts forward a claim that defines sublime consciousness:

> All things, all things,
> all things I know
> all is clear to me now.[59]

What does she know? Her betrayal has taught her that all power is corrupt, it has destroyed Siegfried, and it inhibits natural goodness. What force can overcome this power? What will be the formative agency in the new world where power will be no more? We hear it in the most sweeping of all the *Ring*'s melodies, played only once before when Sieglinde sang in praise of Brünnhilde's selflessness. Wagner simply labeled this melody "Brünnhilde," but generations have rightly sensed it as announcing too the power of unconditional love. As the melody possesses Brünnhilde, the pent-up tensions of the drama are relieved and the singer's breath sounds like the breath of the world.

This is not an ending that can be encompassed by ideology. Wagner knew this and it was the one part of the *Ring* he rewrote. The final solo tells us that the solution to the woes of humanity does not lie in the optimism of Feuerbach, nor in the resigned pessimism of Schopenhauer, nor in the pure naturalism of Rousseau. Instead, it can be found in a concrete world where individual human beings, free from the desire for money and power, act not to further their own interests, but out of compassion for others. We must note especially that, contrary to some assumptions, the conclusion of *Götterdämmerung* does not depict the end of the world and therefore betoken some apocalyptic desire for self-destruction in the whole human race. Only Brünnhilde, Hagen, and the gods, the passing generations, die in the conflagration. Everyone else is left alive in a world where, if they come to understand and live by the values of Brünnhilde's sacrifice, they might do so "safe from dread and dismay." It is a state humans can only achieve when they have freed themselves from greed and lost all fear of the only oppression they can never escape: death. When we no longer fear death, we are resistant to all coercion and are, as Schiller argued, free. Only after humans have willed their deaths can they claim to be free. Brünnhilde is the only character in the *Ring* with that capacity. In willingly dying, she displays a strength that eluded Siegmund, Siegfried, and Wotan. She dies their deaths for them and in so doing shows them how they should have lived.

In returning the ring to the Rhine daughters, Brünnhilde restores the Rhinegold to its proper element so that its primal energy can once again serve as a source of human vitality. But while the title of the cycle, *Der Ring des Nibelungen*, and the repetitive patterns to which all characters but Brünnhilde seem prone suggest that nothing has really changed, the cycle does not end where it began. Compassion as a force that changes people and brings about a less destructive world has triumphed and a utopia has come into view in our imagination if not in actuality. Wagner's belief in that utopia distinguishes him from Rousseau and the entire romantic tradition. Salvation will come about through moral choice not natural volition, through concern for others not through glorification of the self. The free hero, who is ultimately Brünnhilde, is the one who can bring that world about.

5

The last music-dramas: toward the messiah

LAST DRAMAS

If old age is marked by a desire for death as a relief from the rigors of life, then Wagner started aging when he was still quite young, at forty-one, after his first reading of Schopenhauer. Through Schopenhauer he learnt that survival in an antagonistic world comes most effectively through resigned acceptance, which led him to a sensation of profound peace which seemed to cancel his self. As he wrote to Liszt:

His principal idea, the final denial of the will to live, is of terrible seriousness, but it is uniquely redeeming . . . When I think back on the storms that have buffeted my heart and on its convulsive efforts to cling to some hope in life . . . I have now found a sedative which has finally helped me to sleep at night; it is the sincere and heartfelt yearning for death: total unconsciousness, complete annihilation, the end of all dreams – the only ultimate redemption.[1]

Wagner still had twenty-nine years to live and while his letters and personal writings indicate a continuing yearning for death, he spent most of his time living very much in the world, as the contentious, intensely ambitious, cantankerous, visionary individual he had always been. The sensibility of his music-dramas did, however, begin to shift. The first sign of this came when he broke off composition on the *Ring* in 1857. His three last music-dramas, *Tristan und Isolde*, *Die Meistersinger von Nürnberg*, and *Parsifal*, form a unity as in each he explored different aspects of the phenomenon of resignation and of the hero as a conduit between human and natural or numinous planes of being. Romantic and epic heroism in these music-dramas become elided until they are united in the figures of Walther von Stolzing and Parsifal, the sole instances in Wagner's oeuvre of the messianic hero.

While the last music-dramas are thematically related, there are pronounced generic differences between them; *Tristan*, referred to simply as "Eine Handlung" ("an action"), is closest to tragedy, while *Die Meistersinger* is Wagner's sole mature comedy, though he just called it a "music-drama"; and *Parsifal*, a "Bühnenweihfestspiel" ("stage consecration play"), defies categorization. All three music-dramas contain themes that are common to the last plays of tragic dramatists and have a distinctly retrospective dimension, suggesting that Wagner is assessing his life. They center increasingly on resolution and forgiveness, and *Tristan* and *Parsifal* explore planes of consciousness beyond the purely physical, what Kenneth Muir in writing of last plays called "unknown modes of being."[2] In act 3 of *Tristan*, the hero undertakes a harrowing journey through the limbo of his unconscious, but in *Meistersinger* and *Parsifal* Wagner finds a direction for the journey and a meaning for the lives the journey comprises. In doing this, he confronts the question that David Grene found central to many last dramas: "Which is the deeper reality, the standard of 'ordinary' nature or the pattern that man has laid upon it?"[3]

Tristan and *Parsifal* bear many formal marks of being last works. Their action is static, more abstract than in the earlier music-dramas, dialogue is comparatively sparse, reliance is placed on symbolic properties to communicate the immanence of a numinous presence, and throughout there is a sense that humans are not in control of their destiny. The patterns of their lives are delineated in a strikingly unadorned manner. In particular, the repetitive circularity within which most of Wagner's heroes are caught is evinced more starkly, so that the action of his last music-drama, *Parsifal*, can be viewed as nothing but the search of humanity for release from the corrosive state of eternal repetition. Wagner began his career in the company of Byron, Scribe, and Weber, but he ended looking toward the drama of absurdism and Samuel Beckett. The hero in these late dramas is not eclipsed, but his heroism resides less in deeds of bravery and avowals of intense individualism, more in the denial of the self and the cultivation of personal powers that will bring unity to a decayed and disunited world. As the nature of that influence defies easy definition these last works of Wagner arouse disparate, often antagonistic responses.

TRISTAN UND ISOLDE: "THE ENDPOINT OF ROMANTICISM"

This ambivalence is apparent in the reception of *Tristan und Isolde*, which is, perhaps, the supreme expression of romantic love in Western culture. Nevertheless, the self-absorption into which the lovers fall and the death and transfiguration with which the action ends have often been thought of as symptoms of a disease that cankers the human condition. Nietzsche caught *Tristan*'s strangely confusing effect well when he wrote of its "dangerous fascination and . . . gruesome and sweet infinity." He found its allure compelling, even necessary: "the world," he claimed, "is poor for anyone who has never been sick enough for this 'voluptuousness of hell.'"[4] Thomas Mann never missed a performance of "that most sublime and dangerous of Wagner's works" at the Munich Hoftheater,[5] but in his short story, "Tristan," he associates devotion to this music-drama with tuberculosis and unhealthy withdrawal from society. Fascination with the "sickness" of *Tristan* persists today. In the movie *Aria*, Isolde's Liebestod swells over the soundtrack as Bridget Fonda and her lover slit their wrists in a seedy Las Vegas motel and when, some years ago, the Oregon police discovered the bodies of the Kinkle family, slain by their son Kip, a loop of recorded tape was repeatedly playing the final bars of Isolde's transfiguration, an event caught in a macabre police video.

The unease with which generations since Wagner have experienced *Tristan* may arise from uncertainty over its moral framework. As a love-tragedy, *Tristan* is diametrically opposite to that other icon of the genre, *Romeo and Juliet*. In Shakespeare's tragedy, the moral perspective is comparatively lucid: romantic love is a means through which social violence may be stilled. There is a clarity and harshness about the forces that have cut down the young lovers and their pathos is made more painful by the meaninglessness of the conflict that caused it. Punishment is the only harvest of the action. In the words of the Duke:

> See what a scourge is laid upon your hate,
> That heaven finds means to kill your joys with love!
> And I for winking at your discords too
> Have lost a brace of kinsmen. All are punished.[6]

But while there is punishment in *Tristan und Isolde* it does not fall on the heads of the protagonists. For them death is a reward. Tristan dies at a moment of supreme happiness, as if death actually *is* happiness, while Isolde, in rapt contemplation of his body, delivers a song of victory, which announces that freedom exists only beyond human life.

While the philosophical perspective of *Tristan und Isolde* grew from Wagner's devotion to Schopenhauer's philosophy, the conclusion can also be considered as an exercise in Schiller's sublime. The path to Isolde's transfiguration is, however, far from the one either Schopenhauer or Schiller had in mind. For Schopenhauer, union with the noumenal was only achieved after one had rejected the world and proved resistant to the demands of sexual desire, which was the most powerful force tying the individual to the world. Some of Schiller's characters reach sublime consciousness, Wallenstein and

Mary Stuart for example, but in these instances as we have seen sublimity is a fleeting condition, glimpsed briefly before their deaths. It is also a moral state, which they have arrived at only through laborious strife. Some of Wagner's characters touch the sublime when they leave the stage – Lohengrin returns to the utopia of Monsalvat and Brünnhilde, who knows all things, meets her death with sublime fearlessness. But Tristan and Isolde do more than touch the sublime, they inhabit it, and they reach it by the path not of moral travail but of erotic love.[7] Sexuality rather than spirituality or moral excellence is posited as the condition that allows humans to achieve transcendence. While sexual desire had been the central theme of most operas from Monteverdi on, sex had normally been treated as a sign of human secularity, rarely as an agency through which humans gain access to a world beyond the senses, commonly understood to be the exclusive domain of religion. This leads to strikingly contradictory interpretations of the work. Michael Tanner, for example, regards *Tristan* as a "religious" drama, comparable to the *St. Matthew Passion*,[8] while Peter Wapnewski, noting the absence of any supernatural apparatus, sees it as Wagner's "most human work."[9] While these viewpoints can be reconciled, they exemplify the disparate responses *Tristan* can generate. They give some hint too of why *Tristan* caused unease among Wagner's contemporaries and suggest a clue as to why there was an unusual delay of eleven years between its first performance in Munich in 1865 and its second production in Berlin in 1876.

The slowness with which *Tristan* found its way into the repertoire was due to more than the unconventional representation of sexuality. Dramaturgically, it was in accord with few of the canons of nineteenth-century theatre. Wagner wrote it because he wished to produce a work for small provincial theatres that were unable to stage his larger dramas satisfactorily. Although he signally failed in this modest aim, it left some marks that make *Tristan* stand out from his previous work. For a start, the action is extremely simple. Wagner did not so much adapt material from Gottfried von Strassburg's epic poem, *Tristan*, as refine the action to the minimum necessary for stage representation. Gottfried's poem is packed with events: Tristan is a doughty warrior who slays mighty enemies and slaughters a dragon; he and Iseult sustain a lusty, adulterous relationship for several years; King Marke, a somewhat comic character, is kept in the dark by elaborate subterfuges; and Iseult, a morally dubious figure, even considers murdering Brangäne when she thinks she might gain advantage from it. Wagner avoided any complex plot twists and opportunities for spectacle offered by the epic, and moments of dramatic confrontation, which, had he been writing in his earlier vein, would have been drawn out at great length, are reduced to virtually nothing. For example, in *Lohengrin*, the duel between Lohengrin and Telramund provides the extended climax to act 1, but the equally important duel between Tristan and Melot that concludes act 2 of *Tristan* passes with almost no acknowledgment in the score and minimal representation on stage. In performance it can be over before we even notice it has taken place.

Wagner's music-drama is a distillation of the myth of Tristan and Isolde, not a complete representation of it. The action-laden early nineteenth-century drama and opera did not, therefore, provide a suitable model. Thematically, the conflict of love versus honor was suggested by Wagner's reading of Calderón,[10] but, as Francis Fergusson observes, to give his static stage-world form, he referred to Greek tragedy and the neo-classical tragedies of Jean Racine, though with the important rider that *Tristan* is "opposed in almost every way to the tragedy and theatre of reason."[11] The cast of *Tristan* is structured in a strictly Racinean mode, Tristan, Isolde, and Marke each having their confidants in Kurwenal, Brangäne, and Melot. As in Racine, extended passages are devoted to exposition that probes the influence of the past upon the present, and characters declaim in speeches rather than converse in the fluid conversational style characteristic of much of the *Ring* and *Die Meistersinger*. But despite the declamation, *Tristan* has a special intimacy, a quality Wagner only fully understood while rehearsing the work in the confined dimensions of the Cuvilliéstheater in Munich. The proximity of stage and auditorium meant he had never felt so close to his characters. In this space, he wrote to King Ludwig, "everything relates to purely human qualities. The incidents are of a thoroughly internal delicate kind; here a quiver in the face, a blink of an eye is telling."[12] Eventually the size of the orchestra and the King's insistence that *Tristan* be premiered in the Hoftheater meant that Wagner had to abandon the smaller theatre.

Tristan was the first of Wagner's works to be written wholly under the influence of Schopenhauer, whose philosophy led him to acknowledge his own fatalism, so far hidden by his prevailingly optimistic view of the world. This did not intensify his proclivity to depression; on the contrary, as his letter to Liszt attests, he found Schopenhauer's philosophy, which argues that the numinous "will" beyond material appearance is the ultimate reality and that all striving within the human world is vain, to have an oddly tonic effect upon him. Through the journey traveled by Tristan and Isolde, together and separately, into their inner world, Wagner came as close as he ever would to a theatrical realization of the "non-existence" to which Schopenhauer had awoken him.

For Schopenhauer, the end of such a journey was the end of tragedy itself. He granted music a supreme position among the arts as it gave unmediated expression to the power of the will, but tragedy was the preeminent literary genre as its action led to a surrender to the will. This, as we have noted, bears some similarity to Schiller's concept of the sublime. "Thus we see in tragedies the noblest men, after long conflict and suffering, at last renounce the ends they have so keenly followed, and all the pleasures of life, or else freely and joyfully surrender life itself."[13] But Schopenhauer differed from Schiller and most tragedians by arguing that this renunciation does not come best through exceptional situations. Most tragic heroes, he argued, are extraordinary beings who renounce life because of extreme wickedness or the blind workings of chance, but the superior tragedy comes about through "characters of ordinary morality" discovering in the conditions of the world the cause of their suffering. Because these conditions are so ordinary, neither they, nor the audience that witnesses their fate, can complain of injustice. "This last kind of tragedy is also the most difficult of achievement," Schopenhauer insists, "for the greatest effect has to be produced in it with the least use of means and causes of movement."[14] He cites *Clavigo*, *Wallenstein*, and *Hamlet* as notable examples in spoken theatre; among operas, he specifies Bellini's *Norma*.

Wagner also had a special regard for Bellini. As a young man he had had scant respect for contemporary French and Italian opera, but Bellini was the exception. In one of his earliest essays, he praised "his limpid melody, [his] simple, noble, beauteous song" and wrote of *Norma*, "his most successful composition," as a work that reached "the tragic height of the Greeks" through the way in which the music majestically elevates the action.[15] Wagner's musical debt to *Norma* in *Tristan* has already been acknowledged,[16] but there are dramatic similarities also. The configuration of characters in *Tristan* is reminiscent of *Norma*, and Norma and Isolde both recall Medea, Norma in being abandoned by Pollione, Isolde by her immense anger. In both operas it is difficult to identify "plot" as an interlocking series of events; more accurately, each opera presents a basic situation that is resolved. Above all, the climax of *Norma* comprises a personal transformation that has a palpable influence on the entire world of the opera. The betrayal of Norma by Pollione indicates that sexual love has died between them. This does not lead to their separation, however, but to the birth of a compassionate love that prompts them to reveal their past sexual liaison and willingly die on the sacrificial pyre. This reversal is not unexpected. Norma's entrance aria, "Casta diva," is a prayer for peace, which contrasts with the warlike strains of the Gauls, who wish to drive out the Romans.

Later, Norma's love for Pollione prevents her from leading the Gauls in revenge on Rome. Her refined and contemplative vocal line has a pacifying effect upon whoever sings with her; it calms Adalgisa, whose compassion for Norma proves stronger than her love for Pollione, it softens the revengeful cries of the chorus of Gauls, and it convinces Pollione to surrender his life. Dramatic confrontation is avoided and the massive, sorrowful finale expresses unified compassion for Norma, despite nominal hostility in the words of the chorus. Norma's compassion transforms not only her faithless lover but all who are with her, and the agitation that had earlier threatened to overwhelm her is converted into a solemn acceptance of a presence beyond the physical world, a resignation to a force that Schopenhauer identified with the will. This transformation would be recalled in *Tristan und Isolde*, though while in Bellini the powers of Eros have abated, in Wagner they are paramount.

The realm of the will is so present in *Tristan* that it led Wagner to resume the experimental mode that he had initiated in *Holländer* and developed in *Tannhäuser*, where the action represents the inner workings of the protagonists' minds. He had abandoned this in *Lohengrin* and the *Ring*, where the use of realistic scenery is fairly conventional, but in *Tristan* the setting again provides a metaphorical path to the inner life of the lovers, and the drama ends as a representation of that inner life and the numinous will with which that life is unified. It begins with one foot in the world of social and political affairs, but external reality becomes increasingly tangential so that by the end, its incursions into the private, mental realm of Tristan and Isolde seem intrusive and beside the point. The power of the lovers to transform their world becomes the action and determines the way in which we understand the stage. Their submission to romantic love makes them conscious of a universe beyond the perception of human senses, which in turn transforms their and our perception of the normal world. Furthermore, submission to the will in *Tristan* arises, as Schopenhauer wrote of *Norma*, not from "greatest misfortune" caused by extreme acts of wickedness or complex entanglements, but from the simple circumstances of "human action and character."

The public world is felt with particular acuteness early in the music-drama. The boundless seascape of act 1 symbolizes the lovers' lack of direction and dissolution of individual identity once they give way to suppressed passion. The ship, however, confines them, giving order and direction to those sailing in it. The world of concrete action is heard in Kurwenal's stout rhythms, the rough choruses of the sailors, and the perfunctory spectacle of Marke's arrival. Later the public world intrudes with catastrophic effect on the lovers, but despite this its impact becomes progressively muted and its affairs seem increasingly superfluous. The realistic perspective of the *Ring*, through which private emotion is tempered by the public context in which it occurs, is reversed. In *Tristan*, the public world is eventually apprehended exclusively from the standpoint of the subjective self. Thomas Mann's claim for *Tristan* as "a Romantic work, deeply rooted in Romantic thought and sensibility"[17] is well grounded as the subjective viewpoint, that most consistent and central tenet of romanticism, here achieves one of its rare complete manifestations on stage. Its medium is romantic love, which, in contrast to its treatment in the earlier *Holländer* and the later *Die Meistersinger*, is profoundly asocial. Romantic love obliterates the external world, and when consciousness of that world resurfaces, as it does at the end of the love duet, it is transformed but more negligible than it was. Romantic love is problematic, for the action of *Tristan* revolves on the bewildering paradox that at the moment when love is consummated and the lovers most completely celebrate their bodies, they sense themselves closest to death. The interpenetration of love and death, a paradox central to the poetry of Novalis, Byron, and Shelley, has in *Tristan* found a stage to represent it.

The action of *Tristan* has, as we have seen, a formality characteristic of neo-classical drama, but unity does not come through the imposition of neo-Aristotelean principles, nor through a rigorously logical conflict between love and honor, but in exclusive focus on the paradox of love and death. The crisis that Isolde undergoes in the first act is caused only ostensibly by her frustration at being a political pawn between Cornwall and Ireland. Her distress arises from her feelings for Tristan and her sense of having been betrayed by Tristan and herself. Even the origins of her love have betrayed her, because it was engendered as she was nursing Tristan back to life from wounds he had received from Morold. Her love is so intricately associated with the balms she used to cure Tristan's lacerated body and the sword with which he killed Morold, that it seems embedded in the instruments of life and death. The erotic charge of this love defies reason, subverts social loyalty, and threatens her very existence. Its power is apparent the moment she gazes on Tristan – "Mir erkoren" ("Destined to me"). The haunting chromatics of the strings mark the thrill and disturbance of her feelings. "Liebestod" ("Love as death") describes her state of mind from the very start.

It describes Tristan's too. For most of act 1 he is in deep depression, as if the lesions from his earlier encounter with Isolde are still open. There is a striking contrast between his reputation as a hero in the service of the king, boldly announced by Kurwenal and lauded by Brangäne, and the lethargic, introspective character we see on stage, already subdued by his desire for Isolde. Tristan comes to life only when drinking the potion with Isolde, an act that symbolizes the paradox of romantic love, as the lovers only admit to love while they think they are dying. Musically, love spills out of death. As the love draft possesses their bodies, in a strangely graphic passage the lower strings and the theme of the prelude erupt turbulently, followed by a high tremolo, leading to a moment of utter serenity before their passions break out. After this, the single moment of grand operatic spectacle, the arrival of Marke to claim his bride, is no climax, but a violation of their love, which already has a greater reality than the everyday world.

Throughout act 1, the stage has preserved a quasi-realistic status as the site upon which a drama of love against honor, passion against restraint, is played out. But once the lovers have surrendered to their feelings, their emotions also become the filter through which we, the audience, understand the external world. Wagner draws attention to this at the opening of act 2, when Isolde, anticipating the arrival of Tristan, argues with Brangäne about Marke's hunting horns. Have they faded into the distance, hence enabling the lovers to meet, or are they still close? Brangäne warns Isolde

> You are tricked by wishful
> impetuosity
> to notice only what you choose.[18]

but the orchestra does not vindicate Brangäne, because we hear the metamorphosis of the horns into the splashing of the fountain as an expression of Isolde's love. While Brangäne insists on the opposition of subjective and objective, Isolde admits no division. She is possessed by her emotions, and the orchestra and the idyll of a garden at night describe solely her exalted state. Music and stage become her private being. This accompanies a notable change in her character, for she has lost all anger, irony, and mistrust of the world and has given way to feeling.

The love duet expands this mood, first by including Tristan in it, secondly by the lovers moving beyond the physical world to the sublime plane of the will. The celebrated paradoxes of light and dark, nearness and closeness, self and other, indicate that the imaginative sphere the lovers occupy cannot be accounted for by reason. The intensity of their love has given them access to a sublime consciousness, in which earthly relations and the words that describe them are of no moment. It is a realm that subsumes the physical world, when at the crowning moment of the duet, Tristan and Isolde declare themselves to be not of the world, but the world itself. They have become the space that they occupy and the space that we see on stage has become them:

> then myself
> I am the world:
> I engender sublimest bliss,
> I live for holy love,
> never more to waken,
> illusionless,
> sweet, conscious desire.[19]

This transformation is confirmed not denied by Brangäne's warning. Although her words tell that the physical world is threatening them, in performance it is often difficult to distinguish her voice from Isolde's; she neither jars nor disturbs the lovers. Instead, she sounds like an extension of their rapture, singing words of warning in the music of love. The audience sees and hears the world solely through the eyes and ears of Tristan and Isolde.

Although Marke, Melot, and the huntsmen brutally interrupt the lovers, they do not entirely dispel the serenity and sense of being outside the body generated by the love duet. Marke's monologue articulates the deepest sadness and embitterment, but his reproaches are not harsh and vengeful. On the contrary, as his pain grows, so does his compassion. The monologue resolves not on rancor against Tristan, but on questions that point beyond individual responsibility. One might expect that Marke, an aggrieved husband and insulted ruler, should seek instant revenge, thereby inciting a conflict between love and honor, but in spirit he occupies the same mental space as Tristan and Isolde. Despite deep differences, he strives toward harmony with them. The ambience of the duet remains in his monologue, as if it exercises a palpable influence even on one who is nominally opposed to the lovers.

When Wagner wrote a summary of the action of *Tristan*, he confined himself to the first two acts, as if the drama were completed when Tristan and Isolde are united.[20] Certainly, act 3 seems corollary to the action and, as Arthur Groos has pointed out, it is based not on Gottfried's poem, but on his source material.[21] From the perspective of the well-made play, the act is indeed irregular, as Tristan's crisis, which comprises most of its action, has not been anticipated. But *Tristan* is no well-made play, as theme rather than consequential action gives it unity. In act 1, the theme of love and death centers on Isolde as she struggles to understand the nature of her love for Tristan. The tormenting paradox was converted into the ecstasy

of the love duet, but as Marke reaches the end of his soliloquy, the pain
it causes comes to the fore again, focused now on Tristan. It is provided
too with a philosophical apparatus that draws our attention to the larger
question of tragedy that Tristan's condition predicates. Marke asks after
the very conditions of life that have created a betrayal he can hardly
bear:

> why did you give me this hell?
> Misery cannot expiate it;
> Why am I dealt this disgrace?
> There is some unfathomably deep
> secret reason for it.
> Who will reveal it to the world?[22]

Marke is asking after the root cause of tragedy itself. What is it that drives
humans to destroy everything that gives them and others happiness in
everyday life? What impulse leads them to destroy the codes by which they
live? Tristan does not even try to answer, but asks Isolde to accompany him
on a journey to a land where the dimensions of earthly life are null and
void, a realm he identifies explicitly with his mother's womb. Melot's blow
dispatches him there almost before we know it has been inflicted. Tristan
has ostensibly been wounded for his violation of honor, but Wagner has
launched him on a voyage to the heart of tragedy.

Tristan's castle on the coast of Brittany and the dour music that starts
act 3 can be read as metaphors for Tristan's inner world.[23] While Isolde
dominated act 1, act 3 is about Tristan, whose voyage into nullity has been
at devastating cost. Once Isolde has surrendered to her love for Tristan,
her problems are resolved. But the nightmarish journey taken by Tristan
shows his psyche to have been deeply perturbed by his sexual encounter
with Isolde. The act represents Wagner's most penetrating analysis of the
inner life of the romantic hero.

The journey that Tristan takes after being struck down by Melot,
expressed in the prelude, is profoundly dispiriting. As the curtain rises,
the arduous, endless melody of the Shepherd – "Die alte Weise" ("the
old tune") – played on the cor anglais, describes a weary but hopeless travail to escape from encumbrance. Tristan's long monologue, which occupies much of the act and represents this journey, may not drive us mad,
as Wagner feared it might,[24] but it is the most harrowing experience his
music-dramas have to offer. Tristan has been "in the vast realm of universal
night," a timeless expanse before birth and beyond death, void of human
feature, as effective a summation as possible of Schopenhauer's concept of
the nothingness of the will. But it has not provided him with "ultimate

redemption." Instead, Tristan has been forced to flee it, because Isolde is not with him; only in union with her will he find peace. He has therefore returned to the light of day, only to be cruelly disappointed by her absence, which plunges him further into the despair of longing.

While the initial phase of Tristan's journey is described in abstract terms, as he recalls his mother, whom he has associated with nothingness, and his father, memories of pre-existence and childhood become more specific and the focus of dramatic interest fastens on the dynamics of his psychology. Scholars have tried to resist the temptation of applying a Freudian mythology to Tristan,[25] but it is difficult, perhaps pointless to do so, as Tristan's struggle to escape from the influence of his parents, which his encounter with Isolde has opened up to him, is a characteristically Freudian domain. As his mind turns to his parents, the heavy, sinuous "alte Weise" comes back, identified now with their deaths. His father died after conceiving him, his mother as she gave birth to him, so as Tristan advanced into life, he was shadowed by death. At this point he elides in his imagination the circumstance of his birth with Isolde nursing the wound he received from Morold, which then blends into the moment she gave him the love draft. He completes the ellipsis by describing the love draft as brewed by himself from his father's grief and mother's tears.

> Out of my father's distress
> and my mother's pains,
> out of love's tears
> past and future,
> out of laughter and weeping
> ecstasies and wounds,
> for that drink I
> found the poisonous contents.[26]

However incoherent Tristan's ravings might sound, they carry the answer to Marke's question over the "secret reason" for human pain. The prime cause of tragedy is failure of the hero to escape from the grip of the family. For Tristan, growth has been a return to childhood, sexual congress consanguineous with infantile dependency, death has occurred at the moment of birth, and sex has been a defeat, not a fulfillment. It has denied not granted him his freedom. He belongs in the company of Oedipus, Hippolytus, Pentheus, and Hamlet, and figures from the modern drama soon to follow him, Ibsen's Oswald in *Ghosts* and Strindberg's Captain in *The Father*. More pertinently, his predicament recalls the eternal repetition in which Wagner's other heroes were caught. In attempting to escape from the family he finds all roads lead back to it, and in failing to emancipate himself from the night of the womb, he seems destined to suffer like the Dutchman, Tannhäuser,

Lohengrin, Siegmund, and Siegfried. As his predicament becomes clear, Tristan curses himself, reaching a nadir of despair, lower than that of any of Wagner's heroes.

But at this point, a second movement toward the sublime sets in. Tristan's despair and curse are not factors that will henceforth determine his action. As the drama takes place within his psyche, external fiat has no bearing on the action, so his curse on himself has no binding power, as Alberich's curse on the ring had. Rather it is a moment of self-realization, an anagnorisis, which brings about a personal catharsis, for it is followed by his beatific vision of Isolde sailing toward him. The dropping phrases in the high strings which provide some of the most beautiful moments in the score indicate liberation for Tristan. At the moment he recognizes the dreadful circularity of his condition and names it, he acknowledges the futility of human striving and exorcises his need to strive. He dies a free man, his sexuality his own, once more in a state of sublimity. But it is a different sublime than the one he occupied with Isolde during their night of love and different too from Schiller's sublime, as he has earned mental freedom, not through moral struggle, but through an equally momentous fight with what Schopenhauer called the simple circumstances of his own "action and character."

Perhaps we accept too easily the substitution of "Liebestod" for Wagner's description "Verklärung" ("transfiguration") when we speak of Isolde's final solo. Erotic love is not dead, nor is it at the end associated with death. Isolde's ecstatic vision of Tristan's body is engulfed in music that represents intensifying waves of orgasmic passion. Tristan's body is no mere corpse, but is projected upon the stars that, in Isolde's imagination, encircle him. At the same time, Isolde draws the audience's attention to the artistic resources out of which the music-drama has been made. In a moment unique in Wagner, she refers to the very music to which she is singing.

> Do I alone hear
> this tune,
> which so wondrously
> and softly
> wailing for bliss, eloquent of all things,
> gently conciliating
> sounding from within him,
> pours into me,
> leaps up,
> sounds and gloriously
> resounds about me?[27]

At the climax of the solo, as she is united in "supreme bliss" with Tristan, we know that we have seen and heard the romantic transformation of the world, the realization in sound and space of her and Tristan's inner life, projected into the world of the will. Unlike the sublime of the love duet, this second sublime has not been easily won; Tristan in particular has had to overcome all that drew him back to his childhood. But he released himself from constant regression,[28] a condition acknowledged by Isolde's solo, which represents the subjective selves of the lovers transfigured into a universe that was once separate from them. At the end we, as audience, no longer feel any difference between ourselves and the stage. We have become part of the lovers' universe and if we feel, however temporarily, that we have been transfigured, then Wagner's music-drama has done its heroic work on us as well.

DIE MEISTERSINGER VON NÜRNBERG: ARTISTIC UTOPIA

Tristan und Isolde and *Die Meistersinger von Nürnberg* (*The Mastersingers of Nuremberg*), the two great products of Wagner's years of respite from the *Ring*, are frequently thought of as siblings, but if this is so, they are opposites rather than twins. In *Tristan*, the action centers on the emotional life of the lovers, while for much of *Die Meistersinger*, the public world is clamorously in the foreground. *Tristan* eschews the spectacle of conventional theatre, at time almost denies that it is theatre, while *Die Meistersinger*, with its choruses, dances, processions, marches, and plot-devices drawn from a long tradition of comic drama, celebrates theatre. The two music-dramas share a central theme, the overwhelming power of romantic love, but while love in *Tristan* draws one away from the world into night, in *Die Meistersinger* it thrives in the midday sun. Romantic love in Wagner's Nuremberg does not subvert the social and political world, it gives it vitality.

For all its seeming lack of problems, the serene ambience of *Die Meistersinger* has constantly been called into question. Its comedy has been found troubling; Dahlhaus writes of it as "the brainchild of an untrustworthy sense of humor,"[29] while Adorno, throughout his polemic on Wagner, finds in it elements of brutality.[30] Some scholars have pointed out the difference between Wagner's idyll of sixteenth-century Nuremberg and the far more unpleasant reality of its "highly stratified society,"[31] while others find in it a hidden, or not so hidden agenda of anti-Semitism and aggressive nationalism.[32] Even those with few doubts about its integrity often dwell on the darker side of its comedy. Much of John Warrack's volume on *Die Meistersinger* is taken up with the influence of Schopenhauer on the action, so that Sachs' renunciation of Eva becomes the principal event of the drama,[33] a perspective that reminds us that the emotional range of Wagner's comedy is more extensive than was common in the dramatic tradition in which it was written. It is also more heavily laden with dialectic.

The ancestry of most of Wagner's characters can be traced to familiar stereotypes in *commedia dell'arte*, the crucible of much modern comedy. Eva and Walther are the refined young lovers, David and Magdalene their comic counterparts; David, with his constantly empty stomach, reminds us of Harlequin, as, strangely enough, does Sachs, a "Vice" figure, whose ingenuity assures a favorable outcome to the plot. Beckmesser's lineage can be found in Pantalone, the older man who aspires to the hand of a younger woman, while he, Kothner, and other Mastersingers have elements of Dottore, the intellectual who fails to understand the jargon he so readily spouts. The only character who originates mainly from the later sentimental tradition is Eva's father, Pogner. But *Die Meistersinger* is a more capacious work than the comedy of intrigue stemming from *commedia*. While most plays in this tradition had a centripetal action that advanced with little attention to broader contexts, in *Die Meistersinger* the life of Nuremberg demands as much attention as individual characters. Wagner's drama acquires richness from his redistribution of comic functions between the characters, from contrasts between varying modes of comedy, and from scenic, verbal, and musical metaphors of nature and paradise that are interwoven in the action. This occasions a Shakespearean ambience in which pathos and farce, sentimentality and cruelty, age and youth, authority and anarchy, aristocrat, bourgeois, and working people rub against each other. In contrast to the classicism of *Tristan*, *Meistersinger* provides a panorama of life.

In the only drama that Wagner named for a community, it is doubtful whether the experience of one character should be taken as paradigmatic for the whole. The recent critical attention granted to Sachs has deepened our understanding of the thematic complexity of *Die Meistersinger* and drawn attention to his role as guiding spirit of the action. But while his gravity and pessimism modify moods of festivity, nostalgia, and hilarity, they do not determine the prevailing mood of the drama. The comic conclusion can only come about after Sachs has renounced Eva, leaving her free to marry Walther, and it is the values for which Walther stands that prevail at the end.

Wagner, who had conceived of *Die Meistersinger* in 1845, described his comedy as a satyr play to *Tannhäuser*,[34] so he saw *Die Meistersinger* as a comic variation on the theme of the artist and society, in which the two alien entities reach accommodation with each other. Of the early music-dramas, only *Tannhäuser* had been specifically about the creative artist, but Wagner abandoned his focus on the figure halfway through the drama to address other concerns. Here he had represented art as having two purposes: through Elisabeth's response to Tannhäuser's poetry, it appeared as a function of nature, awakening emotions that lead to love and the potential of new life, but the Landgrave, in his earnest solo, expounded on art as a means of creating civil bonds that will unite society. These two accounts of art are not reconciled in *Tannhäuser*, but in *Die Meistersinger* Wagner took up the dialectic once again and elided the natural and social roles of art, and in so doing endowed the artist with a stature that comes closer to the messianic hero than in any of his previous works, foreshadowing the unambiguous shift toward the messianic that will take place in *Parsifal*. Even in the *Ring*, the hero remains a peripheral figure, who inspires others, arouses love, and points toward ideal realms of being, but in *Meistersinger*, he is on the way to becoming institutionalized by finding a place in society and fulfilling a distinct and vital social purpose. To understand this, we should look again at Wagner's ideas on the purpose of art.

Wagner's view of art was pragmatic and romantic. He valued it primarily as the means by which the folk could understand themselves as an entity which "feels a common need and collective want."[35] However, art was also a conduit by which nature challenged organized society, as it aroused the people's sense of their natural origins, giving them a common identity as a folk that lies outside the pale of social life. The folk may not always be aware of their common need or identity, in fact they may only recognize it through the art produced in their name. Wagner went out of his way to insist that the condition of being a folk is potentially there for all people, his initial example of a folk community having been ancient Athens. But modern commercialism, associated in his mind primarily with the French and the Jews, was pursued by people, who by the fact of engaging in commerce, had lost any sense of being a folk. Commercialism was even making inroads into German life, but Wagner, like the romantics before him, still believed the Germans to be the only European people possessed of "folkish" values. In a set of essays, written during the composition of *Die Meistersinger*, "Deutsche Kunst und deutsche Politik" ("German Art and German Politics"), he argues that the German "folk" and their monarchs are still potential bastions against a world corrupted by commercialism. To be German, he claims, is to return to a sense of authenticity, to do "the thing one does for its own sake, for the very joy of doing it."[36] The Germans and their art are marked by down-to-earth, honest qualities and closeness to nature. A few years later, in 1872, in an introduction to the reprint of his essay *Die Kunst und die Revolution*, he cited

Carlyle to support his claim that the Germans are the "heroic-wise" who will return order to a world on the brink of anarchy brought on by the French Revolution.

Wagner's romantic concept of art is at once anarchic and conservative. Through art, humans experience themselves as creatures of nature, which gives them a sense of freedom not available in the social world, but can also acquire a sense of organic unity. "Art is pleasure in itself, in existence, in community," it reverberates with the fundamental rhythms of life.[37] However, in awakening the folk to a sense of their origin in nature, it does not interpret the contemporary world to them, except to point out how the present is a decline from an earlier state of pristine authenticity. Consequently, art has no political content or aim, which led Thomas Mann to argue that *Die Meistersinger* shows a "downright indifference to political structures."[38] Nevertheless, others have found Wagner's conception of art to be acutely political and *Die Meistersinger* in particular to be his most political work. As Mayer has observed, it was composed at precisely the time when German political unity was being constructed under the flag of German art and culture,[39] so even if it has the appearance of being apolitical, art is in fact being used to further the interests of the political.

Although Wagner lauds the capacity of art to implant a sense of freedom in the individual, his dialectic on art makes little accommodation for individuality, and in this it departs from the prevailing ethos of late romanticism. While Byron, the mouthpiece of late romantic individualism, claimed in *Childe Harold's Pilgrimage* that the artist

> in creating live[d]
> A being more intense . . . gaining as we give
> The life we image.[40]

Wagner could only see the folk as gaining intensity from "imaged life." The artist no longer expresses an individual vision of the world, but is a medium between nature and the folk. He finds his material not in the aegis of personal experience, but from his understanding of humans as natural creatures. Indeed, Wagner's writing is constantly informed by the assumption that, however much humanity has been polluted by modern life, its union with nature can be recaptured. In contrast to Rousseau, who had insisted that once this union had been dissolved it could never be regained, Wagner still believed in a utopia of society, and not the individual, at one with nature.

Rarely has art occupied so central a function in human activity as in Wagner's theory and practice. A healthy artistic life is essential to any society, in fact its very survival depends upon it.[41] Only through art can human beings achieve freedom and dignity in the modern world and recognize themselves as a "folk" capable of resisting the corruption of a commercial society. "The wisest constituted states fall through," Wagner wrote in 1867, "the sublimest religions outlive themselves and yield to superstition or unbelief, whilst Art eternally shoots up, renewed and young, from out the ruins of existence."[42] *Die Meistersinger* is about this renewal and survival, achieved through the fusion of the two functions of art that had been separate in *Tannhäuser*.

There is never any question in the Nuremberg of *Die Meistersinger* that art is not the central activity of society. The Mastersingers are dedicated to it and involved deeply in discussions as to its appropriate forms, procedures, and functions, though their vision is largely restricted by smug conservatism. They encounter and at different moments in the action either endorse or reject three different concepts of art: bad art, pragmatic art, and romantic art, which are represented respectively by Beckmesser, Sachs, and Walther von Stolzing.

Wagner's one-time identification of Beckmesser with the Viennese critic Eduard Hanslick has tended to deflect attention from Beckmesser's role as a purveyor of bad art to that of a critic. Hanslick stood in Wagner's mind, unfairly, as the epitome of the critical opposition that had delayed his acceptance into the German operatic world. His resentment is projected onto Beckmesser's disruption of Walther's trial-song with claims that the song violates all the rules of good poetry and music. But Beckmesser is also an artist and for the worst reasons. For him, rules are everything, inspiration and spontaneity nothing. He considers singing a means of gaining social eminence and, through his suit for Eva Pogner, economic security, so he stands for the venal aspects of art Wagner had so persistently attacked in his writings. It is as a critic that Beckmesser causes the mayhem at the end of act 1, but as a bad artist he sparks the riot that concludes act 2. His serenade to Eva is a display of artistic ineptitude, in which words inappropriate for a love song are harnessed to a gauche melody that leads him to violate the common laws of prosody and, with absurd coloratura flourishes, draw attention to the effect of the art, but not its substance.[43] Bad art threatens social peace, which is apparent when the melody of his song becomes the theme of the fugue to which the riot is fought out.

Wagner's treatment of Beckmesser has caused much affront, in his own time and ours. If this dismay arises from the defeat of an unpleasant figure in authority who blocks the union of the young lovers, then it is misplaced. The humiliation of arbitrary and offensive authority and of older people who aspire to the privileges of youth has always been the stuff of comedy, which celebrates the victory of the young over the old, freedom over authority, and "summer over winter."[44] But the mistrust *Die Meistersinger* arouses is occasioned by the suspicion that, in creating an image of Nuremberg as the ideal community of German folk, Wagner isolated, demonized, and excluded the Jews through the figure of Beckmesser. Beckmesser's music, as Barry Millington has argued, satirizes the singing of Jewish cantors, an allusion recognized by Wagner's Jewish contemporaries who demonstrated against performances of *Die Meistersinger*.[45] Objections raised against such accusations of anti-Semitism do nothing to dispel them. Arguments that a Jew would never have been allowed to occupy the position of town clerk in Nuremberg carry no weight, as *Die Meistersinger* is a work of art, not a historical reconstruction, and Wagner's intent was to depict an artistic utopia, so, despite the historical setting, his eyes were set on the future, not the past. It has been claimed that Beckmesser's antecedents are Pantalone and Dottore from the *commedia* tradition, which is true, but does nothing to disprove anti-Semitic associations; rather it might point to anti-Semitic features in the *commedia* stereotypes themselves. A defence can even be mounted on the grounds that the Nazis were not aware of Beckmesser's Jewishness, but the Nazis were hardly noted for the subtlety of their powers of interpretation and, when they did exploit Wagner's works, it was what Hans Rudolf Vaget has called their "atmospheric and liturgical nature" that appealed to them.[46] Ultimately, the extent to which anti-Semitism in the portrayal of Beckmesser compromises the action of the drama must be left to the judgment of each audience member. For those who find it pollutes the entire work, the only solution is to leave *Die Meistersinger* well alone; others should acknowledge the evidence and determine how far it impairs the utopian vision of the drama. But as Wagner had relentlessly identified the corrosive forces of modernity that undermined the unity of the folk with the Jews, it is difficult not to acknowledge anti-Semitic allusions in Beckmesser, who is the antithesis of every value for which the artist-hero stands.

The disquiet at Beckmesser's final exclusion may also have aesthetic grounds, betraying some disjunction between the allegorical aspects of the action and the dramatic-musical milieu. While Wagner's plot owes much to the comedy of intrigue that had employed exaggerated and satirical characterization, he sets it to a generous and hugely agreeable score that leads the audience to identify warmly with all characters, except Beckmesser. Only he is excluded from the general happiness of the end, and because he is Wagner seems to be breaking his own rules, as he had insisted that "mockery" has no place in great art and had caustically criticized those, like Heine, who used it.[47] Nevertheless, in the symbolic landscape of *Die Meistersinger*, Beckmesser's final absence from the stage is essential. As Borchmeyer observes, Beckmesser cannot be reconciled, because the art for which he stands must be banished from the artistic utopia in which the action ends.[48] Symbolic function and the good-humored ambience of the whole are, in the case of Beckmesser, at odds.

While Beckmesser stands for an art that must be rejected, Sachs and Walther personify two functions of art that Wagner prized. Sachs is similar to Beckmesser in one respect: he is both a critic and an artist. As an artist he is, by his own admission, a composer of "street-songs," which are like the shoes he makes as they soften the hard road that people have to travel in life. He has suffered greatly himself, having lost his wife and children, then by renouncing Eva to Walther. Sachs' view of art is a development of that articulated by the Landgrave in *Tannhäuser*: for him, art is the way in which a hard life is made bearable as it augments personal fortitude and holds the community together. Art allows people to recognize the common need that marks their communal identity. In the figure of David, Sachs' apprentice, it also marks the anniversaries and milestones in the life of individuals and society. At the start of the drama, the chorus sings a Bach chorale, and at the end they sing Sachs' poem on Luther, "Wach' auf!" ("Awake!"), again to the melody of a Bach chorale, the most magnificent exemplar imaginable of art serving the function of shoes! We also sense Sachs as a guiding influence on the action because of his respect for well-constructed art. This draws our attention to the tightly wrought structure of *Die Meistersinger*, which, despite its panoramic scale, is no linear, epic drama. Like *Lohengrin*, it is a superior example of the well-made play, with each scene related causally to the preceding action, and each song, chorus, and poetic metaphor contributing directly to the action's central theme. Each are nails firmly holding the elaborate shoe of the drama together.

It is, however, as a critic not an artist that Sachs is of most importance, because he recognizes that Walther's poetry will be the medium by which the energies of romantic art will be released into the community of Nuremberg. Only Sachs can explain to Walther the significance of his own art and in doing this he exercises a crucial function, because as Walther is all intuition and spontaneous feeling, he cannot understand himself. As a result, he is not an especially interesting character. The only time he behaves in a way approximating normal human behavior is when he woos Eva and, in act 2, lashes out in fury against the Mastersingers; otherwise, he is principally the songs he sings. We can hardly expect him to be anything else, because Wagner, in departing from the individualism of late romanticism to adopt the earlier romantic idea of art as an expression of nature, forfeited the possibility of making his artist-hero dramatically interesting. Were he to focus on the artist's inner conflict, as he did in *Tannhäuser*, he would divert attention from the theme of art as an invigorating, natural force. To fulfill the natural function of art, any degree of self-consciousness in the artist endangers its integrity. Hence, Walther's art must be given form by Sachs' understanding so that it can be grasped by all, but the poetry that springs directly from Walther's inspiration remains unaffected.

The power of romantic art is fully explained by Sachs in the long preamble to Walther's composition of the prize-song in act 3. Romantic art keeps the pristine joys of youth alive in middle and old age. Hardship and disappointment are endemic to living, but those who cherish art sustain the memory of youth and alleviate the bitterness that might otherwise possess them. The purpose of the Mastersingers' rules is to preserve that memory.

> It was sorely-troubled Masters,
> spirits oppressed by the cares of life:
> in the desert of their troubles,
> they formed for themselves an image,
> so that to them might remain,
> of youthful love
> a memory, clear and firm,
> in which spring can be recognized.[49]

Sachs' pragmatic art relieves hardship and anxiety, but the romantic art of Walther does more than that because through it people gain the illusion that their strength has been replenished, allowing them to remain, in their imaginations at least, youthful. As a result, they are more capable of withstanding, maybe even of neutralizing life's betrayals. The aesthetic sense is, therefore, the means by which humans endure. This is what Sachs knows, but he also knows that Walther not he can activate it.

While Sachs is the "Vice" of *Die Meistersinger*, Walther's creative vision provides the aural and visual perspective through which we experience the action, so that a successful performance of the music-drama creates, in the audience, a sense of being possessed by the energies of his singing. Given the importance of the community, it is impossible to transform the stage into a reflection of the subjective world of the protagonist, as Wagner had done in *Tristan*, but the gradual dispersal of the influence of Walther's singing through the action allows us to feel how Nuremberg is transformed by his art. This comes about through the distinct idiom of *Die Meister-singer*. Leitmotifs are an important indicator of dramatic meaning, but here they are employed neither as literally nor as frequently as they were in the *Ring*, where they provided a detailed representation and commentary on the action. Instead one leitmotif can serve as the basis for a long sequence and give character to an entire scene. For example, the "Jugendzeit" ("time of youth") scene between Walther and Sachs has a gratifyingly buoyant atmosphere that arises from the gracious melody, first introduced by Sachs, that threads itself through the scene. Such symphonic development purveys fluidity and continuity to the drama, allowing leitmotifs to grow until they seem to possess the stage and guide the action.

The facility of this idiom lends itself most readily to Walther's melodies, which unfold with greater fluency than those of other characters, so that his singing acquires greater presence as the action progresses. In act 1, the Mastersingers, all men who are proud of their social position, are characterized by a variety of rhythms, which are ponderous, authoritative, confident, or irregular, depending on the characters depicted. In contrast, Walther's melodies flow with an effortlessness reminiscent of improvisation. His music is closely associated with nature as an inspiring force, apparent in his first solo, "Am stillen Herd" ("By the quiet hearth"). Walther has grown up close to nature, has learnt to compose in the deep solitude of winter forests, and although there are no literal echoes in his solo of Siegmund and Sieglinde, his swelling music speaks of the coming of spring as both poetic inspiration and the rise of sexual desire. The juncture of nature, sexuality, and creativity is even plainer in his trial song, "Fanget an!" ("Begin!"), in which his physical urges are expressed more graphically. The contrast between his tumescent melody and the harsh scratches of Beckmesser's chalk states baldly how distanced the marker is from the sources of romantic art. Tensions rise to a climax at the end of the act, making evident the disruption that results when the demands of romantic art are not acknowledged. In the complex ensemble, the anarchic delight of the apprentices, the hysterics of Beckmesser, and the worried fulmination of the Mastersingers are kept in a state of precarious unity only by the melody of Walther, which soars above them. After Walther has left the church and everyone has scattered, Sachs alone remains. He is haunted by Walther's song, heard now in a wistful distillation of its melody, played by the oboe above horns and clarinets. The seed of romantic art, an art that is different from his own, has been planted in his mind.

This leitmotif of "spring" is highly fruitful. It obsesses Sachs in act 2 as he sits beneath the linden tree, the first sign of nature in this urban world.

In the *Fliedermonolog* (lilac monologue), Sachs recognizes that Walther's singing expresses passion that makes his own journeyman poetry tame and the memory of it absorbs his senses like the intoxicating perfume of the tree. The leitmotif intensifies the ecstatic atmosphere of Midsummer's Eve; Sachs tries to resist it by singing in his characteristically strong rhythms, but is powerless against it. It floods the orchestra and the stage, leading Sachs into an imaginative realm that he has no way of measuring or understanding. Walther's song, "it sounded so old and was yet so new," connects Sachs to an intuited past and to nature, where he finds renewal. The climax of his solo, "spring's command, sweet necessity," accompanied by the fullest statement of the spring leitmotif in the orchestra, leads him to craft his own new tune. This moment is ushered in by the monotone of a horn-call which, as a pre-echo of the Nightwatchman later in the act, suggests that Sachs' new tune might lead to peace and harmony. The romantic impulse serves rather than subverts society.

Wagner does not overplay the spring leitmotif. It never again occurs with the persistency that it does in the *Fliedermonolog*, but the mood it has established spreads throughout the orchestra in the music of Midsummer's Eve. Even at the most perilous moments of the act, when Eva and Walther are constantly frustrated in their attempt to elope, the rhapsodic playing of the orchestra, while at times seemingly detached from the action, offers an assurance that all will turn out well. Because we hear this music as an extension of Sachs' monologue, we have the aural illusion that the creative forces that Walther's song released in Sachs are guiding the action to its conclusion in the union of Walther and Eva.

The moods of *Die Meistersinger* are alternately bucolic, boisterous, serene, and passionate, not at all unfitting romantic comedy, and even in the representation of the riot, the outbreak of near deadly fury is contained in the form of a fugue, so it remains within the pale of comedy by virtue of that very containment. But the prevailing good humor of *Die Meistersinger* is temporarily dispelled at the start of act 3 by Sachs' meditation on the destruction that lies below the civilized surface, "Wahn! Wahn!" ("Madness! Madness!"). His solo is not long enough to alter the fundamental tone of the drama and though phrases from it linger in the orchestra for the remainder of the scene in his workshop, they have vanished by the time the action moves to the meadows outside the city walls. The monologue effectively calls into question the authenticity of the optimism that has been growing in act 2, but also offers an interpretation of the human condition through which Walther's art appears to be even more imperative for society. Sachs articulates Schopenhauer's dictum that all action is in vain, as it is nothing but humans acting out of pain and so it can only destroy them. He works through his depression by seeing the violence of the riot as the obverse of the Midsummer's Eve magic that prevailed for much of the night. As this atmosphere has already been associated with the magical effect of Walther's singing, the energies released by his song can be read as a counterbalance to the violence. Sachs, once again reflecting Schopenhauer, concludes that poetry has the capacity to heal the pain that drives people to violence.

The alignment of poetry, song, and erotic love, which has been implied in the first two acts, becomes explicit with the composition of the prize-song. In his earlier solos in act 1, Walther had evoked nature through either narrative or relatively uncomplicated images; the prize-song is a more complex affair. Sachs, who provides a constant commentary as Walther composes the song in his workshop, argues that dreams give humans access to the forces of "Wahn" inside themselves from which, as the action of *Die Meistersinger* displays, both violence and love arise. Poetry allows humans to interpret their "Wahn" and discover that it can also offer them means to bind themselves as a folk. Walther is the heroic agent who will achieve this. But does he do it by conveying an impression of unmediated nature or by modifying it? Or, to ask again the question David Grene finds posited in last dramas: "Which is the deeper reality, the standard of 'ordinary' nature or the pattern that man has laid upon it?" The answer is, not surprisingly, uncertain.

The natural world of which Walther dreamt and which provides the landscape for the prize-song is no longer a pristine romantic wilderness, but a lush Pre-Raphaelite Eden, in which, amid heavily scented flowers and luscious fruits, he encounters a woman of great beauty who leads him toward the Tree of Life. She is transformed into a figure of universal harmony, projected onto an astral plane filled with light rather than the darkness of *Tristan*. As Walther puts this exalted vision into words and music, Sachs directs him to be aware of the separate parts of his poem, which seem naturally to fall into the form of the Mastersong, a "bar," which is composed of two stanzas and an aftersong. Under Sachs' guidance, poetic form is no longer an arbitrary imposition but a process similar to falling in love and the birth that follows from it. Poetic creation is cognate with sexual procreation. The unification of poetry and love becomes part of the stage spectacle, when Walther returns, dressed for the singing contest, and is greeted by the sight of Eva, which leads him to compose the final bar, in which through elaborate nature-metaphors he envisages their physical union. Pathos and comic fulfillment are perfectly balanced as the scene reaches its end. Sachs, realizing that the prerogatives of youth are not his and that the well-being of Nuremberg depends on Walther's romantic art, gives up any hope of Eva's hand, and calls in David and Magdalene to celebrate the apprentice's freedom, the anticipated marriages of both couples, and the christening of a new child, the prize-song. The quintet, with its ambivalent tones of pain and ecstasy, both concludes a romantic tragedy of renunciation and completes a romantic comedy of lovers united. It is the climax of the action, and the denouement in the meadows outside the walls of Nuremberg is appropriately a display of the vitalizing power of romantic art.

The setting of this final scene should have a touch of paradise about it. Tumultuous carnival contrasts with the stiff formality of the opening act, the dances and games of the apprentices express the sheer energy of youth that art should sustain, and, in their hymn of praise to Sachs, the people celebrate their sense of community. Bad art is laughed off-stage with Beckmesser, then Walther sings the prize-song. It is shorter and more compact than it was in Sachs' workroom. It is also better constructed, the words are more specific, their metaphorical double-meaning richer, and the contours of the melody clearer. The song, now only one "bar," still provides an abstract of the way in which art is created. The first stanza is about Eva in paradise, both the biblical figure and the woman sitting in front of Walther, the second describes his vision of the muse on Parnassus, and the final stanza brings the two women together, as they will be combined in actuality. As Walther reaches this point of union, the entire chorus joins him. In act 1, the swelling melody of his trial song had been sung only by himself, above the contrary rhythms of the apprentices and Mastersingers, but now the prize-song is sung by everybody. *Meistersinger* ends with the energies of Walther's art filling and transforming Nuremberg, a utopian conclusion that enacts with overwhelming confidence the fulfillment of one the most persistently held ideals of the romantic age, the elevation of the artist-hero to supreme influence over society.

For the first time in Wagner, the hero has achieved messianic status, as society has been regenerated by the power that speaks through his poetry. Their future welfare, even survival, hangs upon Walther's presence. For the first time in the mature music-dramas, the authority embodied in the hero is incorporated into society. Therefore either he runs the danger of committing hubris, which will lead to his downfall, or he will take a position of authority that will require unquestioning loyalty from others. But this is a comedy where tragic categories will not prevail. At the last moment Wagner engineers the action so that Walther's messianic influence and institutional sanction are avoided. As Pogner places the chain of the Mastersingers around Walther's neck, Eva removes the myrtle wreath from Walther's head and places it instead on Sachs'. Social acclaim goes, therefore, to the man whose poetry binds society together, and while romantic art has been recognized by the guild and people of Nuremberg, it still lies, where it should do, outside the limits of authority.

The adrenaline rush brought on by the conclusion of *Die Meistersinger* is designed to dissuade any critical questions. The towering chorus offers one of the most jubilantly comic resolutions in world theatre and celebrates, as romantic comedy does, the creation of new life and the overthrow of the forces that oppose it. But despite this, reservations persist over its reliability. In part these arise from the treatment of Beckmesser, but the disquiet his expulsion arouses is aggravated by the apparently nationalistic tone of Sachs' final peroration to the Nurembergers to revere German culture and protect it from foreign, especially French influences. "No one," Nike Wagner writes, "believes . . . that the conclusion of *Die Meistersinger* is an innocently romantic declaration of the primacy of art over politics."[50] Innocently romantic the ending might not be, but consciously romantic it is, and whether it vitiates the work is questionable. As Mayer has pointed out, *Die Meistersinger* was written at a time when liberal ambitions were being fulfilled in the creation of a united Germany. In fact, in contrast to other works of the time, for example, Lortzing's charming opera *Hans Sachs* with which Wagner was familiar, the nationalism of *Die Meistersinger* is positively subdued. Sachs' protests against "welsch" ("romance") influence were nothing exceptional. Pleas to preserve German opera from "welsch" influence had been common since at least the middle of the eighteenth century,[51] and protests against the French influence over German culture had been standard in Goethe, Lessing, and other writers. Sachs' speech certainly reflects Wagner's own troubled relationship with French culture, but it should be borne in mind that in France the artist occupied a very different position than the one Wagner was representing in *Die Meistersinger*. A comparison of *Die Meistersinger* to another nineteenth-century opera that focuses on the creative artist, Berlioz's *Benvenuto Cellini*, reveals attitudes toward the artist that are so utterly different that they are irreconcilable. In Berlioz's opera, the artistic impulse competes with nature and is used to craft artifacts that offer perfection where nature is lacking; in Wagner's music-drama art and nature are one, art being always at the service of nature. For Wagner art is part of the biology of the mind, it sustains human feelings, intellectual faculties, and imagination, but in Berlioz, art is a means to define oneself in a competitive and authoritarian society, with the end either of binding the individual to the social hierarchy or providing that individual with the opportunity to assert personal identity and freedom in opposition to that hierarchy. Although for Wagner art arises from deeply personal and asocial sources, it is of ultimate value as a cohering force that unites individuals into a community, celebrating their oneness with nature; in Berlioz art drives humans to master the natural and social world. Sachs is not calling for imperialistic expansion but for the sustaining of a romantic artistic tradition that brings renewal and happiness to whoever engages in it. If German art is different from French, it is so for more than purely nationalistic and political reasons.

PARSIFAL: UTOPIA FOUND

In recent decades, *Parsifal* has aroused more disquieting and diverse readings among critics than any other of Wagner's music-dramas. This is not surprising because, like another great final drama, Euripides' *The Bacchae*, *Parsifal* dramatizes fundamental paradoxes of human life in a symbolic framework that seems to invite an infinity of interpretation. At one extreme, *Parsifal* has been declared a vindication of Christian faith,[52] at the other it has been explored as an anti-Semitic diatribe with distinctly homoerotic overtones,[53] and there are a wide variety of interpretations in between. But as there are so few clear pointers as to what actually occurs in the action, it is not easy to disprove interpretations. Few stage-works so clearly demonstrate that the ultimate function of drama may be less the presentation of ideas than the generation of ideas within the audience.

One concern has exercised *Parsifal*'s audiences and critics from its first performance at Bayreuth in 1882: is it drama or ritual? Most critical discussions insist that the action stays within the realm of drama. Michael Tanner, for example, sees it as akin to an Ibsenesque drama on the "psychopathology of religious belief,"[54] while Carl Dahlhaus argues for *Parsifal* as "a document of the nineteenth-century 'religion of art'."[55] But audiences do not always seem to agree. At the end of act 1, a grave silence still usually rules in the auditorium and those innocents who break it will often be indignantly shushed by worshippers at the shrine. More importantly, audiences constantly insist that *Parsifal* exercises a hold on their attentions that is different in quality than that demanded by more common-or-garden operas, including other music-dramas by Wagner.

The theatre and the church are different places and, not infrequently, they have been antagonistic. Theatre provides entertainment that leads us to understand ourselves and the world, the church places us in direct communion with God. Theatre celebrates the secular and, until well into the nineteenth century, had been persistently assailed by the church for arousing sensual desires. But ecclesiastical antipathy to the theatre may have arisen because it sensed in theatre a potential rival to the church. Emotions aroused in the theatre can be as transcendent as those generated by the Christian rite, something that was clearly on Wagner's mind when he began his essay "Religion und Kunst" ("Religion and Art") with the claim that the purpose of art was "to save the spirit of religion by recognizing the figurative value of the mythic symbols which [religion] would have us believe in their literal sense, and revealing their deep and hidden truth through an ideal presentation."[56] To Wagner then, art, for which we may legitimately read theatre, dealt with more fundamental truths than the church did.

The Wagners were in the habit of thinking of the Festspielhaus as a quasi-religious building, in which rituals might not have been inappropriate. Once, after a visit to the construction sight, Cosima wrote of her "grandiose impression, the whole rising up unrestrained like an Assyrian edifice, the pillars ranged like sphinxes below . . . the whole thing seems more past than future,"[57] and several years after the first festival she insisted it was no normal theatre but "dedicated to higher things . . . reminding me of the crib of our Saviour!"[58] Her husband would not have disagreed. The actual audience for *Parsifal*, the only music-drama written specifically for the Festspielhaus, has often been likened to a congregation. Like the people of Nuremberg, they are controlled by illusions,[59] as if they are participants in and not just observers of the performed event. The awkward label for *Parsifal*, "Bühnenweihfestspiel," suggests that Wagner thought his final work to be more than a self-contained drama. There are powerfully ritualistic elements in its action. While no known ritual is completely represented, the Temple scenes with their marches and choral singing, climaxing in the unveiling of the grail, have the impact of a religious rite that summons up the immanence of the divine, and in performance they can affect the audience more as a rite than as climactic moments in a drama. There is even a ritual dimension to the action, which is reminiscent of medieval drama. Because Parsifal's mission has been prophesied and its conclusion preordained, the action unfolds a mystery, much as the medieval mystery play revealed God's purpose on Earth. Parsifal's growth toward becoming a messiah also recalls the medieval morality play. There are also theatrical ritualistic elements. Borchmeyer in a characteristically thorough survey shows how Wagner constructs an "action, language, and thematic writing . . . [of a] hieratic and gnomic character." He draws parallels with those phases of tragedy, Aeschylean and Schilleresque especially, in which action is structured as a ritual, and identifies heroic prototypes for the central characters, seeing in the figures of Parsifal and Amfortas a fusion of Hellenic mythology with Christian legend. Both characters remind us of aspects of Christ and they bear strong resemblance to Heracles and Prometheus respectively.[60]

Wagner had anticipated the composition of *Parsifal* for several decades, knowing it would be the culminating work of his career. Like many final dramas, it avoids a catastrophic conclusion, it is static, and tightly structured. In the two outer acts, there is virtually no development through the interaction of characters. To a greater degree than in *Tristan*, dramatic climaxes are played down. For example, Parsifal's battle with Klingsor's knights is narrated, not shown, the collapse of Klingsor's castle at the end of act 2 is barely indicated in the music, and Parsifal's second arrival in the temple of the grail passes without comment from the orchestra. Overtly theatrical gestures would divert attention from the sublime consciousness toward which the music, in acts 1 and 3 especially, is leading. As for the characters, the poem is singularly uninformative about them. We learn little of Parsifal, his childhood and youth being only minimally recalled and what we do know of him, for example his naïvety, is imparted through the tersest of dialogues. Details necessary for any concrete dramatic action are provided only in Gurnemanz's exposition on the grail brotherhood and its fate, as that is all the audience really needs to know. Like *Tristan*, *Parsifal* has no clear plot line or consequential action. It is composed merely of three events in the life of the hero and what happens to him between them is almost a blank. He fought enemies, restored the purity of the spear, wandered, and suffered, a lifetime of experience that is evoked but not represented in the painful prelude to act 3. *Parsifal* is an abstract of an action rather than an action itself, so Wagner's comment that in *Parsifal* he wished to create "the invisible theatre"[61] may not have been not purely ironic, for the action can only be fully understood on a metaphysical plane that can best be summoned up through ritual and the imaginative construction of a immaterial world. It is hardly surprising then that audiences respond readily to the ritualistic dimensions of its form and action.

But while ritual may be the prime method by which *Parsifal* exercises a hold over the audience, it is also what the drama is about, the subject of the action itself. Ritual is the phenomenon that will ultimately be renewed by Parsifal's redemptive powers, so, as Tanner and Dahlhaus have argued, we should not accept the ceremonial mode of the drama unquestioningly. Far from it, because while ritual can liberate humans by offering them a transcendent experience, it can also imprison them and inhibit their spiritual growth by a dismal rote of repeated figurative action that has no purpose beyond their own performance. The brotherhood, like Wagner's earlier heroes, is caught in the debilitating round of eternal repetition. For them ritual is a force of tragic determination that decays the human spirit. Parsifal will become the only Wagnerian hero to renew the health of that ritual, deny tragic determination, and acquire messianic status.

Parsifal is the most elusive of Wagner's central characters because while he plays a heroic role, he is not distinguished by those qualities customarily associated with heroes. His story first occurred to Wagner as a subject for dramatization during that summer of 1845, when he also conceived of *Lohengrin, Die Meistersinger*, and the *Ring*. Parsifal belongs therefore among those epic heroes whose purpose is the restoration of integrity to a disjointed world by serving as a conduit between humanity and sources of energy in the past, in nature, or an extra-human plane of experience. The initial trajectory of his life is that of the epic hero. Born and reared in obscurity in the forest, he sets out to achieve great deeds in battle. His energies are unruly and lead him to wanton destruction – the shooting of the swan – but then they are channeled toward ends larger than himself, so that his deeds acquire the potential to save the world from the evils that beset it. He overcomes a mighty monster – Klingsor and Kundry – travels through the world, engages in repetitive suffering and error, but continues to champion the ideals symbolized in the spear, and eventually becomes leader of a regenerated society. At this point, his story ends; we know nothing of his rule. In the chronology of Wagner's music-dramas, he is the heir of Lohengrin, though in the myth Lohengrin was his son. He also resembles Siegfried, but he assumes power where neither Siegfried nor Lohengrin could. However, his journey through life is as characteristic of the romantic hero as it is of the epic. The strange amnesia that possesses him on his first entrance recalls Tristan's initial lack of direction, the years of wandering after he has defeated Klingsor align him with the Dutchman and the Wanderer, and his sexual encounter with Kundry stirs up the same treacherous emotional turmoil that overwhelmed Arindal, Tannhäuser, Siegmund, and Tristan. In him, characteristics of all of Wagner's heroes are fused, but where earlier heroes had failed, he survives and succeeds; where they were entrapped by their own weaknesses or the circumstances of the world, he resists. He reverses tragic determination, and, with the exception of Walther in *Die Meistersinger*, becomes the only hero to realize on stage the utopia that in the earlier music-dramas was only glimpsed or lay outside the action.

But in contrast to Wagner's other heroes, Parsifal has little substance. When he first appears as a nameless boy, he is nothing but an empty vessel, and even after he has resisted the temptations of Kundry and the adversities of the world, his travails are not felt as forces that form and individualize him. Parsifal has, on this count, often been thought of as a "passive" hero, but that is misleading because he does live a continuously active life. However, the wisdom and glory he has gained from this never stay with him but pass on to others. His heroism saves others, a condition that is closer to saintliness than previous modes of heroism in Wagner.

Parsifal saves the world by "redemption," a word with several meanings, including winning back something that has been lost, freeing someone from a harmful situation, releasing them from captivity, and liberating them from a burden of blame or debt. "Redemption" is the grace that Senta, Elisabeth, Brünnhilde, and Isolde offered their male partners, but in the instance of *Parsifal*, the entity most in need of redemption is not the hero himself but the brotherhood of the grail. The popular conception of the grail, one that Wagner did much to foster, is the goal of a quest for ultimate truth and perfection. In Wolfram von Eschenbach's *Parzival*, Wagner's main source, the "gral" had a more material function. It was not something to be sought, but a ceremonial stone that guaranteed abundance in the world, and it was revealed not in an austere temple ceremony, but at a sumptuous banquet where it was carried in by fetchingly clad virginal girls. It stood therefore for the bounty of the earth and human fertility. Through the gral, life was prolonged and nourished. Wagner retained aspects of Wolfram's gral, but added several of his own. It is the final manifestation of his idea of an elemental energy that gives vitality and worth to life and is made accessible through the intercession of the hero. It incorporates the perfect unity of the subject and the world, as previously articulated in Lohengrin's narration of the grail, and the ceaseless transformation, spontaneity, sexual potency, and oneness with nature symbolized by the Rhinegold. With a simplicity characteristic of late drama, Wagner baldly states the life-giving properties of the grail through the ceremony, presided over by Amfortas, in which the knights extend their lives by exposure to it. Wagner also lays a heavy load of Christian symbolism onto Wolfram's pagan icon. The grail is also the chalice that caught Christ's blood, shed to redeem humanity, and the spear, which should accompany the grail, is the weapon that once pierced Christ's side on the cross and will now allow the knights to protect the grail and disperse its benefits to humanity. However, as they no longer possess the spear, they cannot disseminate the goodness of the grail, so their rituals have no purpose beyond the mere continuation of their bodily lives. Ritual displays how the knights have become caught in the prison of their own ego.

What is the cause of this disastrous collapse of morale among the knights of the grail? Recent interpretations have argued that in *Parsifal* Wagner was giving vent to his anti-Semitic prejudice. In such a reading, the blood of pure Aryans – the knights of the grail – has been tainted by that of the Jews – Kundry and Klingsor.[62] Given the wide range of reference encouraged by the symbolic framework of the drama, it is not easy to refute this thesis. It stresses the anti-Semitic aspects of "Religion und Kunst," which Wagner wrote while he was completing *Parsifal*, though we must note that in both the stage directions[63] and certain allusions in the dialogue of act I, Klingsor's castle is associated with Moorish Spain, suggesting that the culture that threatens the knights is Islamic, not Judaic. Given Wagner's depth of reading in central Asian cultures, this is no mere quibble. There can be no doubt that the predicament of the brotherhood represents degenerate humanity, and "Religion und Kunst" suggests that this arises from the intermingling of Christian and Jewish religions.[64] But the essay suggests many other reasons for the decline, which are of relevance to *Parsifal* and should not be dismissed as mere fads of an old man, for they identify causes of human decline that we find especially compelling today, including cruelty to animals, destruction of the environment, surrender to the mechanical power of society, and unlimited greed. To insist solely upon a racist interpretation of *Parsifal* reduces Wagner's work, though the racism should, as in *Die Meistersinger*, be understood as part of the dialectic. In fact the stratum of human experience upon which Wagner centers his drama is not that of race but sexuality.

In his intemperate attacks upon *Parsifal*, Nietzsche claimed that Wagner was denying what he had worked for "with all the power of his will . . . the spiritualization and sensualization in his art." Instead, the work displays a "hatred of life. For *Parsifal* is a work of rancour, of revenge, of the most secret concoction of poisons with which to make an end of the first conditions of life – *it is a bad work*. The preaching of chastity remains an incitement to unnaturalness: *Parsifal* [is] an outrage upon morality."[65] Following Nietzsche, it has been widely assumed that the music-drama advocates sexual abstinence, because to be a member of the brotherhood, one must be chaste, but there are fallacies in the argument. First it assumes that Wagner is holding up the rules of the brotherhood as exemplary, which is unlikely, and secondly it presupposes that chastity means the total renunciation of sex, which it does not. Chastity precludes unsanctioned sex, such as spontaneous sexual intercourse or sex for hedonistic purposes alone, but it sanctions sexual relations that ensure social cohesion – one can, for example, be married and chaste. The knights in Wolfram's *Parzival* were encouraged to marry whenever it would ensure peace in the community, but sex for pure pleasure or for the exercise of wanton power over another is explicitly condemned. In Wagner, there is a biological reason why members of the brotherhood should remain chaste, as those who guard the source of life's energy must maintain that energy within themselves. But the brotherhood is ailing as the chastity that binds them has been corrupted and is itself corrupting. Amfortas, their king, has not sustained his chastity. As the most alienated of romantic heroes, he is, as Wagner pointed out, Tristan "inconceivably intensified."[66] By once engaging in intercourse with a beautiful woman, he lost the spear, which Klingsor then turned into a weapon of destruction by wounding him in the side. The festering wound that never heals signifies the consequences of unfettered sexual desire as a force that infects humanity and erodes its energy.[67] Amfortas is a figure immense in his suffering and Wagner was right to fear that he might draw more attention than Parsifal, as his agony is not only theatrically more compelling, but closer to the understanding and experience of the audience than the saintliness by which Parsifal will ultimately redeem him.

But chastity can cause corruption, apparent in the predicament of the brotherhood. For a start, the members of the brotherhood are poor guardians. The opening words of the drama are Gurnemanz's reproach to the squires that they are asleep when they should be watching, as if they perform their duties unwillingly. The squires are also immature, taunting Kundry like callow boys who have just discovered their growing sexuality, and as they cannot come to terms with it, take it out on the woman who arouses desire in them. Their tight vocal lines and sharp rhythms contrast with the easy flow of Gurnemanz's singing, indicating latent violence. As the action moves from the forest into the grail temple, the ominous tolling of the bells arouses an atmosphere of gloom and oppression, which is strengthened as their rhythm transforms into the heavy march of the knights. The movement into the temple is no progression toward the source of primal energy where humanity might find salvation, but a journey into a closed society of men who are weary, harsh, and fearful. The knights of the brotherhood and their squires possess neither the maturity nor generosity to serve as guardians of the grail, and they cling to it for survival rather than nurture it for the well-being of humanity. The soaring voices that end the ritual of act I seem to float above and apart from the knights, as if they articulate a state of mind that the knights, in their hysterical demand for exposure to the grail, can neither be part of nor understand. On Parsifal's return at the end, the atmosphere of intense anxiety has degenerated into rank brutality and terror, the transition music for act 3, in which this is displayed, being the ugliest Wagner ever wrote.

Chastity is, therefore, a double-edged condition, reflecting the intense sexual awareness of the generation for which *Parsifal* was written. The late nineteenth century was acutely conscious of the capacity of sexual desire to destroy personal happiness and undermine social cohesion. As this was paralleled by an ongoing crisis in religious faith, there was no body of belief that could neutralize the fear aroused by this increased knowledge of sex. The literature and drama of Dostoevsky, Ibsen, Strindberg, Tolstoy, and Zola show an acute awareness of the ambivalent nature of sex, which fulfills and destroys, expresses hatred as well as love. Europe was also still in the grip of the widely held belief that the sexual powers of men were limited, while women's sexual appetites were either non-existent or aberrational and insatiable. Woman could therefore threaten the stability of the male. Though man's exercise of his sexual prowess might commonly be considered to indicate his emancipation from the family, as Freud would argue, as sexual desires are manifest in infancy, satisfying them articulates a dependency upon the mother rather than an escape from her, a condition that we have already observed in Tristan and Siegfried. The tragic landscape of sex has rarely been charted as widely and deeply as in late nineteenth-century Europe. Sex, more explicitly than miscegenation, greed, and materialism, is the state from which Parsifal must redeem humankind.

From the little we know, Parsifal's childhood was closer to the natural romanticism of Rousseau than that of any other Wagnerian hero. He was brought up by his mother, Herzeleide, in the desert and kept from all knowledge of the world, especially knighthood and war, which destroyed his father. As a result, he knows nothing of the world nor of himself, so in him the world and self are one. But this state of natural growth is no unqualified idyll, as it does not preclude violence. In retrospect, the serene natural setting of the opening scene can be read as metaphorical for Parsifal's childhood, a quiet world that can offer comfort to those in pain, but its peace is easily shattered, as it is by Parsifal himself when he shoots the swan. A child of nature has violated nature, a meaningless crime which, through Gurnemanz's moving lament, takes on the stature of original sin. Although Parsifal on his first appearance seems identical with Siegfried – his opening line, boasting that he can hit whatever is in flight, sounds just like Siegfried – the two characters follow very different lives. Siegfried pursues a shabby career of moral compromise, Parsifal advances in the opposite direction. After Gurnemanz has reproved him, he throws away his bow, a gesture which, in the spare dramatic ambience of the drama, indicates immediate renunciation of violence and the first stage in Parsifal's moral growth as he learns his difference from the world. His isolation is intensified when he hears from Kundry that his mother is dead. After that he contemplates the world in befuddled silence, witnessing the pain of Amfortas that he cannot yet understand. Growth will occur when understanding dawns on him and he will be moved by the compassion that results from it.

Though Parsifal himself is not passive, his growth is a strangely passive process. We see him grow in just one of his battles, the encounter with Kundry, and here he fights less with the world outside him than with himself. In all he does, he denies himself, and in so doing embodies Schopenhauer's dictum that all action arising from the need to strive is in vain, as it is the cause of alienation, frustration, and pain. Fulfillment lies not in action but acceptance, not in searching for wealth and stature in the world, but in trusting that they will come and in surrendering to that trust. His only motivation can be compassion. In such a way, he will remain a "pure fool," but we should also note that as such he reclaims for himself the innocence of Rousseau's "natural man," for the sole motive that animated this figure's dealings with others was compassion.

Parsifal's encounter with Kundry centers exclusively on sexuality. Kundry is unique in the music-dramas. Despite his metaphorical use of settings, Wagner was fundamentally a realist and only occasionally did he introduce characters whose functions were solely symbolic, the most obvious example being Erda and the Norns in the *Ring*. But with Kundry the aesthetic of the realistic stage is abandoned. She is less a character than an embodiment of female sexuality whose demeanor and even appearance on stage change according to the males with whom she is in company. She is wild and demented in the eyes of the immature squires and the young Parsifal, with Gurnemanz she is the epitome of servitude, while Amfortas sees her, erroneously, as one who can cure him. Klingsor calls her by the names of Herodias and Gundgryggia, figures of omnivorous sexuality. She is a proto-expressionistic figure whose main purpose is to reflect the inner life and desires of the individual she is with. Her figure is granted unity by a single act, laughing at Christ on his way to crucifixion. The mockery of that moment, which is the antithesis of compassion, has alienated her for ever from the world. As one who mocks, she provides a distorted reflection, an ironic comment, to all whom she meets, and condemned, like the Dutchman, to wander for ever, she lives a life of eternal repetition, from which she will be released only when she meets one who can resist her sexual power. That power is expressed in the threat of the rising and falling leitmotif, first heard in the orchestra as Gurnemanz describes how

Titurel found Kundry asleep in the underbrush where the foundations of the castle would be built, which suggests the order is founded upon the suppression of sexuality rather than the incorporation of it into their lives. This leitmotif, a graphic depiction of the swelling and subsiding of sexual desire, dominates the prelude to act 2, where it rampages through the orchestra as a force that will destroy anything that resists it.

This prelude introduces the most desolate scene in Wagner. Klingsor summons up Kundry in her most lurid manifestations, but they are rooted, as Kundry's opening groan makes clear, in deep pain. Kundry is the tool of Klingsor, a lapsed knight of the grail whose overcoming of sexual desire by self-castration, the most violent form of abstinence, has put him beyond redemption. All that Klingsor, the ultimate cynic, touches should be subject to his power or destroyed. His condition is the polar opposite to the ideal state of the grail. Like Amfortas, the knights, and Kundry, he is condemned to endless repetition, ceaselessly reenacting strategies of hatred against the grail and reiterating the tragic nexus in which men betray the idealism of their lives by falling prey to sexual desire. As Parsifal appears outside Klingsor's castle, he too seems to reenact the struggle that maimed Amfortas and the rest of suffering manhood. Kundry is the means by which injury will be done.

Kundry in act 2 has been seen as a representation of pure lust,[68] but she is more than that. The Flower Maidens stand for lust and Wagner encases them in his most saccharine music, reminiscent of the ballets of French grand opera, with their scenes of voluptuous luxury in which the senses, and the senses alone, are charmed. The Flower Maidens are pretty creatures with little capacity to disturb. That Kundry stands for something more powerful is apparent as her voice penetrates and subdues their clamor. This is the moment when Parsifal learns his name and Kundry fulfils one of the most fundamental functions of a mother by giving a child its identity. As she seduces Parsifal, she dwells obsessively on the close physical contact with his mother when he was a baby, so the growing intimacy between them becomes increasingly a reenactment of the physical circumstances of his conception. As Kundry plants on Parsifal the kiss intended to seduce him, to a prolonged statement of the dark leitmotif of sexual desire, the act of seduction is explicitly stated as a recreation of the act that brought him into being. Parsifal is threatened by sexual forces that could engulf him, from a desire that arises from infantile dependence on the mother, the desire that destroyed Amfortas and Tristan. But it does not destroy him. His rejection of Kundry and the maternal sexuality with which she will smother him is the key event of the drama. The moment he achieves this freedom, he is filled with compassion for Amfortas. As he reaches sexual maturity, he acquires moral vision.

But he also gains insight into the paradox at the heart of the drama, as he recognizes that sexual indulgence and asceticism are not unrelated states of being, but closely tied, indicative of a common condition, and therefore requiring salvation in common. This conjunction is first raised in Kundry's reaction to Parsifal's rejection of her advances. She pleads with him to pity her, by telling him of the curse on her for laughing at Christ and insisting that his, Parsifal's, physical love will save her. His response goes to the heart of the tragic dilemma of eternal repetition:

> For evermore
> would you be damned with me
> if for one hour,
> unmindful of my mission,
> I yielded to your embrace!
> For your salvation too I am sent,
> if you will turn aside from your desires.
> The solace to end your sorrows
> comes not from the source from which they flow:
> grace shall never be bestowed on you
> until that source is sealed to you.[69]

Salvation from pain comes only when one does not return to the source from which the pain arose. For Parsifal, sex that arises from infantile experience can only return him to that experience; for Kundry, endless seduction arouses the torments of endless desire – and the balsam that she brought to Amfortas in act 1, coming as it did from Arabia, only aggravated his agony, it did not cure it. More desire does not heal the wounds of desire. Redemption lies in the capacity to escape from the eternal repetition that constantly satisfied desire sets in motion.

The knights too are cursed with repetition. Immediately after Parsifal comes to know the cause of Kundry's pain, he thinks of the knights of the grail:

> Another grace – ah, a different one,
> for which, pitying, I saw the brotherhood
> pining in dire distress,
> scourging and mortifying their flesh.[70]

Extreme self-denial offers no road to salvation either, so the abstinence of the knights is no model to be followed. On the contrary, their misery is as acute as Kundry's because they, like her, are destined to repeat it. This has made them into an obscurantist priesthood that has never been filled with the energy and joy that belief should awaken in the believer. Instead, it extinguishes the faith it is supposed to cherish. Amfortas' ever-increasing pain indicates the relentless degeneration of the knights he leads. When Parsifal returns, the community has disintegrated, reduced to individuals scraping the barest existence from herbs and roots, performing ceremonies that merely put off the end to which they are destined. Like Wotan, the brotherhood lives in terror of death.

In *Parsifal*, Wagner represents in its starkest form the tragic fate faced by all his heroes from *Holländer* on. In the early music-dramas, the hero dies as a result of, or even as a gesture of social alienation, and in the *Ring* the freedom of the hero is progressively determined by the consequences of the acts that he committed to achieve freedom in the first place. But the condition that both betrays and yet defines all heroes, as it is part of their mission, is a perpetual return to origins, a ceaseless drawing back, which can only be broken or redeemed by the sacrifice of a loving woman. Wagner's heroes, however much they are clothed in the exalted trappings of epic heroism or the dark glamour of romantic withdrawal, are also strikingly modern figures. Caught in a vicious circle of everlasting repetition, they prefigure the anti-heroes of Strindberg, Chekhov, and Pirandello, who are condemned endlessly to relive their pasts. Determination lies not so much in the malign effects of the past upon the present, but in the past actually *being* the present, so that no growth is possible. Tragedy is one's incapacity to escape from that vicious circle, from the condition into which one was born.

In redeeming Amfortas, Kundry, and the knights, Parsifal offers a chance of that very escape. He has withstood Kundry's seduction and has avoided the snare of eternal repetition. But what is the new condition that he offers? It is one that is communicated less in the words of the poem than in the music that, in the first scene of act 3, reaches unusual heights of refinement and exaltation: a unique music, penetrating, pathetic, wistful, intensely nostalgic, which in the climax of the Good Friday vision of a meadow of flowers and Gurnemanz's final monologue represents a high point of late romanticism, the most sustained vision of the union of nature and humanity in later nineteenth-century theatre. Nature in *Parsifal* has not been a metaphor for the inner lives of characters as it has been before in previous music-dramas, but a realm of serenity within which humans dwell, but from which they are nonetheless alienated. Nature may alleviate their pain – Amfortas, for example, gains temporary relief from his morning bath in the lake – but humans are essentially separate from nature, a separation symbolized by Parsifal's shooting of the swan. Nature is constant change (and therefore the opposite of eternal repetition), a change articulated in the unceasing chromaticism of the music. Nature in act 2 is lurid, of the hothouse, where it has been cultivated and malformed for human purposes. And although Parsifal has escaped repetition in his denial of Kundry, as the tormenting prelude to act 3 tells us, his life has been wearisome labor within a constantly repetitive world.

When he returns to the domain of the grail, Parsifal once more encounters nature as serenity and constant change, but his sufferings mean he is now at one with it. Compassion, which results from breaking out of eternal repetition, has led to his atonement for the slaying of the swan and now enables him to achieve union with nature. In the Good Friday music and Gurnemanz's monologue, the naturalistic vision of Rousseau from which romanticism stemmed is displayed to its fullest. It envisages humans living at one with nature and never destroying it, bound to each other by compassion, symbolized in the instance of *Parsifal* by the sufferings of Christ on the cross. In the perspective of romanticism, the ring has come full circle, the past is once again repeating itself, but not now to deplete and torment humanity, but to reunite it with the only source from which it can gain energy and life – nature.

Perhaps *Parsifal* should conclude at this point, but the final scene goes beyond it – whether with the intent of questioning the authenticity of romantic union or arguing that it is only a stage toward a messianic utopia is uncertain. The question "Which is the deeper reality, the standard of 'ordinary' nature or the pattern that man has laid upon it?" still remains unanswered. As Parsifal returns to the temple, he displays his power to break eternal repetition and returns again to the issue of ritual. Ritual is one of the principal means by which *Parsifal* speaks to the imagination of its audience, but it is an instance of eternal repetition, in fact the most formal expression imaginable of it. That the ritual of the knights has no more life is apparent as Gurnemanz, Kundry, and Parsifal retrace their steps to the temple. The transformation music of act 1 was heavy and threatening, but in act 3 it is laden with anxiety and barbarism, followed by a hideous chorus of men, desperate for the succor of the grail. Amfortas is in ever deeper agony and the downward spiral of eternal repetition is leading to naked violence. Then Parsifal enters bringing redemption and peace. It is a strange moment, hardly registering in the score, his refusal of Kundry and the Good Friday music having made far stronger impressions. But the absence of concrete action suggests that any further advancement to an ideal world can only take place on a plane beyond the human. To achieve oneness with nature through the exercise of compassion, one must deny the self and all striving must cease. Under these circumstances, no further drama is possible.

The apotheosis of Parsifal in the final scene elevates him to a messianic role, a moment that, at the very end of Wagner's theatrical career, indicates a distinct shift in his attitude toward the hero. Even in *Die Meistersinger*, the hero was ultimately made peripheral, an inspiration to humans rather than an authority over them. He was, reassuringly, unnecessary. But *Parsifal* ends with the hero adopting an absolute relationship to the world around him. By uniting the spear and the grail Parsifal has ensured that the vital energies radiating from the grail may spread through a regenerated humanity as the dysfunctional state of human sexuality has been healed and resolved. But if Parsifal is heralding a utopia, its precise nature is uncertain, and it is difficult to see how it could be anything else, as utopia eludes representation. We know what it will not incorporate – the sex that chastity excludes – but the rest is obscure and must remain so, for any attempt to spell it out would reduce the drama to banality. Nevertheless, one cannot hide from the possibility that the obverse side of the radiance shed by Parsifal's presence might be little more than pure power. In Wagner's previous drama, with the exception of *Die Meistersinger*, the utopian unity of the individual with the world occurred as a result of the death of the hero and the self-sacrifice of the redeeming woman. Now, in his last work, the woman dies but the hero lives. The woman's role as one who loves and is compassionate is dispensable, and the male hero, now a messiah, is absolute to himself.

Kundry's death can, of course, be read as a relief for it concludes almost two thousand years of tormenting repetition. But it is also difficult to avoid the conclusion that, with the demise of female sexuality, the utopia of the grail will be sterile and subject to the same forces that had previously eroded the brotherhood. In the elevation of Parsifal to the sole source of energy and authority, Wagner assigned to the hero an absolute function that, in his previous dramas, he had avoided. But perhaps he did not. Redemption, as the last words of the drama tell us, still has to come to the redeemer. As long as he is in need of redemption, Parsifal's power may not be absolute. Perhaps the last possibility suggested by *Parsifal* is that that final redemption should never come. If it does not, then Wagner did not, finally, endorse a totalitarian view of how our lives should be ordered.

6

Wagner's heroism on stage

Richard Wagner is still with us and it is surprising that he is. For some decades after his death, the theatre developed along lines suggested by his theatrical and dramatic practice and theory, but as the forms and functions of theatre changed in the early decades of the twentieth century, the aesthetic legitimacy of his work was challenged. Not only did the romantic–realistic style in which the music-dramas were conceived become archaic, but the heroic atmosphere and ethos of his work grew increasingly suspect. The notion of heroism as a formative agent in public life, always a questionable assumption, has been more discredited in the latter half of the twentieth century than perhaps at any other time in history. The aphorism of Brecht's Galileo, "Unhappy the land where heroes are needed,"[1] must surely stand as one of our defining mottoes since World War II. But Wagner, for all his championing of the hero, did not disappear. A few years after the defeat of Germany, the music-dramas were reinstated in the international and German operatic repertoire, and although subsequent generations have continued to contest their centrality to German culture, they are as popular as they have ever been. Even smaller European opera-houses now regularly stage the *Ring* and at the Bayreuth Festival applications for tickets, we are told, outweigh availability by a factor of about eight to one. Wagner, it appears, will be with us for several decades to come, probably longer.

WAGNER, FASCISM, AND ANTI-SEMITISM

He has lost none of his capacity to fill audiences with enthusiasm and incite fury in his foes. In each age some find values to be cherished in the music-dramas, while others discover in them advocacy for causes that they abominate. The unending polemic Wagner arouses has its dangers. On the one hand, his hostile critics insist that the meaning of his music-dramas is contained within a narrow range of polemical issues, on the other, many Wagnerians resolutely maintain his work is innocent of all political purpose. Both are wrong. Take, for example, the much-debated question of Wagner and fascism.

There can be little doubt that Wagner, like many other conservative and radical artists and intellectuals of his time and later, laid the groundwork for thinking that led to the nationalist and racist politics of the twentieth century. To refuse to acknowledge this is to fail to recognize one of the reasons why the music-dramas appealed in their time and later. But it is hard to see how his dramas specifically foreshadow the fascism of the 1930s, for if they did they must be interpreted as allegories of world domination by a single race and the mass extermination of those who were not part of it. In actuality, they argue the opposite. Only four of Wagner's heroes, Rienzi, Lohengrin, Wotan, and Siegfried, have political or potentially political careers and each decisively and for different reasons does not achieve the supreme power that fascism would, almost a century later, exalt. A fifth, Parsifal, ends as a leader, but to claim that he assumes totalitarian power in the sense that it was understood in the 1930s is tendentious at best.

Until fairly recently, accusations of fascism in the music-dramas were based on an understanding of dramatic action that was, to put it mildly, incomplete. For example, Peter Viereck[2] and Hans Kohn,[3] noted anti-Wagnerians of the mid-twentieth century, cite isolated incidents and often quote single lines to prove massive points against Wagner, but neither pays any attention to the dramatic situation in which these occur, and context in drama is everything when it comes to determining meaning. So ineffective was the assault on the music-dramas, as opposed to the easier target of the theoretical works, that Wagner's defenders could claim with impunity that they were free of any taint of totalitarian leanings. But Wagnerian polemicists have become more adept at dramatic criticism and it is now difficult to argue that the music-dramas were untouched by his political opinions. In fact, such a claim should never have been made, because as we have seen, Wagner himself insisted at the start of "Eine Mitteilung" that he could not count among his "friends" those "who pretend to love me as an *artist*, yet deem themselves bound to deny me their sympathy as a *man*"[4] – a sentiment repeated by his grandson Wieland when he said that "the life and work of an artist form an organic unity. One must not, even in Wagner's case, say yes to his works and no to his life."[5] Works of art are not produced in a vacuum, but are an expression of the life of their creator.

They also accumulate significance through performance. While artists cannot be blamed for the uses their works are put to after their deaths, their appeal to later generations is a legitimate area of inquiry. Consequently, the fascination Wagner's music-dramas exercised on Hitler and the exploitation of his artistic milieu by the Nazis for their own spectacles is not irrelevant to our understanding of them.[6] Also aspects of their work acquire broader significance for later generations than for those for whom the works were originally written. Hence, in the cultural climate since World War II, greater attention has been directed toward the anti-Semitic aspects of the music-dramas, and studies, which have already been cited, argue persuasively that Wagner's heroes stand opposite characters whose behavioral traits, body language, and physical features were considered, in Wagner's time and later, to characterize the Jews. After reading Marc A. Weiner on anti-Semitic coloring in the characterization and dramatic conflicts of the last seven music-dramas, it is difficult to deny that Wagner's vision was conditioned by a mindset that would contribute to the later development of a philosophy that led to the extermination of millions. But whether Wagner can personally be blamed for later disasters is a matter beyond the reach of rational enquiry.

Wagner's suspect political ideology does not mean his work has no legitimacy on opera stages today or that his heroes should be dismissed as nothing but avatars of a vicious political culture. His work is richer than mere political polemic. Thomas Mann compared the music-dramas to the novels of Zola and Tolstoy, which suggests they comprise a world too massive and various to articulate a single dogma. He also aligned them with the plays of Ibsen,[7] which reminds us that no one character or single set of beliefs provides the viewpoint of drama. Are the negatives in Wagner, therefore, balanced by other factors that we might regard more positively? Certainly. Take the case of his anti-Semitism. First, his anti-Semitic views should be placed in the context of his entire work. For most of his adult life, Wagner was fixated by a hatred for the Jewish race, which, as he grew older, acquired pathological dimensions. However much we might discuss whether his advocacy for "self-annihilation" by the Jews meant spiritual transformation or physical death,[8] his hideous joke about burning all Jews at a performance of *Nathan the Wise*[9] cannot be read ambiguously. Also, the much-vaunted associations he enjoyed with Jewish musicians and intellectuals do not ameliorate but accentuate the pathology of his anti-Semitism, as they display a gratuitous lack of connection between his life and the ideology that should guide it. But not all of his intellectual and creative endeavors should be centered on his anti-Semitic obsession. Paul Lawrence Rose's carefully assembled account of the development of his anti-Semitism from the revolutionary writings of the Vormärz on[10] encourages one to think that anti-Semitism was all he cared about. But in the overall context of his copious essays, diaries, and letters to family members, friends, and associates, anti-Semitic prejudice does not obliterate every other concern. It is a theme, frequently prominent, more often subsidiary, in a life that covered an unusually broad range of intellectual interests, most of which were centered not upon imagining the destruction of those who were racially different, but on the transformative functions of art in a materialistic society. We should also bear in mind that, once stripped of their anti-Semitic associations, many of Wagner's beliefs, and the heroes that stand for them, anticipate modern liberal causes, such as resistance to the industrial-military complex, commitment to ethnic identity, environmentalism, and, always, the arts as an energizing and cohering force in society. Even the supposedly cranky beliefs of his old age – vegetarianism, the humane treatment of animals, and anti-vivisectionism – do not lack followers today.

Just as anti-Semitism does not characterize Wagner's entire thought, it cannot be seen as the sole or even central concern of the music-dramas. There is a difference between using anti-Semitic characteristics in the composition of some dramatic figures and writing a work that is wholly anti-Semitic in intent. Wagner's dramaturgy is driven by his Manichaean tendency to view the world as a product of dualistic conflicts – light versus dark, love versus power, poverty versus wealth, Jew versus Christian, Christian versus heathen, individual versus society, parent versus child. But none of his music-dramas is circumscribed by only one of these conflicts; rather each conflict is complementary to several others implicated in the action. The reading of one conflict alone into the drama limits and misrepresents the whole. Furthermore, while characters such as Beckmesser, Alberich, Mime, Hagen, Kundry, and Klingsor have anti-Semitic characteristics, they are not to be understood as being actually Jewish. Weiner puts it well when he writes that they are "aesthetic construct[s] upon which Wagner and his contemporaries projected and/or in which they recognized diverse signs of difference connoting shared prejudices and fears."[11]

This, however, lets neither Wagner nor Wagnerians off the hook. On the contrary, it complicates matters. There would, after all, be no difficulty in rejecting the music-dramas if they were overtly anti-Semitic. But visual and verbal images, musical phrases, and physical traits used to debase the Jews are incorporated into the dramatic texture and because of this there is a danger the audience will uncritically accept them. It is the duty, therefore, of directors, performing artists, and the audience not to fall prey to that acceptance and to acknowledge that the richest interpretations and fullest appreciation of the music-dramas come about through a process of constantly coming to terms with his work and by not denying that the negative aspects exist. No works in the history of the theatre more effectively demonstrate that the meaning of a work of art lies between the work and the imaginative response of each individual in its audience. So, with regard to anti-Semitism, for someone deeply invested in Jewish culture, the anti-Semitic allusions in a figure such as Beckmesser may so pollute the action that *Meistersinger* can become intolerable and the festive ending be nothing but a display of vicious racism. But for most people this extreme reaction is unlikely. Even then, we must continue to hear Wagner's work with as acute an understanding as possible of its cultural references. We should also have a mature appreciation of how art works upon us. Our bodies, we are told, are what we eat, but our minds are not automatically what we read, see, and hear. Hence when we encounter uncongenial images or ideas of a morally questionable nature in works of art, we should not feel that in this contact we have compromised ourselves and must therefore reject the entire work. Indeed, Wagner, as Laurence Dreyfus aptly puts it, "force[s] us to grow up, to live with the fact that artists are not saints, to admit to the troubled cauldron of ideas and affects that conditions the art work, and to suggest at the same time that these inspired distillations of humanity are indispensable to an enriched and examined life."[12]

THE MIXED APPEAL OF WAGNER

The recent history of Wagnerian production can be read as a continuing attempt to achieve a reckoning with his multivalent work and, in recent decades especially, with the darker implications identified above. But there is much even in the brighter aspects of his music-dramas, particularly in his depiction of heroism, that contradicts the liberal ethos that has, in the last fifty to sixty years especially, imbued European and American theatre. The elevation of the hero sanctions the privilege of the individual over the collective, while the idea of the hero as a conduit for forces of energy beyond the plane of everyday life is largely suspect in today's material world. So too is the intense admiration demanded by the colossal apparatus surrounding Wagner's heroes, which amplifies our sense of extra-human forces lying behind them. If heroes are treated with too much glory, the villainous figures opposing them seem as if they can be cast aside without question, and so the music-dramas are transformed from tragedy into grandiose melodrama, whose purpose is to argue for the rightness of a certain philosophy or world-view, rather than to represent cycles of human self-destruction and renewal. We often sense that Wagner's work grips us like first-rate melodrama does. Nietzsche claimed that Wagner "wanted to conquer and rule as no artist had done before"[13] and it is not at all unusual at a performance of one of his music-dramas for us to feel as if there is no escape from the insistent momentum of the action or the encompassing spectacle. But a signal achievement of the modern theatre has been to open up the multiple strains of his music-dramas, thus allowing us a greater freedom in our response to his work, a deeper appreciation of its dramatic complexity, and a respite from the totalizing tendencies of the *Gesamtkunstwerk*.

However, this has required radical changes in how the music-dramas are staged and designed, and these changes themselves have become cause for great division among audiences. Wagner is unusual in theatre history because not only were his works methodically canonized by an institution, the Bayreuth Festival under Cosima's direction, but they were given the imprimatur of a specific style of design and staging. This in itself was not problematic, for it was useful to have a series of well-planned productions of his major works in the style in which he originally envisaged them. But the mystique of these productions, that they represented the only way in which the music-dramas should be staged, had a regressive effect on their production elsewhere in Germany and abroad. For a good forty years after his death his music-dramas were denied the rejuvenation changing theatrical styles can bring and this would certainly not have been his wish. While Wagner had insisted that all theatrical elements should contribute to the action, he was, as his direction of the 1876 *Ring* revealed, aware that each moment could be realized in a variety of ways.[14] Despite this, the idea of there being only one way to perform the music-dramas not only initially limited interpretative opportunities, but has dogged reception ever since. Even now innovations in staging arouse greater controversy in connection with Wagner than other composers or dramatists.

Division of opinions among critics and audiences over the staging of Wagner arises from the unusually broad spectrum of expectations the music-dramas are called upon to meet. This was apparent in Wagner's day, for his popularity was based on the appeal he had both for those who wanted the theatre to be a pleasant escape from everyday life and for those who looked for entertainment that was challenging and transformative. Few stage-works of the time catered so completely to the escapist desires of audiences as *Tannhäuser, Lohengrin*, and *Meistersinger*. The detail of the spectacle and the opulence of the music created the illusion that the past was being materialized on stage with unprecedented vividness and totality. This was what appealed so profoundly to Ludwig II, for whom the music-dramas embodied a heroic paradise in which the divine right of kings was never challenged and the appeal of sensuous art never sullied by contact with the banality of modern life. In his artistic tastes, Ludwig was not mad, he merely took the popular culture of his time more literally than anyone else. But Wagner also spoke to those for whom this culture was anathema, to none more than Nietzsche, who dismissed historicist art as "antiquarian" and evidence that the nineteenth century had no culture of its own. "When the historical sense no longer conserves life but mummifies it," he wrote, "then the tree gradually dies from the top downwards to the roots – and in the end the roots themselves usually perish too. Antiquarian history itself degenerates from the moment it is no longer animated and inspired by the fresh life of the present."[15] The young Nietzsche considered Wagner to be precisely the one to bring "fresh life" into the airless historicist culture of the nineteenth century. He would restore theatre as the articulator of the great myths of humanity and reawaken in audiences a sense of themselves as natural and changeable beings, enabling them to understand the present and face the future with confidence. So, in one and the same work, Wagner could nurture the dreams of those who wished to retreat into a changeless paradise and arouse in others the illusion of humanity advancing toward higher consciousness.

Today, Wagner arouses equally diverse expectations, which also have their roots in the nineteenth century. Even though the modern Bayreuth Festival has been to the fore in sponsoring experimental productions of Wagner's work, the very existence of a festival devoted to one artist encourages him to be thought of in quasi-divine terms. There are still those who would echo Heinrich Porges' encomium of Bayreuth as a place where audiences should be saved from the "greed for sensation" that is a common reason for them to visit the theatre. They would agree with Porges that "for all the many signs of spiritual degradation," Bayreuth still gives evidence that "the feeling amongst the people for what is good and noble has not been lost."[16] But this mandarin view of commercial entertainment as a symptom of "spiritual degeneration" is no longer essential to an appreciation of Wagner. In fact the music-dramas have proved to be more amenable to "sensational" stage treatment than many operas, and such effects widen the potential audience for them. The existence of Bayreuth also propagates the romantic myth of the hero-artist whose work can only be satisfactorily performed when, again in Porges' words, "a number of artists share the conviction that a divine creative power has found paramount expression in one single individual, and accordingly regard it as their mission to give material form to the ideal images which this genius had hitherto conceived of only as possibilities."[17] But performers, at Bayreuth and elsewhere, are no longer required to be acolytes of the works they perform: they can even be critical of them and let this show in their performance. Production is now no longer devoted to realizing the vision of one man, Richard Wagner, but to presenting his work as a document in the social and political life of his time, our own, or of periods in between.

Although pleas to return to the "original" sets and stage directions in Wagner can still occasionally be heard, the production history of the music-dramas, over the last fifty years especially, has been dynamic and varied. The art of theatre is transient; like fashion, it is constantly changing. As Peter Brook put it, "truth in the theatre is always on the move."[18] Vital interpretation of the theatre of the past does not lie in deferential imitation of revered models, but in discovering contemporary relevance. If one is to find one unchanging "truth" in Wagner, it may be that there is no absolute truth; rather truth *is* constant transformation, and the work of art survives precisely because it is able to appeal to different generations by allowing them to see their own hopes and anxieties, beliefs and fears, reflected in it.

"THE CURSE OF RIDICULOUSNESS"

There is much evidence that Wagner had little faith in the production he mounted of the *Ring* in 1876. About a week after its final performance, he was in deep depression. "Costumes, scenery, everything must be done anew for the repeat performances," Cosima wrote in her diary. "R. is very sad, says he wishes he could die!"[19] Wagner's moods were extremely changeable – in the next sentence Cosima reports him making a harsh joke – but his doubts over the quality of the Bayreuth production and the suitability of the theatrical style to the work he had composed were well founded. While critical opinion was divided on the distinction of the score, it was acknowledged that the orchestra and several singers had performed the *Ring* with great understanding and sympathy. Theatrically, however, its full potential was not realized, a failure particularly galling to Wagner, as he had boasted that the Bayreuth Festival would provide model performances of his works, with regard to staging as well as music, something his more hostile critics were quick to pick up on.[20] His disillusion led him, for the moment at least, to abandon all further theatre projects. As he wrote to Ludwig: "The enormous effort to create a performance of my *Nibelung* work in the best possible taste has utterly exhausted me as it only led in the end to a common child of the theatre; I have built nothing with it, nothing but an unoccupied shell."[21]

Wagner had never been content with the treatment of his works in the theatre, but his ire had generally been directed against sloppiness in stage management, inappropriate design, thoughtless staging, and singers engaging in routine rhetorical gestures with no attention to the character they were playing. But he had had few problems with the theatrical style in which his music-dramas were produced, and when he did have the opportunity to craft model productions of his works in Munich during the 1860s, he found the impeccably detailed, historicist designs of Angelo II Quaglio and Heinrich Döll to be highly appropriate.[22] With regard to theatre, Wagner was, as we have seen, a thoroughgoing realist. He could have been little else. Romantic–realism, which utilized settings of purportedly historical accuracy, was the universal style in which opera, Shakespeare, the classics, and contemporary historical drama were performed. In accordance with the prevailing myth of realism, Wagner considered a theatrical performance to be successful to the degree that it erases the audience's consciousness of being in the theatre at all: "Art ceases to be art," he wrote in his essay "Über Schauspieler und Sänger" ("On Actors and Singers," 1872), "the moment it presents itself as art to our reflecting consciousness."[23] He insisted performers subject themselves entirely to the work, obliterating concern for self-exhibition and resisting all temptation to display virtuoso skills, for if they did, the illusion that lifts the audience "entirely outside themselves" was broken. So steeped was Wagner in the aesthetic of realism that his famous remark about creating an "invisible theatre"[24] has been taken to refer to the desire not to eliminate the physical stage, but to create the fullest illusion of reality.[25] The configuration of the stage and auditorium in the Festspielhaus, whereby the audience senses that it is seated within an expanded proscenium arch, makes the possibility of achieving that illusion greater.[26] But the realities of theatrical production militated against it. Although Joseph Hoffmann's sets for the *Ring* were admired as picturesque, the inadequate technology of the Bayreuth stage not only drew attention to the fact of performance, but reduced moments of high drama to bathos, in particular when the rainbow to Valhalla looked like a garden-bridge, the Valkyries bounced ineffectively, and the notoriously laughable dragon failed to arouse terror.[27] Unfortunately Richard Fricke's fear that the production would be dogged by "the curse of ridiculousness"[28] was frequently confirmed.

But inadequacy of staging points to a more intrinsic problem. The fundamental assumption of realism is that on stage the relationship between character and setting is similar to that in life, where human beings live and interact in an environment unrelated to their inner life. The Bayreuth *Ring*s of both 1876 and 1896 were staged on sets constructed by the Brückner brothers who also built the scenery for the company of the Duke of

Saxe-Meiningen, which, between 1874 and 1890, represented the acme of the theatre of realistic spectacle and ensemble. Such a style was suited to the exploration of neither the mental and emotional life of the individual nor the internal dynamics of heroic action. As early as *Holländer*, Wagner had been aware of how setting could be metaphorical for the inner life of his protagonist and he exploited this scenic capacity in *Tannhäuser* as well. In *Lohengrin* setting has an objective status; indeed, the point of that drama is that a human environment does not and cannot have bearing on the mental state of an epic hero such as Lohengrin. It is difficult to interpret the *Ring* as a drama occurring within the psyche of its characters, though one of the most celebrated modern analyses attempts to do this.[29] Nevertheless throughout the cycle there are passages in which the natural setting reflects the characters' inner lives, and the scenic environment of the cycle is frequently invested with a symbolic meaning, which controverts the aesthetics of realism. For Wagner, the mythical dimensions of the action articulated truths, but these could best be realized through non-realistic design and staging. Among the later music-dramas, only *Die Meistersinger* fitted easily into contemporary realistic scenic and production practices of the time.

Realism was particularly inappropriate for drama centered on heroic action, be it romantic, epic, or messianic heroism. When the romantic hero occupies the center of the drama, focus is primarily on his psychic condition, but realistic scenery insists upon its own presence, detached from character. Realistic scenery can generate a poetic atmosphere – and there is much evidence that the 1876 *Ring* sets were quite atmospheric – but it is difficult for it to be a conduit between the audience and the mental world of the characters. It might even do the opposite and become a barrier. Hence the centripetal energies by which romantic heroes draw the world to themselves and transform it so that the world is understood as a projection of their consciousness cannot be realized on the realistic stage. The energies of the epic or messianic hero cannot be felt effectively either. These are centrifugal as they radiate a warmth that energizes others and transforms a society that is constricted, worn, and exhausted or torn by greed and the lust for power. But the effect of the epic hero is reduced by realistic scenery, for the clear lines of the body that can provide a visual complement to the "inwardly secure being" of the hero are obscured against a detailed setting. The material presence of the objective world rather than the energies of the individual prevails on the realistic stage.

Neither Wagner nor Cosima was at ease with the design for the 1876 *Ring*. On seeing Joseph Hoffmann's first sketches, Cosima commented on "the downgrading of the dramatic intentions in favor of an elaboration of the scenery," while Wagner insisted they should turn away from "all outward pomp" so as "to present human beings without any conventional frills."[30] Up to the opening of the production, Cosima had severe doubts about Emil Doepler's costumes, which she dismissed as "much conventionalism, little inventiveness, lack of beauty . . . too much ornateness . . . [and] provincial tastelessness."[31] Nevertheless, once she had taken over the reins of the Festival, far from rescuing the music-dramas from the straitjacket of realism, she bound them more closely within it. Her declared purpose of enshrining the music-dramas by staging them as Wagner had originally envisaged them meant that in the forty-year stasis following his death, most productions were designed and staged in a style that failed to represent the heroic aspects of the action effectively and did nothing to come to terms with their dramatic conflicts. Style was privileged over content and performance was an act of reverence to the Master, not a meeting between the work and modern sensibilities. It is even questionable whether Cosima was faithful to Wagner's intentions. There are significant differences between the sets for the 1876 *Ring* and the ones commissioned for the 1896 production, and contemporary photos suggest the latter were heavier and even more of the material world than the earlier sets. Those who revered the original productions of the *Ring* and *Parsifal* were irked by the changes Cosima introduced.[32] Unlike her husband, who prized improvisation and spontaneity, she was one of those directors who cannot abide unpredictability. Every move and gesture had to be determined before performance. She also introduced onto the Bayreuth stage a literalness in acting that had been current in Germany since the late eighteenth century, a style that insisted that each feeling or emotion had a finite expression in characteristic poses and gestures. Once the actor had mastered these, the performance was considered complete. The Bayreuth style in which word, tone, mien, and gesture were bound to each other in unchanging unity robbed the music-dramas of much life and spontaneity. Although George Bernard Shaw in retrospect praised Cosima's productions as "the utmost perfection of the pictorial stage," his reports from the Festival suggest that the performances lacked energy, because the singing-actors failed to express "overwhelming crises of emotion . . . which occur in the minds of the spectator . . . [and are] supported with most powerful sympathy by the orchestra."[33] Ultimately, Shaw admitted that his "favorite way of enjoying a performance of the *Ring* is to sit at the back of a box, comfortable on two chairs, feet up, and listen without looking."[34]

CLEARING THE STAGE: SYMBOLISM

Cosima's urge to preserve the music-dramas in their "original" theatrical form came at the wrong time, as romantic–realism was in serious decline by the end of the century, a decline in part initiated by the theories of one of Wagner's most zealous disciples, Adolphe Appia. Most of Appia's innovations, which transformed direction and scenography in European theatre, were introduced in the name of Wagnerian music-drama and led to a mode of performance in which heroic experience came to the fore. But when Cosima refused Appia the opportunity to work at Bayreuth, she did so on the grounds that there was no relation between Wagner's visual concept of the music-dramas and Appia's abstract settings. By the end of his life, however, Wagner was becoming aware of the shortcomings of romantic–realism. As early as 1872, in "Schauspieler," he had written of the open stage of the Elizabethan theatre as a space where actors can perform with a freedom unattainable on realistic stages, where they implant "the representation of scenic incidents"[35] solely in the imagination of the audience. He considered Shakespeare's greatness lay in his ability to use every detail – "storm winds, the song of a fool, the sight of a dagger" – to intensify his drama, which was vastly preferable to the "flat and naked" sensationalism of Victor Hugo.[36] In his own theatre-work he became aware that in theatre less suggests more; in coaching the actors in *Parsifal*, he discovered "that a half-uplifting of one arm . . . a characteristic movement of the hand, the head, was quite enough to emphasize a somewhat heightened feeling."[37] He had already seen beyond the emphatic literalism of the Bayreuth productions that followed his death. Had Wagner lived to read Appia's theories, he may not have acknowledged any kinship between them and the music-dramas, but in retrospect he was finding his way toward a theatre that Appia would later imagine, if not actualize.

Wagner's music-dramas stimulated Appia to his most consequential insights. Appia understood instantly what others did not fully grasp, that Wagner was "torn between the all-powerful intensity of his genius and the inadequacy of his means of representation."[38] Accordingly, stage expression had to be raised to an expressive power equal to that of the drama. Appia acknowledged that seamless harmony in which all elements of the action are interrelated is the essence of Wagner's *Gesamtkunstwerk*, but insisted that realism is not essential to this conception, as it disturbs rather than promotes harmony. But his most striking insight was that Wagnerian music-drama is not driven by external events. As the action of *Parsifal* is nothing but the spiritual transformation of its hero, duration and sequence on stage are determined solely by his psychological growth. This means that time passes differently in *Parsifal* than in reality and the events of the action do not follow the sequence of cause and effect as in conventional drama. Everything that does not directly apprehend Parsifal's psychology must be omitted. All relationships between characters are ideal ones in that they have "no material analogy to those set up by real life."[39]

Some of the music-dramas are easier to submit to this treatment than others: the dramatic space in *Holländer* and *Tristan* especially is an extension of the consciousness of their heroes. But even in the *Ring*, where space is treated realistically and action is driven by cause and effect, the focus is on the impact of events on the psychology of the characters, so, as in the more subjectively oriented music-dramas, settings should express those changes that occur in the mental and emotional lives of the characters and the actor and setting should seem to be one. The stage-space must therefore be abstract, allowing the imagination of the audience free rein, for, as Appia observed, it "tacitly imposes the exterior form it needs in order to be convinced of the drama's inner life."[40] The changes in the drama are registered in the constantly modulating light, which Appia thought of as the scenic equivalent to the music, and, as it works directly on the mood of the audience, it is the most effective means of conveying the inner life of the drama.

Appia's symbolism brought the romantic dimensions of Wagnerian music-drama to the fore as had not been possible with realistic productions. It provided a simplicity of setting that gave actors the stature they had lacked on the realistic stage. Not only were sets and actor at one, the contrast between the abstract linearity of the sets and the rounded natural lines of the actor's body, apparent in many of Appia's designs, enhanced and gave emphasis to the body, which now dominated the stage. In the realistic theatre, it had too frequently been lost in the details.

Appia offered more of an inspiration than an example. The few opportunities he had to stage Wagner, *Tristan* at La Scala in 1923, and *Das Rheingold* and *Die Walküre* in Basle in 1924–25, were highly controversial. *Tristan* failed because the audience was unwilling to contemplate non-realistic sets. There were signs that the first two *Ring* music-dramas in Basle might have been successful with audiences, but their cubist sets created such furious reaction among conservative Wagnerians that production of the last two works was suspended.[41] Elsewhere in Europe, abstract sets did not automatically meet with rejection. *Tristan* was the music-drama most open to experimentation: Alfred Roller's celebrated Secessionist designs for *Tristan* (Vienna,

1903) allowed the material world to disappear during the love duet, the stage becoming entirely a representation of the "endlessness" of the lovers' emotions,[42] while Vsevolod Meyerhold (St. Petersburg, 1909), in rejecting the principle of recreating every detail of the score in acting and design, centered the design of each act on a single element and insisted that his singers act in accordance with the music rather than try to repeat in gesture the meaning of the words. This production was, according to Meyerhold's biographer, "probably the first attempt to free the composer's conception of the *Gesamtkunstwerk* from the banal conventions of the nineteenth century and give it credible theatrical form."[43] There were experimental productions during the expressionist period: Ludwig Sievert's mythical landscapes for the *Ring*, seen in a number of German opera-houses in the 1910s and 1920s, showed how the hero could dominate the scene on a stage cleared of all realistic clutter. Even Bayreuth, after Cosima and Siegfried Wagner's deaths, proved open to innovation; the sets of Emil Preetorius for the new production of the *Ring* (1933–34) were copybook Appia.

So when Wieland Wagner reopened the Festival after World War II in 1951 with his abstract *Parsifal*, he was not setting out on a completely unexplored path. Although he was reticent to admit any influence, a pamphlet he published at the time indicates how Appia had influenced his thought about theatre. Wieland argued that Wagner's stage directions indicated "inner visions rather than practical demands," he favored the "illuminated space [in place of] the lighted canvas," and quoted his grandfather that setting was of no importance in itself, but served as "a silent facilitating background and setting for a certain dramatic situation."[44] In actuality, Wieland went further than this. Ernest Newman's much-quoted review of *Parsifal* – "we felt the forest rather than saw it, a legendary forest that was of no time and no place, and one, moreover, over which mystery and sorrow and pain seem to have brooded long"[45] – suggests that the audience became absorbed into the production in the way Wagner's romantic characters had absorbed the environment into themselves. The gap that romanticism strove to bridge, between subject and object, self and other, was closed in the imaginative meeting of audience and stage.

The mesmeric hold of this production of *Parsifal* over the audience, perhaps the most complete realization ever of Appia's abstract theatre, seems rarely to have been equaled in Wieland's later career, but, during the 1950s, he made the flight from realism a permanent feature of Wagnerian production. As a minimalist, he cleared the stage of realistic clutter, conceiving of it as an architect rather than a painter. His productions were often considered monumental, closer to oratorio than conventionally staged opera.

He drew from the ancient Greek theatre, a major inspiration for his grand-father, more than from contemporary modes of performance, and in his first production of the *Ring* in 1951 distanced the work from its sources in Germanic mythology by emphasizing its kinship with classical Greek myth.[46] He did not abandon the romantic view of Wagner, one of his most contested productions being *Die Meistersinger* in 1956 where the realistic environment was entirely erased – though reintroduced in impressionist details in later years – to represent the creative process that produces song, rather than the community that song can create. Audiences were held by the impeccable precision and beauty of his blocking, which clarified the tensions of the drama. In his 1954–55 production of *Tannhäuser*, the masses of the chorus isolated Tannhäuser as a social pariah, while the contrast between the Venusberg and Wartburg reflected the inner division of the artist. But while Wieland brought to fruition romantic aspects of Wagner's music-dramas, the ideal aspects of character, those open to the appeal of the epic hero, were reduced. The statuesque dimensions of his *Ring* as Greek tragedy, staged on top of a rounded disc that suggested the globe, encouraged one to consider the universal implications of the action, but Wieland countered the symbolic leanings of the production by crafting a drama centered around human failings. While Wotan appeared with the grandeur of a god, he was portrayed as a man "whose downfall is the result of his own weaknesses rather than the cunning of his enemies."[47]

While the minimalist productions of Wieland and Wolfgang Wagner aroused the ire of traditional Wagnerians, they can now be seen as an extension of the aesthetic of the *Gesamtkunstwerk* rather than a repudiation of it. The ideal of the seamless whole, in which each element of the per-formance complemented and strengthened all others, worked best when the visual elements of the production played directly on audience emotions without any attempt to make the stage historically or geographically spe-cific. Under these circumstances, the romantic–heroic aspects of the drama were fully realized. But, like the earlier phase of romantic–realism, mini-malism did not attempt to come to terms with the ideological aspects of Wagner's music-dramas. Indeed, the Wagner brothers actively discouraged any discussion of the political implications of their grandfather's work in the opening festivals.[48] Wagner was still a cultural icon whose work went unquestioned.

DRAMAS OF GREED AND POWER

The centenary production of the *Ring* at Bayreuth, directed by Patrice Chéreau, was greeted, initially, with howls of derision, as if the barbarians had not only stormed the Master's bastion, but were dismantling the foundations as well. In fact, the citadel had been threatened long before 1976, when the Klemperer/Fehling production of *Holländer* at the Kroll Oper in Berlin in 1929 had eschewed traditional folkloric settings for a concrete social environment and a plain style of acting that invited little sympathy for the characters.[49] But further exploration in this direction was cut off by the Nazis. Once again, it was Wieland Wagner who took up an experiment from the past and initiated a mode of stage-direction that countered the aesthetic principles of the *Gesamtkunstwerk*.

The ideal of seamlessness was probably only fully achieved in Wieland's productions of the 1950s. But seamlessness can palliate conflict and encourage the audience to indulge in the beauty of the scene, often at the expense of the drama. Performance under these circumstances can become more an act of hagiography than an interpretation of a dramatic action. It was with his 1963 production of *Die Meistersinger* that Wieland decisively turned away from the ethos of the *Gesamtkunstwerk*. In this production, his Nuremberg was a community of aggressive, vain, and greedy citizens – even Eva, a conceited teenager, was antipathetic. The setting, far from conjuring up hallowed memories of a cozy German community, was reminiscent of the stage of an Elizabethan theatre, one which brought to mind less the romantic comedies of Shakespeare, more the rough citizen comedies of Thomas Dekker. The guiding spirit of the production was Brecht, whose theories and practice of theatre had been developed in hostile reaction to the mesmeric theatre of Wagner. None of Wieland's productions was as controversial as this, and none was booed more roundly.[50]

In retrospect, however, there is a good case to be made for Wieland's *Die Meistersinger* and his production of the *Ring* the following year as being decisive for the survival of Wagner in the modern theatre. They freed the music-dramas from a theatrical style that invited audiences to sympathize with the work through unquestioningly admiring its heroes and their values. Furthermore, they allowed audiences' attention to be drawn toward symbolic realms that, in Wieland's earlier productions, had been signified in the vast abstraction of the sets. They also indicated that the stage was not an arena for the propagation or surreptitious transmission of ideas, but the site for an action in which ideas are in conflict with other ideas, are acknowledged as contingent rather than absolute, are not mystical in origin, and are formed in and formative of social life. On such a stage, Wotan, for example, does not embody or "stand for" Schopenhauer's ideas, but through him we understand the efficacy of those ideas and judge how effective they are as a description of life. Heroism is no longer an assumed virtue, but a facet of being that can either destroy or work to the advantage of whoever possesses it and is affected by it. By emphasizing dramatic difference, by representing all characters, good and evil, sympathetic and uncongenial, with objectivity, and by centering audience attention on purely human affairs in a material world, these productions opened the music-dramas to the debate over Wagner's beliefs about politics, race, and sexuality that had so far been confined to critical writing and polemic.

Although Chéreau's *Ring* was just one example of the widespread revolution in Wagnerian staging during the 1970s and 1980s, as the centenary production at Bayreuth it attracted much attention and became symbolic of changes already initiated not only by Wieland Wagner, but by Ulrich Melchinger, Götz Friedrich, Joachim Herz, Harry Kupfer, and others. It was also the first *Ring* to be internationally televised and, later, distributed in various video formats, so it has been seen by an unusually wide audience and acquired for Wagner an unprecedentedly large audience. It rejected, however, the *Gesamtkunstwerk* and eschewed any attempt to use the stage as a means of enchanting the audience. In Chéreau's production, word, tone, and the array of expressive means available to the singing-actor, designer, and director, do not necessarily complement each other. Dissonance of artistic elements is even appropriate, for a clash between theatrical elements reflects dislocation in the dramatic action. Seamlessness in contrast is no virtue, for it tends to hide rather than disclose conflict.

Chéreau discounts the entire hypothesis upon which Wagner's constructs of heroism are based.[51] The source of energy symbolized by the Rhinegold is no scintillating emanation of nature but lumps of matter in the turbines of a dam, to be read as electricity itself. This deprives the hero of his function as a conduit of natural energy. When nature makes its belated appearance on stage, mainly in *Siegfried*, it is not a nurturing environment for a growing adolescent, but a dark tangle of twigs and thorns that confounds human senses. Siegfried's bodily strength is no longer a crucial agent in the action, as Nothung is forged by a machine, not his muscles. This is a *Ring* in which any irony that throws heroic action into question is played to the maximum, and mechanical power not the strength of the human mind or body drives society. There is a heroic aura about the settings, but it is an urban heroism, reminiscent of the novels of Balzac and Dickens. The façade of Valhalla is menacing rather than impressive and its imperialist architectural motifs from the eighteenth and nineteenth centuries are appropriately repeated in the courtyard of Hunding's mansion and the hall of the Gibichungs, houses of misery where the oppression symbolized by Valhalla is replicated. There is one scenic acknowledgement of a heroic past in Brünnhilde's mountain peak, where the impressive open tower refers to both a

bombed-out factory and a medieval castle keep, but this breadth of infer-
ence is rare. Chéreau's *Ring* does not encompass the whole of human history
but is emphatically a fable of modern life, of the growth of a capitalist society from the revolutionary years of the late Enlightenment to those of the
early twentieth century.

The relationship between the orchestra and the stage is often fraught
with irony. One of Wagner's weaknesses as a composer of music-drama
had been his tendency to allow his capacity to write music of great power
to overwhelm the dramatic situation, so that some climactic moments –
for example, the gods' entrance into Valhalla, the Ride of the Valkyries,
Siegfried's forging of the sword, and the summoning of the vassals – sound as
celebrations of their subject rather than explorations of a complex dramatic
situation and the emotions of those implicated in it. Chéreau's staging
possibly overcompensated for this: Wotan pulls a string of unwilling and
terrified gods into Valhalla, the Valkyries haul corpses with disconcerting
exuberance, a machine does Siegfried's work for him, and the vassals in
Götterdämmerung are mainly discontented workmen. At these, and other
points in the action, the stage treats the orchestra as ironic commentary
rather than an excuse to aggrandize the action.

This does not trivialize the *Ring*, but intensifies its drama, highlighting
its tragedy and eliminating any potential for melodramatic polarization
that was endemic in romantic–realistic staging. Wotan, in *Das Rheingold*,
is possessed by the need for power, and, in showing no compunction about
using violence whenever it suits him, is as repellent as Alberich. In *Die
Walküre* his tragic stature does not endow him with nobility, because as he
comes to realize how he is determined by the consequences of his action, he
also sees how he has been caught by his own corruption and self-ignorance.
If his claim to be acting impartially is a façade, so too is his withdrawal from
the world. As the Wanderer, he brings on the mechanical forge Siegfried
will use to make his sword and hangs the caged Woodbird on the branch of
a tree. Each moment of Siegfried's progress toward the sleeping Brünnhilde
has been carefully planned, so that the ideal of the heroic will, free from
coercion, aspiring for a utopia of social and political freedom, is a fallacy.
Even if such a utopia were possible, Siegfried would not be the man to
accomplish it. The Wanderer's guardianship means Siegfried is not self-
reliant, and the manufacturing of Nothung is reminiscent of the turbines
of the dam that lodged the Rhinegold. His forging of the sword does not,
therefore, look to a new world, but decisively repeats the old. Siegfried
is an appealing figure, he even has stray moments of affection for Mime,
but their relationship is so driven by the resentments they arouse in each

other that there is nothing arbitrary about Siegfried killing Mime. It is a grim but logical end, one more manifestation of the relentless destruction brought about by greed. Siegfried is a creature of the women he encounters, closer to a child than a conquering hero with Brünnhilde, helpless slave of his passion with Gutrune. Throughout the production, the sharply etched dramatic conflicts, the ugly extremes in characterization, and the avoidance of any attempt to idealize the characters reveal the caustic ironic vein that Wieland Wagner in his productions a decade prior to Chéreau's *Ring* had only started to mine.

Chéreau's *Ring* was neither definitive nor authentic, in fact it challenged any notion that definitiveness and authenticity are either possible or desirable in Wagner. The dramatic landscape of this *Ring*, and the politically oriented productions of Wagner by other directors, also made clear that no single production can hope to articulate any work's entire meaning. Wagner's music-dramas, like Shakespeare's plays, have now become sites for constant experimentation. As a result, Wagnerian production at the beginning of the twenty-first century is more diverse than it has ever been. Past styles have been neither superseded nor eliminated by newer styles. Despite occasional complaints that one never sees Wagner in an approximation of the style in which his work was originally performed, romantic–realistic productions are not uncommon. When such a production finds a compelling *raison d'être*, as did Steven Wadsworth's production of the *Ring* in Seattle in 2001, it succeeds not because it recalls early Bayreuth, but because it allows for a rethinking of the purposes of nature and the workings of compassion in the cycle's dramatic pattern. The mannerist productions of Robert Wilson call to mind Wieland Wagner's minimalism, though with a heightened attention to the hieratic elements in the action. There is still much energy in those productions that find themes that speak to our own concerns. The scrupulously directed *Das Rheingold* in Robert Carsen's production of the *Ring* (Cologne, 2000) fastens upon union disputes and, with unexpected comedy, on the arrogance of inordinate corporate wealth, while the wintry *Walküre* (Cologne, 2001) takes place in a war-torn landscape reminiscent of recent conflicts in the Balkans. An ultra-modern setting such as this robs the drama of neither poetry nor warmth. Siegmund and Sieglinde, engulfed in a blizzard, close their eyes for the spring song, and their love gains rather than loses in poignancy when it founders in a hostile setting that starkly fails to reflect their emotions. Love in such an environment has an added intensity, for it will always be a symptom of loneliness in a world that has no place for it. In even the most objective of settings, the isolation of the romantic hero can be felt as a palpable force.

IMAGIST AND ABSURDIST WAGNER

While the use of Wagner as a polemic against contemporary ills employs the stage in a way different from that envisaged in the theory of the *Gesamtkunst-werk*, it is not entirely alien to the nineteenth-century dramaturgy of the music-dramas. Chéreau, Carsen, Friedrich, and other directors generally acknowledge a purpose and forward movement in the dramas. Even if the bleak conclusion of Chéreau's *Ring* presents few reasons for Brünnhilde's self-sacrifice, the blank faces of the chorus staring out into the auditorium after the immolation awaken in the audience concern over the injustice brought about by greed and the desire for power. In such an instance, transformation does not take place in the heroic individual but through the people as represented in the chorus, and then in the audience itself. But more radical experiments in Wagnerian production have abandoned progressive dramaturgy, realism, and symbolism in staging and design for readings that display fundamental and unchanging conditions of being that lie beneath actions of social debate and psychological motivation.

With remarkable frequency, from the early 1990s on, program notes to productions of Wagner have cited the name of Samuel Beckett. Beckett had little tolerance for opera and his concept of theatre was antipodal to that of the *Gesamtkunstwerk*. Furthermore, his dramas do not record change and progress in the human condition, but represent, in unadorned form, the human condition as one of endless repetition. Salvation, if there is any, lies in the hope of cessation. Beckett's dramas do not tell stories that begin and end, but are centered around images within which the characters' lives are grounded and through which we come to understand how all action is a repetition of what has come before. Despite the formal distance between Beckettian minimalism and the Wagnerian *Gesamtkunstwerk*, Beckett's view of the human condition has much in common with that of the Wagnerian hero, from the Dutchman to Parsifal.

An imagist approach to Wagner, which evinces the static condition of humanity, is perhaps most suited to *Tristan* – Meyerhold was the first to stage this music-drama around single images. Wieland Wagner, the source of most modern experimentation in staging the music-dramas, adopted a similar approach. His celebrated *Tristan* of 1962, which has been described as a mystery play about "the power of *eros thanatos*, the destructive force of love,"[52] was set among forbidding totemic symbols, which combined Celtic and erotic images suggestive of maternity, sexual violation, and alienation. While Wieland's production recalled early twentieth-century symbolism, Samuel Beckett was directly alluded to in Heiner Müller's haunting *Tristan* at Bayreuth in 1992, in which the dusty set and the obese and recumbent shepherd of act 3 recalled *Endgame* and Tristan's return to his childhood was enacted as but one instance of an agonizing journey, endlessly repeated. Harry Kupfer (Berlin, 2000) staged the intimate drama of *Tristan* on the broken statue of an angel, fallen from a great height, so his lovers seemed imprisoned by a lost innocence, paralleled in the downfall of an imperial society of which they had once been a part.

The underlying condition of life as repetition is basic to absurdism, in which human action has no efficacy. It is a view antithetical to that of the dramaturgy of the nineteenth-century well-made play, but even those works of Wagner written in this vein have been mined for their absurdist potential. The action of David Alden's weird but compelling *Tannhäuser* (Munich, 1995) is seen solely through the consciousness of Tannhäuser and is therefore effectively a representation of the inner condition of the romantic hero. This surreal extravaganza, akin to dream and utilizing images reminiscent of a Fellini movie, takes place amid broken classical pediments and scenic fragments referring to Germany's imperial and Nazi past. Tannhäuser, wandering in confusion through this bizarre landscape, is torn neither between promiscuous and monogamous love, nor between sensual love and religious asceticism. Rather he is driven mad by his failure to reconcile his desire for sex with his terror of it, a grotesque conflict that seems to afflict the hysterical denizens of both the Venusberg and the Wartburg. The singers are aging and no attempt is made to hide this, so Wagner's tale of youthful rebellion becomes an exhibition of middle-aged anxiety and fear. Political authority is nothing more than brute force and religious devotion is delirium, a sublimation of disturbed sexuality. It is a production that denies all possibility of salvation. When the pope's flowering staff is carried on by a rejoicing chorus, it is already encased in glass, a lifeless relic and an apt symbol for the sclerotic world Alden has placed on stage.

Epic heroism has no place in Alden's *Tannhäuser*. If it exists, it is a mere illusion, a fantasy of deluded minds. The same is true of Keith Warner's production of *Lohengrin* (Bayreuth, 1999), where society is in an advanced state of demoralization and decay. In this grim production, water, or, more accurately, the lack of it, is key to meaning. Warner discards ethereal blue and silver for darker hues, an impression of black on black. The peculiar juxtaposition of King Henry's fully armored troops on a platform above gloomy Brabant, which is a saline desert inhabited by a devitalized population in quasi-Victorian clothing, suggests the production might be a parable on Wagner's own time – a meditation, perhaps, on Nietzsche's view of nineteenth-century society crippled by its obsession with history. The swan does not appear on a broad river but in a muddy pool into which, at the end of act 1, Elsa invites Lohengrin to engage in a wan sexual revel. Water becomes an ever more precious commodity, washed away for good when Elsa asks the forbidden question and the platform on which the bedroom scene is staged is tipped forward and water sluices out of channels at its side. At the end, King Henry dies along with everyone else on stage. Only the young Gottfried survives, carrying a dead swan. Lohengrin descends into a dry hole once filled with water. This forbidding production, epitomized by a permanent eclipse that set in during the course of the wedding, takes Wagner's initial thesis of the world's insensitivity to the artist to its furthest extreme, so that it becomes a myth of the year-god reversed. Lohengrin offers a dying world the possibility of love, imagination, and sexual vitality, but the world is incapable of responding and cannot survive. Elsa's tragedy becomes the predicament of all.

Productions in the absurdist vein tend to reverse Wagner's optimism, though it is difficult to claim this as a misrepresentation of his work because an attribute of tightly constructed dramas such as *Lohengrin*, in which each element complements the whole, is that the action can represent diametrically opposed themes and points-of-view. The more negative the action, the greater the irony of the lush orchestral music or, in the case of Warner's *Lohengrin* especially, the greater its poignancy, as it articulates a longing for a utopian state slipping ever further from human grasp.

WAGNER: POST-SPECTACLE

Absurdism not only posits the view that human action is meaningless and repetitive, it employs techniques that are literally absurd, in which high pathos is replaced by a staging that is trite, farcical, and downright bathetic. This approach can be dangerous as the performance runs the danger of doing nothing but arousing the ire of the audience, a trivial ambition unworthy of a serious artist. But in the hands of some directors, notably Peter Konwitschny, the most controversial opera director in contemporary German music-theatre, the debunking of canonical works can open surprising perspectives on them; in the case of Wagner it can, against expectations, recoup some of the heroic dimensions of the drama. Konwitschny, like many contemporary directors, has a suspicion of spectacle, as if it hides the issues and ideology of the drama rather than explicates them. He also denies any possibility of grandeur to the work. His *Lohengrin* (Hamburg, 1999) is set in a late nineteenth-century schoolroom, in which the Brabantians and the Saxon army are schoolchildren flinging spitballs at each other, under the ineffective discipline of the monitor, the Herald, and their teacher, King Henry. His *Tristan* (Munich, 1998) begins in a similarly disconcerting manner as the lovers, on a luxury cruise, play arch sexual games like participants in a Noel Coward comedy. Even the love duet starts in an ungraceful, anti-romantic vein as Tristan drags a sofa on stage. As for *Parsifal* (Munich, 1995), Kundry appears as a Beckettian clown and Parsifal as an absurd lampoon of Rousseau's "natural man"; both seem designed to destroy all credibility in the music-drama.

While Konwitschny's opening acts seem little more than instances of *épater les Wagneriens*, they have a serious purpose. Not only do they alienate the audience by making them see an accustomed action from a startling new viewpoint, but their comic idiom serves as a foil that intensifies the pathos of the later phases of the music-drama. In each case, comedy is suddenly checked by a moment of striking beauty. The mayhem in *Lohengrin* is silenced by the magical rise of a seedy-looking man through the floor, with a boy in front of him waving his arms like swan's wings. The children's awe at this extraordinary occurrence underlines, in a way no period or mythologically oriented production can, the genuine shock that the advent of extra-human forces can have on our imagination. In *Tristan*, the apparatus of comedy of manners and naïve children's theatre recedes as Tristan and Isolde advance into their night of love, and when it returns in the figure of Mark, it strikes us as tacky and scant, representing a world entirely incommensurate with the warmth the lovers have found in themselves. In *Parsifal*, the knights of the grail, ashen and depleted nature worshippers gathering in an underground chamber around the roots of a dying tree, are hysterical for whatever crumb of nourishment they can find. The grail is Kundry herself, radiant and sexually potent, framed in a kitsch Nazarene altar-piece, exercising over the knights a physical attraction that literally draws them after her. The sexual and religious impulses at the center of the work are fused in one figure.

The effect of Konwitschny's approach is to nullify polemical aspects of the drama, allowing the agencies at contention in the action to be equally balanced and defined with clarity. *Lohengrin* centers with increasing exclusivity on the nature of power, be it the loutish bullying by Ortrud and Telramund or the no less disquieting charisma that Lohengrin exercises on the besotted children. As Elsa accepts Lohengrin's hand to enter a minster created by the children's imagination, she does so in utter terror of the figure her plight has conjured up, and the disaster of the wedding night that follows arises not from her demand to know Lohengrin's name, but from her fear of sex. The conceit of this schoolroom *Lohengrin* is not watertight – it is difficult to imagine any school in the nineteenth, twentieth, or twenty-first centuries allowing a student to engage in sex with a stranger so as to educate children in the facts of life – but its impact is unnerving nonetheless. The theme of the production is how children form partisan loyalties and hatreds by responding to heroic myths. But the battle between Ortrud and Lohengrin for the favor of the children does not result in a favorable victory for Lohengrin, for Gottfried when he crawls out of a hole in the schoolyard is no innocent boy on a swan, but a soldier with helmet and machine-gun, an epitome of the ugly violence that has been growing relentlessly throughout the production. He is a symbol for a society that generates violence and constructs an educational system that fuels it. This does not totally reverse Wagner's intent with *Lohengrin* because the titular knight does incite the troops to violence for the cause of Germany, but Konwitschny reveals the darkness we know lies in all violence and the awful damage belief in heroism can wreak, a damage that Wagner, in his less optimistic moments, would have had no difficulty in acknowledging.

Modern versions of Wagner tend to be deeply pessimistic. Konwitschny's *Parsifal* is no exception. The off-white setting demystifies the action, which is symbolized by the death of the tree at which the knights worship. By act 3 it is nothing but a charred pillar, an oppressive hulk at the back of the stage, standing for the tyranny of those who are old and for the exhaustion of the green forces of life. Whatever is green is embodied in Kundry, no maternal seducer, but a fund of sexual energy that Parsifal resists. Klingsor attempts to pierce him in the side, but he cannot, because Parsifal is resistant to all sexual temptation. From this point, the production deliberately loses energy. The scenery closes in, ceremony drops away, and spectacle is abandoned. Parsifal's victory over himself devitalizes him, and when he and Kundry enter the temple, she carries the spear. The knights, terrified of her, kill her. Parsifal is left to rule a dying world of sexually ossified men.

Konwitschny does not always deny heroism, at least not romantic heroism. His *Tristan* ends on a wave of optimism that strengthens rather than nullifies the aura of the sublime, but in an unorthodox way. The essence of the Wagnerian *Gesamtkunstwerk* is to create an illusion that the stage is its own world and to nullify any tendency of the audience to think of it as a stage. Konwitschny, in *Tristan*, does the opposite and follows Brecht by highlighting the artificiality of the stage and its technology, most of the drama taking place on a stage within a stage. In act 1 this draws attention to the artificiality of the games of the lovers, in act 2 it reveals the physical world as a place the lovers would do best to leave, in act 3 it represents a cramped, unfurnished hospital ward, an apt image for Tristan's desolate state of mind, captured poignantly by slides he shows himself of his mother and childhood. The diminutive stage becomes increasingly claustrophobic, even comically cluttered when Marke's men rush in after Tristan's death. At this point, Tristan returns to life and leaves the stage with Isolde, both of them closing the curtains on its chaos. Isolde then sings the Liebestod directly to those to whom Wagner's words suggest it is addressed, the audience. As she finishes, the curtain of the inner stage opens on the graves of the two lovers, but they, still alive for us, walk off stage in triumph. As they do, we realize the world has been well lost. Romantic heroism has returned to Wagner's stage with rare strength, confidence, and even invigorating wit. At the end, we no longer see the numinous world through the filter of the physical, but occupy it ourselves, and from this viewpoint the physical world seems eminently dispensable. Wagner's sublime tragedy has been converted into a utopian comedy.

To mark the millennium, the Stuttgart Opera staged a *Ring* the intent of which was to demonstrate the obsolescence of Wagner's utopia and the distance between the art and ideals of his time and those of Europe at the end of the twentieth century.[53] To highlight discontinuity in the *Ring*, each music-drama was staged by a different director, who did not consult any other of the directors. Under such circumstances, little unity could be expected. Nonetheless, a common theme did emerge, which was an intense suspicion of the very act of theatre. In all four productions, which were stylistically distinct, any gesture, incident, emotional climax, or spectacular event that had the potential to be enlarged by theatrical means was either rigorously underplayed or exaggerated to the level of absurdity. This approach is not unique, but reflects trends at large in the European theatre of the early twenty-first century where spectacle is increasingly eschewed and the contours of dramatic structure are flattened until they disappear. Any element that calls for the emotional engagement of the audience through the exercise of illusion is suppressed. It is a mode of theatrical fundamentalism, more rigorously anti-theatrical than any of Appia's innovations had been and even more determined in insisting on the artifice of performance than Brecht was. It is a theatre that stands for everything that the lushly scored, amply theatrical *Ring* does not. Nevertheless, the Stuttgart *Ring* does not destroy Wagner's *Ring*. Oddly, it enhances it. The gap between stage and orchestra, already tangible in productions that center on material conflict, becomes so wide that one listens to the music anew, finding in it new accents of violence and passages of lyricism that unexpectedly complement or actively controvert the action on stage.

Das Rheingold, directed by Joachim Schlömer, is set in the hall of a spa whose waters dry up after Alberich steals the Rhinegold. Here all space is the same, be it the depths of the Rhine, Earth, Nibelheim, or Valhalla, and when at the end the gods leave their place of torment they only reappear in the place they had left a few moments before. The nimbus of evil that repetition arouses is close to unbearable, and no salvation is possible, be it through the epic hero or even the event of cessation. *Die Walküre*, directed by Christof Nel, is effectively the thesis production of the cycle, as it devolves not on the painful separation of father and daughter, but on Wotan as a cynical powermonger, using the media, in this case closed-circuit television, to torment his daughter and distance himself from any emotional engagement with the world. *Siegfried* is directed by Jossi Wieler and Sergio Morabito as a social drama, set in the slums of a modern city, a claustrophobic landscape of fear and hopelessness that abrogates the comic arc of Siegfried's ascent and centers attention on all of Wagner's characters as wanderers in a world without anchor. Finally, Peter Konwitschny's *Götterdämmerung*, much of which is directed with surprising effectiveness as farce, is disquietingly double-focused. On the one hand, the comedy serves as a deceptive overlay of the brutality that drives the action, to have it burst forth that much more furiously in the scene with the vassals and Siegfried's murder; on the other, the apparatus of the theatre is displayed to such a degree that it becomes thematic, and as the stage directions for the final conflagration are projected onto a screen instead of being represented on stage, one meditates upon how theatre speaks to and, perhaps, deceives our imagination.

The Stuttgart *Ring* makes no allowances for heroism. Wotan's three separate manifestations never achieve tragic stature; in *Das Rheingold* and *Die Walküre* he is weak or despicable, in *Siegfried*, a bully in a leather jacket. Siegfried does not rise above his lowly origins, while in *Götterdämmerung* he is, strikingly, an aimless charmer, another figure from Noel Coward, serving as Everyman to the drama in which he is caught; there was not a breath of heroism about him, even in retrospect. What therefore is left of Wagner? In fact, much. The music-dramas continue to be compelling, even when theatre does all it can to repudiate their heroic dimensions; in such circumstances, the human imperatives that Wagner's characters represent have more rather than less strength, and the diabolical power of the score, under Lothar Zagrosek's direction, is intensified rather than lessened. Most remarkably, the one experience never open to question is that of romantic love, in both its sexual and compassionate aspects. The emotional center of this disparate *Ring* never shifts and is never alienated or placed in a context that raises doubts about it. It rests in the surprisingly moving, possibly mutual affection between Freia and Fasolt in *Das Rheingold*, in the erotic encounter of Siegmund and Sieglinde, and in Sieglinde's hymn of praise for Brünnhilde and, by implication, her unborn son. It arises unexpectedly in the grappling of Siegfried and Brünnhilde over an unmade bed, and most surprisingly, it is felt in the agony of Gutrune's love for Siegfried, a minor theme in most interpretations, but here raised to the most striking statement of *Götterdämmerung*. Of course, the directors' intense self-consciousness over the rhetorical appeal of their craft does not allow them to develop these moments so as to influence or modify the prevailingly prosaic stagings, but they do remind us that it is in the emotional depths of the romantic hero and romantic love that freedom resides. In this respect at least Wagner would have found something in common with his modern interpreters.

Love prevails over all heroic impulse, or is, more accurately, the end toward which that impulse is leading. Our time is much at odds over whether love has the power to save and regenerate humanity. Konwitschny's *Parsifal* ends with a slain Kundry and a timorous Parsifal gathering around him a group of terrified knights, an apt image, one surmises, for the cause of so much of the oppression and slaughter that has marked our history since Wagner. But love can prevail, as in the moving reinterpretation of the closing act in Nikolaus Lehnhoff's much-contested production of *Parsifal* (San Francisco, 2000).[54] On a sparse stage, religious icons are not represented literally, but through abstract space and light. References to nature are erased in the bleak set, which represents the world after a holocaust. The visual sparseness of the production centers attention exclusively on personal relationships, in which suppressed violence, sexual dysfunction, and communal fear of the outsider are most apparent. The production eschews any ritualistic appeal, the action unfolding in terms of human experience alone.

This gives the final act a consequential action that clearly contrasts to Wagner's vaguer dramaturgy. Not a note of the music nor a word of the poem is rewritten. Only the stage directions are altered. The Good Friday music, which symbolizes a renewed bond between humanity and nature, is not complemented by views of fields blooming with spring flowers, but by something more moving, which Wagner himself referred to when he wrote of "the representation of scenic incidents" taking place within the minds of the actors and the imagination of the audience: Parsifal and Kundry fall in love. When they arrive at the temple, the reunification of grail and spear, which normally has only symbolic meaning, now has human, individual relevance. Sexual dysfunction has been healed. Parsifal returns the spear to

Gurnemanz, and Amfortas dies as he gives the crown to Parsifal, an event that arouses our compassion and may even gratify us, as his longing for death has been excruciating and acute. Parsifal then places the crown on the body of the dead Titurel, indicating thereby that its power is of the past, so it is a symbol to be set aside. Most knights gather tightly around Gurnemanz, figures of the old order, still resistant to those from outside, but with some hope restored to them by Parsifal's moral authority and strength. Kundry then leads Parsifal slowly off-stage, followed uncertainly by one or two of the knights. They walk out into a stream of light. The refined beauty of the closing music describes not a renewal of the old, of the brotherhood of the grail, but the birth of a world that is potentially different. The final, enigmatic words of Wagner's poem, "Erlösung dem Erlöser" – "Redemption to the Redeemer" – are invested with an unfamiliar clarity as it is apparent this redemption will come, literally, from physical birth, the creation of new life. However much Wagner's heroes have failed, new life has always been their goal and promise. In this rereading of Wagner, it is a tangible goal that might actually be achieved.

Notes

INTRODUCTION

1. *The Essential Writings of Ralph Waldo Emerson*, ed. Brooks Atkinson (New York: Modern Library, 2000), p. 233.
2. Max Nordau, *Degeneration* (New York: Appleton, 1895), p. 171.
3. Peter Viereck, *Metapolitics: The Roots of the Nazi Mind* (New York: Capricorn, 1961), p. 91.
4. Thomas Mann, *Pro and Contra Wagner*, tr. Allan Blunden (London: Faber, 1985), p. 123.
5. Herbert Lindenberger, *Opera: The Extravagant Art* (Ithaca: Cornell University Press, 1985), p. 285.
6. Throughout I follow Wagner in applying the term "music-drama" to all his stage-works from *Holländer* on.

1 MODES OF HEROISM IN THE EARLY NINETEENTH CENTURY

1. Virgil Nemoianu, *The Taming of Romanticism* (Cambridge, MA: Harvard University Press, 1984), pp. 6–12.
2. James J. Sheehan, *German History: 1770–1866* (Oxford: Clarendon, 1989), p. 452.
3. Thomas Nipperdey, *Germany from Napoleon to Bismarck, 1800–1866*, tr. Daniel Nolan (Princeton: Princeton University Press, 1996), p. 263.
4. Nipperdey, *Germany*, p. 265.
5. Hans Kohn, *The Mind of Germany* (London: Macmillan, 1960), p. 51.
6. Lilian R. Furst, *Romanticism in Perspective* (London: Macmillan, 1969), p. 58.
7. Louis Bredvold, *The Natural History of Sensibility* (Detroit: Wayne State University Press, 1962), pp. 53–73.
8. *Rousseau's Political Writings*, ed. Alan Ritter and Julia Conaway Bondanella (New York: Norton, 1988), p. 26.
9. Jean Starobinski, *Jean-Jacques Rousseau*, tr. Arthur Goldhammer (Chicago: University of Chicago Press, 1988), p. 295.
10. Jean-Jacques Rousseau, *Reveries of a Solitary Walker*, tr. Peter France (Harmondsworth: Penguin, 1979), p. 88.

11. Frederick Garber, "Self, Society, Value, and the Romantic Hero," *Comparative Literature* 19/4 (Fall 1967), 321.

12. Novalis, *Werke*, ed. Gerhard Schulz (Munich: Beck, n.d.), p. 147.

13. Garber, "Hero," 321–22.

14. René de Chateaubriand, *René*, tr. Irving Putter (Berkeley: University of California Press, 1980), p. 85.

15. Chateaubriand, *René*, p. 87.

16. [Prince Pückler-Muskau], *Tour in England, Ireland, and France in the Years 1828 and 1829* (Philadelphia: Carey & Lea, 1833), p. 389.

17. Peter Thorslev, *The Byronic Hero* (Minneapolis: University of Minnesota Press, 1962), p. 185.

18. Furst, *Romanticism*, p. 64.

19. Mario Praz, *The Romantic Agony*, tr. Angus Davidson, 2nd edn. (London: Oxford University Press, 1970), pp. 59–83 and 111–66.

20. Lilian R. Furst, *The Contours of European Romanticism* (Lincoln: University of Nebraska Press, 1979), p. 44.

21. Walter L. Reed, *Meditations on the Hero* (New Haven: Yale University Press, 1974), p. 5.

22. *GS*, vi, pp. 55–67. See note on abbreviations of sources (p. x) for details of editions of Wagner's writings.

23. James D. Wilson, *The Romantic Heroic Ideal* (Baton Rouge: Louisiana State University Press, 1982), p. 19.

24. Richard Wagner, *My Life*, tr. Andrew Gray (Cambridge: Cambridge University Press, 1983), p. 208.

25. Wagner, *Life*, pp. 210–13.

26. Elizabeth Magee, *Richard Wagner and the Nibelungs* (Oxford: Clarendon, 1990), p. 12.

27. Peter Wapnewski, "The Operas as Literary Works," in Ulrich Müller and Peter Wapnewski (eds.), *Wagner Handbook*, ed. Eng. tr. John Deathridge (Cambridge, MA: Harvard University Press, 1992), pp. 30, 75, and 85.

28. Hans-Joachim Bauer, *Richard Wagner Lexikon* (Bergisch Gladbach: Lübbe, 1988), p. 126.

29. *GS*, xii, p. 13; *PW*, iv, p. 14. See note on abbreviations of sources (p. x) for details of editions of Wagner's writings.

30. *GS*, vi, p. 139.

31. John Lash, *The Hero: Manhood and Power* (London: Thames & Hudson, 1995), p. 11.

32. Jan De Vries, *Heroic Song and Heroic Legend*, tr. B. J. Timmer (London: Oxford University Press, 1963), p. 225.

33. De Vries, *Heroic Song*, p. 235.

34. Lash, *Hero*, p. 11.

35. De Vries, *Heroic Song*, p. 183.

36. Maurice Bowra, *Heroic Poetry* (London: Macmillan, 1952), p. 105.

37. Lord Raglan, *The Hero* (New York: Oxford University Press, 1937), pp. 180–89.

38. Joseph Campbell, *The Hero with a Thousand Faces* (Cleveland: Meridian, 1956), p. 337.
39. *PW*, I, p. 21.
40. *CD*, II, p. 291. See note on abbreviations of sources for details (p. x).
41. Thomas Carlyle, *On Heroes, Hero-Worship and the Heroic in History*, ed. Carl Niemeyer (London: University of Nebraska Press, 1966), p. 112.
42. Carlyle, *Heroes*, p. 115.
43. Carlyle, *Heroes*, p. 123.
44. Eric Bentley, *The Cult of the Superman* (London: Robert Hale, 1947), p. 54.
45. Carlyle, *Heroes*, p. 11.
46. Carlyle, *Heroes*, p. 196.
47. Lash, *Hero*, p. 29.
48. *CD*, II, p. 850.

2 WAGNER AND THE EARLY NINETEENTH-CENTURY THEATRE

1. *GS*, VII, p. 17; *PW*, VIII, p. 66.
2. *GS*, VII, p. 66; *PW*, VII, p. 111.
3. *GS*, VII, pp. 165–68; *PW*, VIII, pp. 78–81.
4. *GS*, VII, p. 209; *PW*, VIII, p. 121.
5. *GS*, VII, p. 202; *PW*, VIII, p. 114.
6. *GS*, X, p. 24; *PW*, I, p. 142.
7. *GS*, X, p. 16; *PW*, I, p. 34.
8. *GS*, X, p. 19; *PW*, I, p. 37.
9. *GS*, X, p. 25; *PW*, I, p. 43.
10. See especially Wagner's discussion of myth in *Oper und Drama*, *GS*, XI, pp. 138–61; *PW*, III, pp. 152–78.
11. Hans Knudsen, *Deutsche Theater-Geschichte* (Stuttgart: Kröner, 1959), p. 269.
12. *GS*, XII, pp. 106–07; *PW*, VII, p. 324.
13. Friedrich Schiller, *Complete Works*, 8 vols. (New York: Collier, 1902), VIII, p. 342.
14. Ute Daniel, *Hoftheater* (Stuttgart: Klett-Cotta, 1995), pp. 127–31.
15. Ulrich Parenth, *Wie Goethes Faust auf die Bühne kam* (Brunswick: Holtzmeyer, 1986), pp. 52–53.
16. Carl Dahlhaus, "Wagner's Place in the History of Music," Müller and Wapnewski (eds.), *Handbook*, p. 108.
17. Richard Wagner, *Selected Letters*, ed. Stewart Spencer and Barry Millington (London: Dent, 1987), p. 24.
18. Aubrey S. Garlington, Jr., "German Romantic Opera and the Problem of Origins," *Musical Quarterly* 63/2 (April 1977), 251–52.
19. J. E. Bernard, *Faust: Romantische Oper in zwei Aufzügen* (Vienna: Wallishauser, 1814), p. 2.

20. John Warrack, *Carl Maria von Weber*, 2nd edn. (Cambridge: Cambridge University Press, 1976), pp. 234–35.

21. Wagner's debt to and use of Marschner's operas will be discussed in the next chapter, in connection with *Holländer* and *Lohengrin*.

22. Hedwig Hoffman Rusack, *Gozzi in Germany* (New York: AMS, 1966), pp. 72–103.

23. *CD*, I, p. 505.

24. *GS*, VIII, p. 129; *PW*, V, p. 41.

25. *GS*, VIII, p. 73; *PW*, VIII, p. 180.

26. *GS*, VII, p. 57.

27. *GS*, VIII, p. 64; *PW*, VII, p. 219.

28. *GS*, VII, p. 261; *PW*, VIII, p. 170.

29. Simon Williams, "The Well-Made Play," *European Writers*, ed. Jacques Barzun and George Stade, vol. VII (New York: Scribners, 1985), p. 1914.

30. *GS*, XI, p. 94; *PW*, II, pp. 98–99.

31. Anselm Gerhard, *The Urbanization of Opera*, tr. Mary Whittall (Chicago: University of Chicago Press, 1998), p. 174.

32. Ludwig Finscher, "Wagner der Opernkomponist. Von den *Feen* zum *Rienzi*," *Richard Wagner: Von der Oper zum Musikdrama* (Berne: Francke, 1978), p. 33.

33. *GS*, I, pp. 86–87; *PW*, I, pp. 299–300.

34. *GS*, I, p. 85; *PW*, I, p. 298.

35. Joachim Fest, "Richard Wagner – Das Werk neben dem Werk," in Saul Friedlander and Jörn Rüsen (eds.), *Richard Wagner im Dritten Reich* (Munich: Beck, 2000), pp. 32–33.

36. Theodor Adorno, *In Search of Wagner*, tr. Rodney Livingstone (Trowbridge: NLB, 1981), p. 14.

37. John Deathridge, *Wagner's* Rienzi (Oxford: Clarendon, 1977), pp. 35–36.

3 EARLY MUSIC-DRAMA: THE ISOLATED HERO

1. *GS*, I, pp. 58–59; *PW*, I, pp. 269–70.

2. Sieghart Döhring and Sabine Henze-Döhring, *Oper und Musikdrama im 19. Jahrhundert* (Laaber: Laaber-Verlag, 1997), pp. 176–79.

3. Dieter Borchmeyer, *Richard Wagner: Theory and Theatre*, tr. Stewart Spencer (Oxford: Clarendon, 1991), pp. 190–215.

4. Thorslev, *Byronic Hero*, p. 128.

5. Attila Csampai and Dietmar Holland (eds.), *Der fliegende Holländer* (Reinbek bei Hamburg: Rowohlt, 1982), p. 136.

6. Wagner, *Life*, p. 74.

7. Helmut Kirchmeyer, *Situationsgeschichte der Musikkritik und des musikalischen Pressewesens in Deutschland*, IV, *Das zeitgenössische Wagner-Bild*, 2 (Regensburg: Bosse, *c.* 1960), p. 78.

8. Heinrich Pfitzner (ed.), "Vorwort," Heinrich Marschner, *Der Vampyr* (Berlin: Fürstner, 1925), n.p.n.

9. *GS*, IX, p. 45; *PW*, III, p. 209.

10. Carolyn Abbate, *Unsung Voices* (Princeton: Princeton University Press, 1991), pp. 85–87.
11. Richard Wagner, *The Flying Dutchman*, tr. Charles Osborne in Frank Granville-Barker, *The Flying Dutchman: A Guide to the Opera* (London: Barrie & Jenkins, 1979), p. 132.
12. Wagner, *Dutchman*, p. 133.
13. *GS*, IX, p. 52; *PW*, III, p. 216.
14. Thomas Grey, *Richard Wagner: Der fliegende Holländer* (Cambridge: Cambridge University Press, 2000), p. 64.
15. Carolyn Abbate, "The Parisian 'Venus' and the 'Paris' *Tannhäuser*," *Journal of the American Musicological Society* 36 (1983), 73.
16. *CD*, II, p. 996.
17. *GS*, IX, p. 37; *PW*, III, p. 198.
18. Reinhard Strom, "Dramatic Time and Operatic Form in *Tannhäuser*," *Proceedings of the Royal Musical Association* 104 (1977–8), 6–7.
19. *GS*, IX, p. 42; *PW*, III, p. 203.
20. Charles Baudelaire, "Richard Wagner and *Tannhäuser* in Paris," in *The Painter of Modern Life and Other Essays*, tr. and ed. Jonathan Mayne (London: Phaidon, 1964), p. 126.
21. Marion Bless, *Richard Wagners Oper Tannhäuser im Speigel seiner geistigen Entwicklung* (Eisenach: Karl Dieter Wagner, 1997), pp. 71–76.
22. Nike Wagner, *The Wagners: The Dramas of a Musical Dynasty*, tr. Ewald Osers and Michael Downes (Princeton: Princeton University Press, 2000), p. 29.
23. Borchmeyer, *Theory and Theatre*, pp. 198–200.
24. Hans Mayer, *Richard Wagner: Mitwelt und Nachwelt* (Stuttgart and Zurich: Bleser, 1979), pp. 57–58.
25. Richard Wagner, *Tannhäuser*, ed. Nicholas Jahn, tr. Rodney Blumer (London: Calder, 1988), p. 74.
26. Franz Liszt, *Lohengrin und Tannhäuser von Richard Wagner*, *Sämtliche Schriften* IV (Wiesbaden: Breitkopf & Härtel, 1989), p. 129.
27. Wagner, *Tannhäuser*, p. 76.
28. Carl Dahlhaus, *Nineteenth-Century Music*, tr. J. Bradford Robinson (Berkeley: University of California Press, 1989), p. 131.
29. Liszt, *Lohengrin/Tannhäuser*, pp. 83–85.
30. Döhring, *Oper und Musikdrama*, p. 176.
31. Reinhold Brinkmann, "Wunder, Realität und die Figur der Grenzüberschreitung," in Attila Csampai and Dietmar Holland (eds.), *Lohengrin: Texte, Materialien, Kommentare* (Reinbek bei Hamburg: Rowohlt, 1989), pp. 255–58.
32. Anthony Arblaster, *Viva la Liberta! Politics in Opera* (London: Verso, 1992), p. 157.
33. Mayer, *Wagner*, pp. 69–70.
34. Liszt, *Lohengrin/Tannhäuser*, p. 35.
35. *GS*, I, p. 117; *PW*, I, p. 333.

36. *GS*, III, p. 209; my translation.
37. *GS*, I, p. 130; *PW*, I, p. 347.
38. Carl Dahlhaus, *Richard Wagner's Music Dramas*, tr. Mary Whittall (Cambridge: Cambridge University Press), p. 41.
39. *GS*, III, p. 235; my translation.

4 HEROISM, TRAGEDY, AND THE *RING*

1. Richard Wagner, *Selected Letters of Richard Wagner*, tr. and ed. Stewart Spencer and Barry Millington (London: Dent, 1987), p. 233.
2. Borchmeyer, *Theory and Theatre*, pp. 287–325.
3. Michael Ewans, *Wagner and Aeschylus: The Ring and the Oresteia* (Cambridge: Cambridge University Press, 1982).
4. George Steiner, *The Death of Tragedy* (New York: Knopf, 1968), p. 127.
5. Hugh Lloyd-Jones, *Blood for the Ghosts: Classical Influences in the Nineteenth and Twentieth Centuries* (London: Duckworth, 1982), p. 142.
6. Quoted in Albin Lesky, *Greek Tragedy*, tr. H. A. Frankfort (London: Benn, 1967), p. 8.
7. Dorothea Krook, *Elements of Tragedy* (New Haven: Yale University Press, 1969), p. 41.
8. I. A. Richards, *Principles of Literary Criticism* (London: Paul, Trench & Trübner, 1924), p. 246.
9. Steiner, *Death*, pp. 124–27.
10. A. W. Schlegel, "Ancient and Modern Tragedy," tr. R. P and I. F. Draper in *Tragedy: Developments in Criticism*, ed. R. P. Draper (London: Macmillan, 1980), p. 103.
11. Johann Friedrich Schiller, "On the Art of Tragedy," in *Essays*, ed. Walter Hinderer and Daniel O. Dahlstrom, The German Library, vol. XVII (New York: Continuum, 1995), p. 9.
12. Arthur Schopenhauer, *The World as Will and Idea*, tr. R. B. Haldane and J. Kemp, 3 vols. (London: Routledge & Kegan Paul, 1883), III, p. 213.
13. Schopenhauer, *World*, I, p. 215.
14. Terry Eagleton, *Sweet Violence: The Idea of the Tragic* (Oxford: Blackwell, 2003), p. xvi.
15. Borchmeyer, *Theory and Theatre*, p. 290.
16. *GS*, I, p. 141; *PW*, I, p. 358.
17. *GS*, X, p. 25; *PW*, I, p. 43.
18. Henry Hatfield, *Clashing Myths in German Literature* (Cambridge, MA: Harvard University Press, 1974), p. 72.
19. Thomas Mann, *Pro and Contra*, p. 192.
20. Anthony Winterbourne, *Speaking to Our Condition: Moral Frameworks in Wagner's Ring of the Nibelung* (Cranbury, NJ: Associated University Presses, 2000), p. 78.
21. *GS*, X, p. 19; *PW*, I, p. 37.

22. *Richard Wagner's Letters to August Roeckel*, tr. Eleonor C. Sellar (Bristol: Arrowsmith, n.d.), p. 96.
23. Jean-Jacques Rousseau, *Reveries of a Solitary Walker*, p. 88.
24. *Letters to Roeckel*, p. 95.
25. Dahlhaus, *Music Dramas*, p. 99.
26. Stewart Spencer and Barry Millington (eds.), *Wagner's Ring of the Nibelung: A Companion* (London: Thames & Hudson, 2000), pp. 105–06. All further quotations from the *Ring* are taken from this edition.
27. Jeffrey L. Buller, *Classically Romantic: Classical Form and Meaning in Wagner's Ring* (Xlibris, 2001), p. 42.
28. *Ring*, p. 116.
29. *Letters to Roeckel*, p. 96.
30. Carlyle, *Heroes*, pp. 31–32.
31. *Letters to Roeckel*, p. 83.
32. *Ring*, p. 137.
33. *Ring*, p. 137.
34. Deryck Cooke, *I Saw the World End* (Oxford: Clarendon, 1979), p. 336.
35. *CD*, I, p. 88.
36. Dietrich Mack, "Zur Dramaturgie des *Ring*," *Richard Wagner: Werk und Wirkung*, ed. Carl Dahlhaus (Regensburg: Bosse, 1971), p. 61.
37. Thorslev, *Byronic Hero*, pp. 30–31.
38. Peter Wapnewski, *Der traurige Gott: Richard Wagner in seinen Helden* (Munich: Beck, 1978), p. 167.
39. De Vries, *Heroic Song*, pp. 211–16.
40. *Correspondence of Wagner and Liszt*, tr. Francis Hueffer, 2nd edn., rev. William Ashton Ellis, 2 vols. (New York: Vienna House, 1973), II, p. 204.
41. *Letters to Roeckel*, pp. 149–50.
42. *Selected Letters*, p. 323.
43. Winterbourne, *Condition*, pp. 107–09.
44. *Ring*, p. 230.
45. *Ring*, p. 152.
46. *Ring*, p. 155.
47. *Ring*, p. 256.
48. Ernest Newman, *The Wagner Operas* (New York: Knopf, 1949), p. 582.
49. *Ring*, p. 258.
50. Weiner, *Anti-Semitic Imagination*, p. 199.
51. *Ring*, p. 268.
52. George Bernard Shaw, *The Perfect Wagnerite: A Commentary on the Nibelung's Ring*, 4th edn. (London: Constable, 1923), pp. 87–94.
53. *Letters to Roeckel*, p. 102.
54. Mayer, *Wagner*, p. 238.
55. *Ring*, p. 348.
56. Elizabeth Magee, *Richard Wagner and the Nibelungs*, pp. 176–77.
57. *Ring*, p. 304.

58. *Letters to Roeckel*, p. 97.
59. *Ring*, p. 349.

5 THE LAST MUSIC-DRAMAS: TOWARD THE MESSIAH

1. Wagner, *Selected Letters*, p. 323.
2. Kenneth Muir, *Last Periods of Shakespeare, Racine, Ibsen* (Detroit: Wayne State University Press, 1961), p. 3.
3. David Grene, *Reality and the Heroic Pattern* (Chicago: University of Chicago Press, 1967), p. viii.
4. Friedrich Nietzsche, *On the Genealogy of Morals*, tr. Walter Kaufmann (New York: Vintage, 1989), p. 250.
5. Thomas Mann, *Pro and Contra*, pp. 88–89.
6. William Shakespeare, *Romeo and Juliet*, ed. G. Blakemore Evans (Cambridge: Cambridge University Press, 1984), p. 194.
7. Linda and Michael Hutcheon, "Death Drive: Eros and Thanatos in Wagner's *Tristan und Isolde*," *Cambridge Opera Journal* 11/3 (November 1999), 281–82.
8. Michael Tanner, *Wagner* (London: HarperCollins, 1996), pp. 152–54.
9. Peter Wapnewski, *Tristan der Held Richard Wagners* (Berlin: Severin & Siedler, 1981), p. 109.
10. Wapnewski, *Tristan*, pp. 90–94.
11. Francis Fergusson, *The Idea of a Theater* (Princeton: Princeton University Press, 1949), p. 68.
12. *König Ludwig II und Richard Wagner: Briefwechsel*, ed. Otto Strobel, 5 vols. (Karlsruhe: Braun, 1936), I, p. 86.
13. Schopenhauer, *World*, I, p. 327.
14. Schopenhauer, *World*, I, p. 329.
15. *GS*, VII, pp. 28–29; *PW*, VIII, pp. 68–69.
16. Dahlhaus, *Nineteenth-Century Music*, p. 117.
17. Mann, *Pro and Contra*, p. 125.
18. Richard Wagner, *Tristan and Isolde*, tr. William Mann (London: Friends of Covent Garden: Dutton, 1968), p. 63. All further quotations from this edition.
19. Wagner, *Tristan*, p. 85.
20. Dahlhaus, *Music Dramas*, p. 50.
21. Arthur Groos, "Appropriation in Wagner's *Tristan* Libretto," in *Reading Opera*, ed. Arthur Groos and Roger Parker (Princeton: Princeton University Press, 1988), p. 18.
22. Wagner, *Tristan*, p. 99.
23. Wapnewski, *Tristan*, pp. 112–13.
24. *Richard Wagner to Mathilde Wesendonck*, tr. William Ashton Ellis, 2nd edn. (New York: Vienna House, 1972), p. 119.
25. Joseph Kerman, *Opera and Drama* (Berkeley: University of California Press, 1988), p. 164.
26. Wagner, *Tristan*, p. 119.

27. Wagner, *Tristan*, p. 137.
28. That one can read the ending as a projection of Tristan's consciousness only strengthens this reading. See Slavoj Žižek and Mladen Dolar, *Opera's Second Death* (New York: Routledge, 2002), pp. 127–31.
29. Dahlhaus, *Music Dramas*, p. 65.
30. Adorno, *In Search of Wagner*.
31. Peter Uwe Hohendahl, "Reworking History: Wagner's German Myth of Nuremberg," in *Rereading Wagner*, ed. Reinhold Grimm and Jost Hermand (Madison: University of Wisconsin Press, 1993), p. 49.
32. Barry Millington, "Nuremberg Trail: Is There Anti-Semitism in *Die Meistersinger?*" *Cambridge Opera Journal* 3/3 (November 1991), 247–60.
33. See especially Lucy Beckett, "Sachs and Schopenhauer," in John Warrack, *Richard Wagner: Die Meistersinger von Nürnberg* (Cambridge: Cambridge University Press, 1994), pp. 66–82.
34. *GS*, I, p. 113; *PW*, I, p. 329.
35. *GS*, X, p. 55; *PW*, I, p. 75.
36. *GS*, XIV, p. 101; *PW*, IV, p. 107.
37. *GS*, X, p. 19; *PW*, I, p. 37.
38. Mann, *Pro and Contra*, p. 141.
39. Mayer, *Wagner*, p. 141.
40. Lord Byron, *Selected Poems*, ed. Susan J. Wolfson and Peter J. Manning (Harmondsworth: Penguin, 1996), p. 416.
41. Paul Robinson reaches the same conclusion through an analysis of Ruskin's theories of art, in *Opera and Ideas: From Mozart to Strauss* (New York: Harper & Row, 1985), p. 225.
42. *GS*, XIV, p. 75; *PW*, IV, p. 80.
43. Frank W. Glass, *The Fertilizing Seed: Wagner's Concept of the Poetic Intent* (Michigan: University of Michigan Press, 1983), pp. 171–78.
44. Northrop Frye, *An Anatomy of Criticism: Four Essays* (Princeton: Princeton University Press, 1971), pp. 180–84.
45. Millington, "Nuremberg Trial," pp. 259–60.
46. Hans Rudolf Vaget, "Wagner-Kult und nationalsozialistische Herrschaft," in *Richard Wagner in Dritten Reich*, ed. Saul Friedlander and Jörn Rüsen (Munich: Beck, 2000), p. 270.
47. *GS*, XIV, p. 64; *PW*, IV, p. 68.
48. Borchmeyer, *Theory and Theatre*, p. 279.
49. Richard Wagner, *Die Meistersinger von Nürnberg*, tr. Peter Branscombe (Decca Records 452 606–2, 1997), pp. 297–99.
50. Nike Wagner, *The Wagners*, p. 104.
51. John Warrack, *German Opera: From the Beginnings to Wagner* (Cambridge: Cambridge University Press, 2001), p. 85.
52. Lucy Beckett, *Parsifal* (Cambridge: Cambridge University Press, 1981), pp. 129–49.
53. Robert Gutman, *Richard Wagner: The Man, His Mind and His Music* (Harmondsworth: Penguin, 1971), pp. 589–616.

54. Michael Tanner, "The Total Work of Art," in *The Wagner Companion*, ed. Peter Burbridge and Richard Sutton (Cambridge: Cambridge University Press, 1979), p. 209.
55. Dahlhaus, *Music Dramas*, p. 144.
56. *GS*, XIV, p. 130; *PW*, VI, p. 213.
57. *CD*, I, p. 713.
58. *CD*, II, p. 357.
59. Robert Raphael, *Richard Wagner* (New York: Twayne, 1969), p. 96.
60. Borchmeyer, *Theory and Theatre*, pp. 384–85.
61. *CD*, I, p. 154.
62. Gutman, *Wagner*, pp. 595 and 597.
63. *GS*, V, p. 183.
64. *GS*, XIV, pp. 149–54; *PW*, VI, pp. 232–36.
65. Friedrich Nietzsche, *Nietzsche contra Wagner*, *The Complete Works of Friedrich Nietzsche*, tr. J. M. Kennedy (New York: Russell & Russell, 1964), VIII, pp. 72–73.
66. *Selected Letters*, p. 457.
67. It is appropriately identified with syphilis in Linda and Michael Hutcheon, *Opera: Desire, Disease, Death* (Lincoln: University of Nebraska Press, 1996), pp. 62–68.
68. Barry Millington, *Wagner*, p. 267.
69. Richard Wagner, *Parsifal* (Philips Classics, 416 390–2, 1962), p. 144.
70. Wagner, *Parsifal*, p. 144.

6 WAGNER'S HEROISM ON STAGE

1. Bertolt Brecht, *Life of Galileo*, tr. John Willett (New York: Arcade, 1994), p. 98.
2. Peter Viereck, *Metapolitics*, pp. 90–125.
3. Hans Kohn, *The Mind of Germany*, pp. 189–221.
4. *GS*, I, pp. 58–59; *PW*, I, pp. 269–70.
5. Quoted in Geoffrey Skelton, *Wieland Wagner: The Positive Sceptic* (London: Gollancz, 1971), p. 195.
6. See especially Reinhold Brinkmann, "Wagners Aktualität für den Nationalsozialismus," Saul Friedländer, "Hitler and Wagner," and Hans Rudolf Vaget, "Wagner-Kult und nationalsozialistische Herrschaft," in Friedlander and Rüsen (ed.), *Dritten Reich*, pp. 109–41, 165–78, and 264–82.
7. Mann, *Pro and Contra*, pp. 84–86.
8. Dieter Borchmeyer, "The Question of Anti-Semitism," in *Wagner Handbook*, pp. 173–76.
9. *CD*, II, p. 773.
10. Paul Lawrence Rose, *Wagner, Race, and Revolution* (New Haven: Yale University Press, 1992).
11. Weiner, *Anti-Semitic Imagination*, p. 327.

12. Laurence Dreyfus, "Hermann Levi's Shame and *Parsifal*'s Guilt: A Critique of Essentialism in Biography and Criticism," *Cambridge Opera Journal* 6/2 (July 1994), 145.
13. Friedrich Nietzsche, *Untimely Meditations*, tr. R. J. Hollingdale (Cambridge: Cambridge University Press, 1983), p. 227.
14. *Wagner in Rehearsal, 1875–1876: The Diaries of Richard Fricke*, tr. George R. Fricke (Stuyvesant, NY: Pendragon, 1998), pp. 67–68.
15. Nietzsche, *Untimely Meditations*, p. 75.
16. Heinrich Porges, *Wagner Rehearsing the* Ring, tr. Robert A. Jacobs (Cambridge: Cambridge University Press, 1983), p. 1.
17. Porges, *Wagner Rehearsing*, p. 2.
18. Peter Brook, *The Empty Space* (New York: Athenaeum, 1969), p. 140.
19. *CD*, I, p. 922.
20. See for example, Heinrich Ehrlich's review in *Bayreuth in der deutschen Presse*, ed. Susanna Großmann-Vendrey, 4 vols. (Regensburg: Bosse, 1977), I, pp. 146–47.
21. *König Ludwig und Richard Wagner. Briefwechsel*, V, p. 158.
22. See Detta and Michael Petzet, *Die Richard Wagner Bühne König Ludwigs II* (Munich: Prestel, 1970).
23. *GS*, XII, pp. 315–16; *PW*, V, p. 162.
24. *CD*, II, p. 154.
25. Dietrich Mack, *Der Bayreuther Inszenierungsstil* (Munich: Prestel, 1976), p. 16.
26. Simon Williams, *Richard Wagner and Festival Theatre* (Westport: Praeger, 1994), pp. 116–21.
27. Details of inadequacies of staging can be found in essays by Grieg and Hanslick in Robert Hartford (ed.), *Bayreuth: The Early Years* (London: Victor Gollancz, 1980), pp. 68 and 84–85.
28. Fricke, *Rehearsal*, p. 65.
29. Robert Donington, *Wagner's* Ring *and Its Symbols: The Music and the Myth* (London: Faber & Faber, 1974).
30. *CD*, I, p. 704.
31. *CD*, I, p. 917.
32. See, for example, Lilli Lehmann's account of the 1896 cycle in which she sang Brünnhilde in Hartford, *Early Years*, pp. 212–18.
33. Hartford, *Early Years*, p. 225.
34. Hartford, *Early Years*, p. 238.
35. *GS*, XII, p. 349; *PW*, V, p. 193. See Borchmeyer, *Theory and Theatre*, chapters 3 and 4, for a full discussion of Wagner's thoughts on non-illusionistic theatre.
36. *CD*, I, p. 522.
37. *GS*, II, p. 373; *PW*, VI, p. 307.
38. Adolphe Appia, *Music and the Art of the Theatre*, tr. Robert W. Corrigan and Mary Douglas Dirks (Coral Gables: University of Miami Press, 1962), p. 112.
39. Appia, *Music*, p. 126.
40. Adolphe Appia, *Staging Wagnerian Drama*, tr. Peter Loeffler (Basle: Birkhäuser, 1982), p. 51.

41. Richard Beacham, *Adolphe Appia: Theatre Artist* (Cambridge: Cambridge University Press, 1987), pp. 118–37.

42. Max Mell, *Alfred Roller* (Vienna: Wiener Literarische Anstalt, 1922), p. 23.

43. Edward Braun, *A Revolution in Theatre* (Iowa City: University of Iowa Press, 1995), p. 95.

44. Quoted in Skelton, *Wieland Wagner*, pp. 94–95.

45. Quoted by Penelope Turing, *New Bayreuth* (St. Martin, Jersey: Jersey Artists, 1969), p. 6.

46. Mack, *Inszenierungsstil*, p. 13.

47. Skelton, *Wieland Wagner*, p. 110.

48. Joachim Fest, "Richard Wagner – Das Werk neben dem Werk," in Friedländer and Rüsen (ed.), *Dritten Reich*, p. 26.

49. Hans Curjel, *Experiment Krolloper 1927–1931* (Munich: Prestel, 1975), p. 253.

50. Frederic Spotts, *Bayreuth: A History of the Wagner Festival* (New Haven: Yale University Press, 1994), p. 226.

51. My discussion is based on the DVD recording (070 407–9) of the production distributed by Philips in 2002.

52. Oswald Georg Bauer, *Richard Wagner: The Stage Designs and Productions from the Premieres to the Present* (New York: Rizzoli, 1982), p. 160.

53. Klaus Zehelin, "Zum Stuttgarter Ring, 1999/2000," in A. T. Schaefer, *Der Stuttgarter Ring* (Mönchengladbach: Kühlen, 2000), p. 5.

54. First staged at the English National Opera in 1999 and, subsequent to the San Francisco production, in Chicago in 2002.

Bibliography

Abbate, Carolyn, *In Search of Opera*, Princeton: Princeton University Press, 2001.
    "The Parisian 'Venus' and the 'Paris' *Tannhäuser*," *Journal of the American Musicological Society* 36 (1983), 73–123.
    Unsung Voices: Opera and Musical Narrative in the Nineteenth Century, Princeton: Princeton University Press, 1991.
Adorno, Theodor, *In Search of Wagner*, tr. Rodney Livingstone, Trowbridge: NLB, 1981.
Appia, Adolphe, *Music and the Art of the Theatre*, tr. Robert W. Corrigan and Mary Douglas Dirks, Coral Gables: University of Miami Press, 1962.
Arblaster, Anthony, *Viva la Liberta! Politics in Opera*, London: Verso, 1992.
Barth, Herbert (ed.), *Bayreuther Dramaturgie: Der Ring des Nibelungen*, Stuttgart and Zurich: Belser, 1980.
    Richard Wagner: Life, Work, Festspielhaus, Bayreuth: Festspielleitung, 1952.
Baudelaire, Charles, "Richard Wagner and *Tannhäuser* in Paris," in *The Painter of Modern Life and Other Essays*, tr. and ed. Jonathan Mayne, London: Phaidon, 1964, pp. 111–46.
Bauer, Hans-Joachim, *Richard Wagner Lexikon*, Bergisch Gladbach: Lübbe, 1988.
Bauer, Oswald George, *Richard Wagner: The Stage Designs and Productions from the Premieres to the Present*, New York: Rizzoli, 1983.
    Richard Wagner Goes to the Theatre: Impressions, Experience and Reflections on the Road to Bayreuth, tr. Stewart Spencer, Bayreuth Festival, n.d.
Beckett, Lucy, *Richard Wagner: Parsifal*, Cambridge: Cambridge University Press, 1981.
Bekker, Paul, *Richard Wagner: His Life in His Work*, tr. M. M. Bozman, Freeport: Books for Libraries, 1931.
Bentley, Eric, *The Cult of the Superman: A Study of the Idea of Heroism in Carlyle and Nietzsche*, London: Hale, 1947.
Bless, Marion, *Richard Wagners Oper Tannhäuser im Speigel seiner gesitigen Entwicklung*, Eisenach: Dieter, 1997.
Borchmeyer, Dieter, *Richard Wagner: Theory and Theatre*, tr. Stewart Spencer, Oxford: Clarendon, 1991.
    Das Theater Richard Wagners: Idee – Dichtung – Wirkung, Stuttgart: Reclam, 1982.

Bowra, Maurice, *Heroic Poetry*, London: Macmillan, 1952.

Bredvold, Louis, *The Natural History of Sensibility*, Detroit: Wayne State University Press, 1962.

Buller, Jeffrey L., *Classically Romantic: Classical Form and Meaning in Wagner's Ring*, Xlibris, 2001.

Campbell, Joseph, *The Hero with a Thousand Faces*, Cleveland: World Publishing Co., 1956.

Carlyle, Thomas, *On Heroes, Hero-Worship and the Heroic in History*, rep. Lincoln: University of Nebraska Press, 1966.

Cicora, Mary A., *Modern Myths and Wagnerian Deconstructions: Hermeneutic Approaches to Wagner's Music-Dramas*, Westport, CT: Greenwood, 2000.

Cooke, Deryck, *I Saw the World End*, London: Oxford University Press, 1979.

Corse, Sandra, *Wagner and the New Consciousness: Language and Love in the* Ring, Cranbury, NJ: Associated University Presses, 1990.

Csampai, Attila, and Holland, Dietmar (eds.), *Der fliegende Holländer*, Reinbek bei Hamburg: Rowohlt, 1982.

Lohengrin, Reinbek bei Hamburg: Rowohlt, 1989.

Tannhäuser, Reinbek bei Hamburg: Rowohlt, 1986.

Dahlhaus, Carl, *Nineteenth-Century Music*, tr. J. Bradford Robinson, Berkeley: University of California Press, 1989.

Richard Wagner's Music Dramas, tr. Mary Whittall, Cambridge: Cambridge University Press, 1979.

Dahlhaus, Carl (ed.), *Richard Wagner Werk und Wirkung*, Regensburg: Bosse, 1971.

Dahlhaus, Carl, and Voss, Egon (eds.), *Wagnerliteratur – Wagnerforschung*, Mainz: Schott, 1985.

Deathridge, John, *Wagner's* Rienzi, Oxford: Clarendon, 1977.

De Vries, Jan, *Heroic Song and Heroic Legend*, tr. B. J. Timmer, New York: Arno, 1963.

Döhring, Sieghart, and Henze-Döhring, Sabine, *Oper und Musikdrama im 19. Jahrhundert*, Handbuch der musikalischen Gattungen 13, Laaber: Laaber-Verlag, 1997.

Dreyfus, Laurence, "Hermann Levi's Shame and *Parsifal*'s Guilt: A Critique of Essentialism in Biography and Criticism," *Cambridge Opera Journal* 6/2 (July 1994), 125–45.

Eagleton, Terry, *Sweet Violence: The Idea of the Tragic*, Oxford: Blackwell, 2003.

Ewans, Michael, *Wagner and Aeschylus*, Cambridge: Cambridge University Press, 1983.

Fergusson, Francis, *The Idea of a Theater*, Princeton: Princeton University Press, 1949.

Fischer-Lichte, E. *Kurze Geschichte des deutschen Theaters*, Tübingen and Basle: Franke, 1993.

Fricke, Richard, *Wagner in Rehearsal, 1875–1876: The Diaries of Richard Fricke*, Franz Liszt Studies 7, tr. George R. Fricke, Stuyvesant, NY: Pendragon, 1998.

Friedlander, Saul, and Rüsen, Jörn (eds.), *Richard Wagner im Dritten Reich*, Munich: Beck, 2000.

Furst, Lilian R., *Romanticism in Perspective: A Comparative Study of Aspects of the Romantic Movement in England, France and Germany*, London: Macmillan, 1969.

The Contours of Romanticism, Lincoln: University of Nebraska Press, 1979.

Garber, Frederick, "Self, Society, Value, and the Romantic Hero," *Comparative Literature* 19/4 (Fall 1967), 321–33.

Gerhard, Anselm, *The Urbanization of Opera: Music Theater in Paris in the Nineteenth Century*, tr. Mary Whittall, Chicago: University of Chicago Press, 1998.

Glass, Frank W., *The Fertilizing Seed: Wagner's Concept of the Poetic Intent*, Ann Arbor: UMI Research Press, 1983.

Granville-Barker, Frank, *The Flying Dutchman: A Guide to the Opera*, London: Barrie & Jenkins, 1979.

Gregor-Dellin, Martin, *Richard Wagner: His Life, His Work, His Century*, tr. J. Maxwell Brownjohn, San Diego: Harcourt Brace Jovanovich, 1983.

Grene, David, *Reality and the Heroic Pattern: Last Plays of Ibsen, Shakespeare and Sophocles*, Chicago: University of Chicago Press, 1967.

Grey, Thomas, *Richard Wagner: Der fliegende Holländer*, Cambridge: Cambridge University Press, 2000.

Grimm, Reinhold, and Hermand, Jost (eds.), *Re-Reading Wagner*, Madison: University of Wisconsin Press, 1993.

Groos, Arthur, "Appropriation in Wagner's *Tristan* Libretto," in *Reading Opera*, ed. Arthur Groos and Roger Parker, Princeton: Princeton University Press, 1988.

"Back to the Future: Hermeneutic Fantasies in *Der fliegende Holländer*," *19th-Century Music* 19/2 (1995), 191–211.

Großmann-Vendrey, Susanna, *Bayreuth in der deutschen Presse: Beiträge zur Rezeptionsgeschichte Richard Wagners und seiner Festspiele*, 3 vols., Regensburg: Bosse, 1977.

Gutman, Robert, *Richard Wagner: The Man, His Mind, and His Music*, Harmondsworth: Penguin, 1971.

Hartford, Robert (ed.), *Bayreuth: The Early Years*, Cambridge: Cambridge University Press, 1980.

Hatfield, Henry, *Clashing Myths in German Literature*, Cambridge, MA: Harvard University Press, 1974.

Heldt, Brigitte, *Richard Wagner, Tristan und Isolde: Das Werk und seine Inszenierung*, Laaber: Laaber-Verlag, 1994.

Holman, J. K., *Wagner's Ring: A Listener's Companion and Concordance*, Portland, OR: Amadeus, 1996.

Hutcheon, Linda and Michael, "Death Drive: Eros and Thanatos in Wagner's *Tristan und Isolde*," *Cambridge Opera Journal*, 11/3 (November 1999), 267–93.

Opera: Desire, Disease, Death, Lincoln: University of Nebraska Press, 1996.

Kämpfer, Frank (ed.), *Musiktheater heute: Peter Konwitschny, Regisseur*, Hamburg: Europäische Verlagsanstalt, 2001.

Kerman, Joseph, *Opera and Drama*, new and rev. edn., Berkeley: University of California Press, 1988.

Kirchmeyer, Helmut (ed.), *Situationsgeschichte der Musikkritik und des musikalischen Pressewesens in Deutschland*, IV *Das zeitgenössische Wagner-Bild*, 2, Regensburg: Bosse, 1967.

Knudsen, Hans, *Deutsche Theatergeschichte*, Stuttgart: Kröner, 1959.

Kohn, Hans, *The Mind of Germany: The Education of a Nation*, London: Macmillan, 1962.

Kunze, Stefan (ed.), *Richard Wagner: Von der Oper zum Musikdrama*, Bern and Munich: Franke, 1978.

Large, David C., and Weber, William (eds.), *Wagnerism in European Culture and Politics*, Ithaca: Cornell University Press, 1984.

Lash, John, *The Hero: Manhood and Power*, London: Thames & Hudson, 1995.

Lindenberger, Herbert, *Opera: The Extravagant Art*, Ithaca: Cornell University Press, 1984.

Liszt, Franz, *Lohengrin und Tannhäuser von Richard Wagner. Sämtliche Schriften* IV, ed. Detlev Altenberg, Wiesbaden: Breitkopf & Härtel, 1989.

Lloyd-Jones, Hugh, *Blood for the Ghosts: Classical Influences in the Nineteenth and Twentieth Centuries*, London: Duckworth, 1982.

Mack, Dietrich, *Der Bayreuther Inszenierungsstil*, Munich: Prestel, 1976.

Mann, Thomas, *Pro and Contra Wagner*, tr. Allan Blunden, London: Faber & Faber, 1985.

Mayer, Hans, *Richard Wagner: Mitwelt und Nachwelt*, Stuttgart and Zurich: Belser, 1978.

Magee, Bryan, *Aspects of Wagner*, rev. and enl. edn., London: Oxford University Press, 1988.

Wagner and Philosophy, London: Allen Lane, 2000.

Magee, Elizabeth, *Richard Wagner and the Nibelungs*, Oxford: Clarendon, 1990.

McCreless, Patrick, *Wagner's Siegfried: Its Drama, History, and Music*, Ann Arbor: UMI Research Press, 1982.

Millington, Barry, "Nuremberg Trial: Is There Anti-Semitism in *Die Meistersinger?*" *Cambridge Opera Journal* 3/3 (November 1991), 247–60.

Wagner, Princeton: Princeton University Press, 1992.

Millington, Barry (ed.), *The Wagner Compendium: A Guide to Wagner's Life and Music*, New York: Schirmer, 1992.

Millington, Barry, and Spencer, Stewart (eds.), *Selected Letters of Richard Wagner*, London: Dent, 1987.

Wagner in Performance, New Haven: Yale University Press, 1992.

Müller, Ulrich and Peter Wapnewski (eds.), *Wagner Handbook*, ed. Eng. trans. John Deathridge, Cambridge, MA: Harvard University Press, 1992.

Nattiez, Jean-Jacques, *Wagner Androgyne*, tr. Stewart Spencer, Princeton: Princeton University Press, 1993.

Nemoianu, Virgil, *The Taming of Romanticism*, Cambridge, MA.: Harvard University Press, 1984.

Newman, Ernest, *The Wagner Operas*, New York: Knopf, 1949.

Nietzsche, Friedrich, *Nietzsche contra Wagner*, vol. VIII, *The Complete Works of Friedrich Nietzsche*, tr. J. M. Kennedy, New York: Russell & Russell, 1964.

On the Genealogy of Morals and Ecce Homo, ed. and tr. Walter Kaufmann, New York: Vintage, 1989.

Untimely Meditations, tr. R. J. Hollingdale, Cambridge: Cambridge University Press, 1983

Nipperdey, Thomas, *Germany from Napoleon to Bismarck, 1800–1866*, tr. Daniel Nolan, Princeton: Princeton University Press, 1996.

Nordau, Max, *Degeneration*, New York: Appleton, 1897.

Peckham, Morse, *Beyond the Tragic Vision: The Quest for Identity in the Nineteenth Century*, New York: Brazillier, 1962.

Petzet, Detta and Michael, *Die Richard Wagner-Bühne König Ludwigs II, München, Bayreuth*, Munich: Prestel, 1970.

Pfitzner, Heinrich (ed.), "Vorwort" to *Der Vampyr*, Berlin: Fürstner, 1925.

Porges, Heinrich, *Wagner Rehearsing the* Ring, tr. Robert L. Jacobs, Cambridge: Cambridge University Press, 1983.

Praz, Mario, *The Romantic Agony*, 2nd edn., tr. Angus Davidson, London: Oxford University Press, 1970.

Raglan, Lord, *The Hero*, New York: Oxford University Press, 1937.

Raphael, Robert, *Richard Wagner*, New York: Twayne, 1969.

Rather, L. J., *The Dream of Self-Destruction: Wagner's* Ring *and the Modern World*, Baton Rouge: Louisiana State University Press, 1979.

Reed, Walter L., *Meditations on the Hero: A Study of the Romantic Hero in Nineteenth Century Fiction*, New Haven: Yale University Press, 1974.

Robinson, Paul, *Opera and Ideas: From Mozart to Strauss*, New York: Harper & Row, 1985.

Rose, Paul Lawrence, *Wagner, Race and Revolution*, New Haven: Yale University Press, 1992.

Salmu, Hannu, *Imagined Germany: Richard Wagner's National Utopia*, New York: Peter Lang, 1999.

Schaefer, A. T., *Der Stuttgarter Ring: Staatsoper Stuttgart 1999/2000*, Mönchengladbach: Kühlen, n.d.

Shaw, George Bernard, *The Perfect Wagnerite: A Commentary on the Nibelung's* Ring, 4th edn., London: Constable, 1923.

Sheehan, James J., *German History: 1770–1866*, Oxford: Clarendon, 1989.

Skelton, Geoffrey, *Wieland Wagner: The Positive Sceptic*, London: Gollancz, 1971.

Spencer, Stewart, and Millington, Barry, *Wagner's Ring of the Nibelung: A Companion*, London: Thames & Hudson, 1993.

Spotts, Frederic, *Bayreuth: A History of the Wagner Festival*, New Haven: Yale University Press, 1994.

Steiner, George, *The Death of Tragedy*, New York: Knopf, 1968.

Strohm, Reinhart, "Dramatic Time and Operatic Form in *Tannhäuser*," *Proceedings of the Royal Musical Association* 104 (1977–78), 1–10.

Tanner, Michael, "The Total Work of Art," in *The Wagner Companion*, ed. Peter Burbridge and Richard Sutton, Cambridge: Cambridge University Press, 1979.

Wagner, London: HarperCollins, 1996.

Thorslev, Peter L., Jr., *The Byronic Hero: Types and Prototypes*, Minneapolis: University of Minnesota Press, 1962.

Viereck, Peter, *Metapolitics: The Roots of the Nazi Mind*, New York: Capricorn, 1961.

Wagner, Cosima, *Cosima Wagner's Diaries*, 2 vols., tr. Geoffrey Skelton, New York: Harcourt Brace Jovanovich, 1977 and 1980.

Wagner, Nike, *The Wagners: The Dramas of a Musical Dynasty*, tr. Ewald Osers and Michael Downes, Princeton: Princeton University Press, 1998.

Wagner, Richard, *Correspondence of Wagner and Liszt*, tr. Francis Hueffer, new rev. edn. by W. Ashton Ellis, New York: Haskell House, 1969.

Gesammelte Schriften, ed. Julius Kapp, 14 vols., Leipzig: Hesse, 1914.

Letters to August Roeckel, tr. Eleanor C. Sellar, Bristol: Arrowsmith, 1897.

The Mastersingers of Nuremberg, tr. Peter Branscombe, Decca Records, 1997.

My Life, tr. Andrew Gray, Cambridge: Cambridge University Press, 1983.

Parsifal, Philips Classics, 1962.

Prose Works, 8 vols., tr. William Ashton Ellis, London: Paul, Trench, Trübner, 1893.

Richard Wagner to Mathilde Wesendonck, ed. and tr. William Ashton Ellis, New York: Vienna House, 1905.

Tannhäuser, ed. Nicholas Jahn, tr. Rodney Blumer, London: Calder, 1988.

Tristan and Isolde, tr. William Mann, London: Friends of Covent Garden: Dutton, 1968.

Wapnewski, Peter, *Der traurige Gott: Richard Wagner in seinen Helden*, Munich: Beck, 1978.

Tristan der Held Richard Wagners, Berlin: Severin and Siedler, 1981.

Warrack, John, *German Opera: From the Beginnings to Wagner*, Cambridge: Cambridge University Press, 2001.

Richard Wagner: Die Meistersinger von Nürnberg, Cambridge: Cambridge University Press, 1994.

Weiner, Marc A., *Richard Wagner and the Anti-Semitic Imagination*, Lincoln: University of Nebraska Press, 1997.

Wessling, Berndt W., *Wieland Wagner: Der Enkel*, Köln-Rodenkirchen: Tonger, 1997.

Williams, Simon, "The Well-Made Play," in *European Writers: The Romantic Century*, vol. VII, ed. Jacques Barzun and George Stade, New York: Scribners, 1985.

Richard Wagner and Festival Theatre, Westport: Praeger, 1994.

Wilson, James D., *The Romantic Heroic Ideal*, Baton Rouge: Louisiana State University Press, 1982.

Winterbourne, Anthony, *Speaking to Our Condition: Moral Frameworks in Wagner's Ring of the Nibelung*, Cranbury, NJ: Associated University Presses, 2000.

Žižek, Slavoj, and Dolar, Mladen, *Opera's Second Death*, New York: Routledge, 2002.

Zuckerman, Elliott, *The First Hundred Years of Wagner's* Tristan, Columbia: Columbia University Press, 1964.

Index